Maureen Stapleton
& Jane Scovell

A
Hell *of*
a Life

AN AUTOBIOGRAPHY

Simon & Schuster

New York London Toronto Sydney Tokyo Singapore

SIMON & SCHUSTER
Rockefeller Center
1230 Avenue of the Americas
New York, NY 10020

SIMON & SCHUSTER and colophon are registered trademarks
of Simon & Schuster Inc.

Designed by Elina D. Nudelman

Manufactured in the United States of America

10 9 8 7 6 5 4 3 2 1

Library of Congress Cataloging-in-Publication Data
Stapleton, Maureen.
    A hell of a life : an autobiography / Maureen Stapleton & Jane Scovell.
    p.   cm.
    1. Stapleton, Maureen.   2. Actors—United States—Biography.
I. Scovell, Jane, date.   II. Title.
PN2287.S675A3   1995
792'.028'092—dc20
[B]   95-11064   CIP
ISBN 0-684-81092-1

This book is dedicated
to each person who buys it.

Introduction

Because I don't mince words and have always called things as I've seen them, lots of stories about me are circulated in the entertainment world. Here's a perfect example.

In 1962 I went to Hollywood to appear in the screen version of the popular Broadway musical *Bye Bye Birdie.* Although I was still in my thirties, I was cast as Dick Van Dyke's mother—like Beulah Bondi before me, I portrayed older ladies throughout my younger life. Allegedly, at a wrap-up party for the cast and crew of *Bye Bye Birdie,* the producer got up and told everyone he was thrilled to be associated with such a superb film and so many fabulous people, especially Ann-Margret, the singing-dancing ingenue. The director then rose, paid tribute to the company and ended by saying he, too, was thrilled to work with Ann-Margret. Next, Dick Van Dyke got up, praised everyone and finished by, once again, singling out Ann-Margret. Finally, I stood up and said, "Well, it looks like I'm the only one on this picture who didn't try to fuck Ann-Margret."

I hate to disillusion anyone, but that's not what happened. Actually, we were at a party at somebody's home, and I noticed that

Ann-Margret was sitting on a couch surrounded by a bunch of guys coming on to her. About an hour later she was in the same place. I was on my way to the buffet table and called over to her. "Annie, why don't you come and sit with me? I'm the only one here who doesn't want to fuck you." That's the true story, and I wouldn't care how it was told except that I like Ann-Margret and the first version makes it sound like I was putting her down. Much later, I was back in Hollywood and ran into Ann-Margret, whom I hadn't seen since *Birdie*. I repeated the screwed-up account of the party. "Honey," I apologized at the end, "I'm gonna get this thing straightened out if it's the last thing I do." Annie smiled, patted my hand, and said, "Leave the story alone, Maureen, it's a classic."

Ann-Margret's probably right; you shouldn't mess with a "classic," even a dubious one. What the hell, there are plenty of *accurate* stories I can tell about my fifty years in show business, so I might as well begin right now.

Chapter One

There's a place called Troy on the east bank of the Hudson River. If you want to know me, you have to know where I come from, and Troy is my hometown. I still feel more welcome there than any other place on earth. Troy's kind of faded now, but it was once big in the iron and steel industry and later became a manufacturing center for clothing, especially men's shirts. Do you like trivia? I love it. I'm a *Jeopardy* freak and watch it every day. I'm just waiting to get on the show and have Alex Trebek say, "The American city where the detachable collar for men's shirts was designed." Troy also is home to some pretty fine schools, like Rensselaer Polytechnic, Russell Sage College, and the Emma Willard School for Girls.

With all due respect to industry and education, as far as I was concerned, however, Troy was the greatest city in the world to have grown up in, not because of the iron and steel and clothing industries or the good schools, but because Troy contained five, count 'em, five! movie theaters. They were the Troy, Proctor's, the American, the Lincoln, and the Griswald, and on almost any given day of the week, you could be sure of finding Maureen

Stapleton in one or another of those picture palaces. I'm nuts about movies. I've been in plenty of them myself, yet I remain an unabashed fan. Movies were the magic that got me through my childhood.

I was born on June 21, 1925, to John P. and Irene Walsh Stapleton. My full name is Lois Maureen Stapleton. I never was known as Lois; the only person to call me that was my maternal grandmother, and she only used it when she was angry. I knew I'd done something wrong when I'd hear her cry out, "Lois Maureen, I want to talk to you." My parents were practicing Roman Catholics of Irish descent. Luckily for me, neither side sprang from the kings of Ireland. I'm peasant stock and proud of it; that iron constitution's kept me going. I've always said, if I'd been born a princess I'd be dead already.

My arrival was not exactly a model of good timing. The Great Depression was around the corner for the nation and in our house the Great Battle between my mother and father had already begun. Most of my childhood memories are of arguments, and I'm not talking about debates. These were knock-down, drag-out fights punctuated by cries, screams, shouts, and blows. Jack Stapleton was a stereotypical Irishman who drank morning, noon, and night. What his demons were, I don't know; the reasons never were discussed; we dealt only with the results—his drunkenness, his savage behavior, and his inability to care for his family. I'm sure his condition was caused by a lot of things. There was no money and though he tried to work, to my knowledge he never held a steady job. My aunts tell me he was employed by the railroad when my mother married him and that he was well-liked. At the time he seemed like a fine match. That period of grace was long gone when I arrived. By then, my father had become a prodigious drinker and his boozing permeated our lives. I can recall him having only two jobs: running a speakeasy in a garage behind our place, and later, after he had separated from my mother, tending bar in a joint way out on the city limits. There's an obvious trend here—both jobs were alcohol oriented.

I don't know much about my father's family; I assume my

paternal grandparents died before I was born. The only relatives of his with whom we had any contact were his older sister, Rosamund, and their cousin, Monie, who lived together in South Troy; I saw them once a week or so when I was little. Monie was an elderly woman, a terrific lady who died when I was quite young. My dad wasn't close to his sister, and I completely lost track of her when I left Troy. Even if I had wanted to keep up with her, I wasn't about to ask my mother how Dad's family was doing.

My mother's family, the Walshes, dominated. We're talking Irish here, and any which way you look at it, this was a one-hundred-percent solid matriarchy ruled by my grandmother, Mary Walsh. Everyone called her Momma, and she was, indeed, the mother of us all. When Momma Walsh passed on, she was succeeded by her oldest child, my mother, Irene. I suppose you could call me the latest in the line of matriarchs; I'll have to inform my kids, as if they didn't know already. My grandpa, Martin Walsh, was a sweetheart of a man and, considering that he died when I was barely six, I remember him quite well. One memory, in fact, especially stands out. Grandpa Walsh took me for a stroll to the corner pub one sunny afternoon. He hoisted me onto the shiny mahogany bar and while I stood there looking around, called out to the bartender, "Let's have a sarsaparilla for my little granddaughter." And so, I had my first drink in public.

Grandpa came from County Cork; Grandma was from County Mayo. They met and married over there, immigrated here and, since Grandpa was an ironmonger, probably wound up in Troy because of the iron and steel industry. When Grandpa retired, he liked to while away the hours at the local saloon. He wasn't a mean drinker like my dad, just a good-natured old-fashioned social imbiber. My grandmother was a born actress and could tell a story like nobody's business, especially ones about her childhood in Ireland. When I was older I'd go back home just to hear her spin those tales. As she talked, she became a little girl again and the whole emerald scene came alive. Mary Walsh definitely had the gift, a gift that my mother inherited to a degree; she loved to recite poetry aloud. My girlfriends remember being enthralled by my mother's recitations of long narrative poems, many of which she knew by heart.

My grandparents had quite a few children who died before I was born. The survivors were Irene, Martin, Jeanette, Julie, Anna Mae, and Vincent. I said my mother, Irene, was the oldest and (forgive me, Ma) I'm sure she was—not that she'd admit it. Age was never discussed in the family, and God help anyone who ever brought up the subject in front of my mother and/or my aunts. To them, telling your age was a no-no, a mortal sin. It was the one thing they seem to have been given special dispensation to lie about. All their fibbing drove me crazy, so I went completely the other way. Today, I'm liable to walk up to someone, shake hands, and say, "Hi, I'm Maureen and I'm seventy years old."

When I was out in California, I had to fill out some forms for an actors' directory. I can't remember if I was too busy working or going out of town or what, but I had the papers sent to my mother so they'd be completed before the deadline. I prepped her real good for the task. "You can lie all you want about *your* age, Mom, but this is important for me and it's no skin off your arm, so don't fool around with my birth date. Put it down right."

"Sure, sure, sure," my mother said.

Months later when the directory came out, I received my copy and turned the pages till I came to my picture and bio. Mother had lied about my birth date by *one* stinking year. For her own wacky reason, she simply could not put down the correct figure.

I swear I don't know how old my mother was when she died. There was so much hedging going on, I can't even be certain how old I am! I'm pretty sure I'm seventy, but who knows? Who cares? What's the big deal about age? You can't change it, and it seems ridiculous to hide it. Why the Walsh women cared so much, I don't know. All that secrecy, and yet, there may have been some mystical power to it. My aunts always looked younger than I did; Jeanette and Julie still do! God bless them, they've been younger than springtime forever.

• • •

A Hell of a Life

My parents and I lived in a four-story house at 183 First Street in Troy, across the street from my grandparents. We never had a peaceful household, but by the time my brother John was born in 1929, life in that top-floor apartment had become unbearable. I've never wanted to talk about my early childhood, and, at this point, nobody else seems to remember it with my degree of anxiety. As I said, all my memories were of those horrendous fights, most of which were about money. Whatever the topic, my parents would get physical and bash each other around. I didn't take one side or the other, though I certainly was more sympathetic toward my mother and would have sided with her if I'd been forced to make a choice.

When both my parents were shrieking and fighting, however, I wasn't concerned about taking sides, I just wanted them to stop. I stood by and watched, often screaming myself in hopes that they'd quit. They never even heard me, of course; they probably didn't realize I was there. In desperation, I'd run down to our landlord or across the street to my grandparents, trying to find someone to help. I came late to school virtually every day because of the ferocious action at night. Peace and quiet descended only during those times when my father had raging D.T.'s and my mother called to have him carted off to a hospital outside Troy. The tranquillity would be short-lived, however, because when he came back the whole screaming mess would start all over again. Every night was fight night. I'm sure it's one of the reasons why, to this day, I go very far out of my way to avoid confrontation. I can't handle it.

Everyone on the block knew about the turmoil at 183 First Street. Ethnically and religiously, our neighbors were a very mixed group, but they were all good people and most of us had one thing in common—we were poor. Everyone knew one another's problems and supported one another in troubled times.

Finally, my mom had had enough. I don't think there was any one particular incident that caused her to call it quits, it just happened. Her family damn well knew it wasn't Blondie-and-Dagwood time at our place, and I'm pretty sure they'd been urging her all along to get rid of her husband. The decision was a long time coming, but once she made up her mind she never faltered.

One morning, at her request, Cousin George, a six-foot-plus state trooper, arrived at our door all decked out in his uniform, the very picture of the law. Mom let George in, and while she and I stood by and my baby brother lay on the sofa, my father was given the old heave-ho. Cousin George told him to pack his stuff and get out . . . for good. My father didn't quite grasp what was happening and blustered. He tried to make light of the situation and bring it down to a family level, just another foolish little skirmish to be passed over. But my mother wouldn't budge and neither would George. He stood with his arms folded, his jaw locked, and his eyes staring straight ahead. The scene was like something straight out of *East Lynne*—almost that melodramatic.

At long last, Jack Stapleton got the message, gave up his efforts, and got his belongings together. George marched him out the door. And that was it. He was gone. I can't remember if he even said good-bye. All I can recall feeling as I watched him leave was a profound sense of relief. Now the fighting would stop. After he left, I didn't miss him. I had such mixed feelings about this dark man. I still do. I'm not sure I liked him, but he was my father, and when you come from a religious background where you're taught to *honor* your parent from day one, it's hard to break with the tradition, no matter what. However I may have felt about my father, I know I didn't want to hear people talking against him. They did, of course—my mother, my grandmother, my uncles, my aunts all put in their two-cents; no one had a good word to say for Jack Stapleton. My mother ranted on until I told her to cut it out.

"Look," I said, "I'm sure I'll find plenty of reasons to hate Dad. I want to hate him on my own terms, though, not anybody else's."

Years later, I found my reasons.

I've never spoken about some of them before, not even to those closest to me, not even to the therapists I saw for umpteen thousand years or the doctors in the funny farm I wound up in back in the sixties. The memory was too painful, and I shoved it away. Like all bad memories, however, it resurfaced. I'm not so crazy about discussing it now, either, and I wouldn't except for the fact that I've been told it's relevant and necessary. So here goes.

After my parents separated, I'd visit with my father on an occasional afternoon or evening. Sometimes he'd be waiting for me after school, and we'd go off together. Other times, I'd meet him at the bar where he worked. I never stayed overnight with him; our appointments always were limited to a few hours for a meal or a movie or a picnic. I was about eleven or twelve on a particular Saturday when he took me to a movie matinee. We sat in the darkened theater and he had his arm around me. Then it happened. He must have been very drunk—he had to have been drunk—because, even though I didn't know much, I did know that what happened was wrong, terribly, terribly wrong. He began to fondle me, and as I shrank from this loathsome invasion I thought, "Holy Mary, what if Mother finds out." I knew better than to tell her, because she'd have killed him. Here I was, being violated, and what worried me most was not that my father was molesting me but what would happen to him if he were caught.

That incident alone, however, didn't turn me completely against him. I was a kid, and though his actions upset me and unnerved me, I refused to look at the full implications and held on to the "honor thy father" routine. I had to believe it was a stupid, drunken mistake. I buried my hurt and hate simply because I couldn't deal with them; I'm good at doing that. I was able to coast along because I didn't see that much of my father during my adolescence. Later, when I moved out of Troy, we clashed.

I'd been in New York City for a while and was doing okay in the theater. My father called me now and again and even came down to New York on a few occasions. I'd usually take him out to some jazz joint or nightclub. I had a friend who was a comic, and one night we went to see him. My friend was a funny, funny guy, and I started laughing my head off. I'm not what you call a "refined" giggler, I'm a no-holds-barred laugher; when I'm enjoying myself, I really enjoy myself. You know what my father did? He kept hushing me, saying, "Shh, keep it down, Maureen. Don't laugh so loud, you're laughing too loud. You're making a spectacle of yourself." The irony of it really struck me. My father, who was capable of the most repulsive behavior and whose drunken actions had destroyed our family and who had mortified me throughout my childhood, was ashamed by my exuberance. All of a sudden, Jack the Ripper became the arbiter of taste. Because I couldn't shake off the deeply embedded belief that my parent somehow had to be honored, I still didn't turn my back on him. Money, a lot of money, passed between us, and it was a one-way toss from my end to his. In the mid-fifties, he went into the hospital and asked me to pay his bills. I sent enough to cover everything and then some. A little later, he called again and said he needed more.

"I sent you the money for the hospital," I answered.

"Well, it wasn't enough," he countered. "Something came up and I had to spend it."

"How could you use the money I sent you for the hospital on something else?" I replied. I knew damn well he'd probably blown the dough on booze or gambling or anything else he felt like. I went a little nuts and told him I wouldn't give him another red cent. He paused. His breathing quickened and he announced in this kind of mealy-mouthed way, "You know it wouldn't look nice if I told the newspapers that the big actress Maureen Stapleton refused to pay her father's hospital bills. It wouldn't look nice at all."

That did it. I went bananas. I started screaming. I stood there stiff as a board with the phone in my hand and shrieked my head off. At the time, I was married to my second husband, David Rayfiel, and he came over, took the receiver out of my hand, and hung it up. I was shaking violently. I couldn't believe it; my own father threatened to blackmail me.

I wouldn't talk to him for a long time after that.

"What's the matter with Maureen? Why doesn't she send me

money anymore?" he'd complain to my brother. I don't know what my brother told him, and I sure as hell didn't care.

The last time I saw my father was in 1961. I was appearing on Broadway in *Toys in the Attic* and late one afternoon, before I took off for the theater, Althea Brown, the lady who worked for me, came into my bedroom and said, "Your father's here."

I went into the living room and there he was, big as life and twice as needy.

"I came by to see the children," he said cheerily. "When do they get home from school?" He'd never seen his grandchildren, *never;* now he claimed to have made a pilgrimage to call on them.

"It's August, Dad," I said calmly, "there's no school in August. The kids are away for the summer. What do you want, Dad?"

Naturally, he wanted money. I said "no" a few times; then he got down on his knees in front of me and began begging. "Don't do that!" I screamed at him. But it was no use. He cried and beseeched, and finally, just to shut him up and get him out of there, I gave him the fucking money. I turned around and stormed out of the room, slamming the door so hard that the top molding fell off. Somewhere inside of me, in that crazy Irish pit of my stomach, I'd known this was going to happen. I had to play Cordelia to a guy who didn't even deserve a Goneril or a Regan.

It's hard to believe, but I truly felt more rage about the attempted blackmail and extortion than I ever did about the incident in the movie theater. It might have been because I was grown up and could understand and deal with my father on an adult level, whereas the childhood episode was beyond my understanding. Am I being naive? According to current theory, I went through a traumatic episode of child abuse. What do I know? I only know my father used me shamelessly on many, many occasions. To this day, I'm still trying to resolve the conflict. The truth is, I didn't like him a lot, and I don't like feeling that way. I *hate* feeling that way. I really don't want to dislike anyone and at this point in my life I really don't dislike anyone, including my ex-husbands. This hatred—and dammit, I do have to use that word—for my father is the only thing sticking in my craw, and I'm trying real hard to find forgiveness in my heart for the man. It ain't easy.

When Dad got the boot, Mom took over. She was one smart cookie; my aunts always said she was the brightest of the lot. Mom knew she had to pull things together for her children. As for herself, since she was a practicing Catholic, her only solace lay in religion, because she couldn't be divorced. I don't think being without a man bothered my mother. If she was consigned to life without a mate, so what. You see, Irene Stapleton was a bit pathological on the subject of sex. Mother and I were as close as could be, and yet while she was wonderful and rational about practically everything else, she went berserk-o when it came to the subject of the physical relationship between men and women. And since that subject came up with particular frequency in my life, my mother and I had our share of dissension.

Dad was gone and Mom had no income. She couldn't pay the rent on the apartment, so when I was about eight, she moved us lock, meager stock, and barrel across the street to my grandmother's house, which was already full of assorted uncles and aunts ranging in age from early teens to late twenties. Although my relatives were kind, I felt like a charity case. Mom, Jack, and I had a room on the top floor. We shared one small bed, and Jack and I took turns sleeping at the bottom. Not only was it uncomfortable; worse still, both of us were bedwetters. I don't know how the hell we got through it, especially my mother. When I was twelve, Mom got a permanent job and could afford to pay rent. We moved down to the second floor and each of us had our own bedroom. It was glorious.

The youngest Walsh relative was my darling uncle Vincent. I absolutely adored that man. There's a certain time when you have one friend who sheds some light on life; for me, that one friend was my uncle Vincent. When I was around him I never felt like a fat jerk, because he made me feel wanted. I wasn't afraid to tell him anything, even though he always spoke the truth no matter how harsh. Vincent was in the Navy and away from home a lot. He returned to Troy a few times a year, and each time it was "Christmas" for me. I looked forward to seeing him as much as I looked forward to going to the movies. One time, this blinding love for him caused a bit of a scene.

I was about six years old and Mom and I were walking in downtown Troy. We reached the county courthouse just as a bunch of men began walking down the steps. I looked over and saw, in the middle of the group, a tall, attractive, skinny man; from a distance he looked exactly like my uncle Vincent. I took off like a shot and began running away from Mother towards the men. "Come back, Maureen," cried my mother. "Where are you going? Come back here this instant." I paid no attention. I ran up the courthouse stairs, pushed my way through the others, reached my "uncle" and hugged him around the knees. He reached down and patted my curls. "Hi, honey," he said in an unfamiliar voice. I looked up and realized I had my arms wrapped around a stranger. I should have known it couldn't have been my uncle, because this guy was wearing a suit and tie and my uncle didn't wear suits. I wasn't checking the clothes, though; I was intent upon reaching my adored Vincent. A thousand cops appeared from nowhere, and as Mother reached us, one of the officers passed me over to her. The men moved on down the steps and got into a big black car. Just before he got in, my "uncle" looked back, waved, and smiled. I waved back. I thought he was darling; the police thought otherwise. It seems I had thrown myself at the feet of Jack "Legs" Diamond, who was shot dead the next day in Albany. Legs Diamond will never get any bad press from me, though. He couldn't have been nicer and seemed real glad to see me . . . just like my uncle.

My beloved uncle Vincent died in his early thirties. I've never gotten over his death. To this day, when I need to cry for acting scenes, I think of him and the tears flow. Vincent was my idol and love because he was genuinely affectionate toward me and, equally important, never disparaged me. The other family members might dismiss my aspirations; not him. And I did have aspirations. I started dreaming about being an actress when I was barely five years old and by the time I was twelve, I definitely had made up my mind—it was to be an actor's life for me—and the movies had brought me to my destiny.

In those depression days, the only way out of the daily heartache was losing yourself in the grand doings on the silver screen. Oh God, I loved the movies and did anything to get into them. By hook or by crook, I'd scrape together enough change, pay my money, go into the theater, plunk down in the seat, and dream myself right onto the screen. A ticket cost ten cents, a sum that could be raised with a little maneuvering. If you brought ten pounds of paper, like newspapers or magazines, to the salvage place, you'd get two cents. It took fifty pounds of paper to get you a movie ticket. That's a helluva lot of paper. Nevertheless, I'd lug my bits and pieces in to be weighed. The guy would put them on the scale, check the figure, and fish into his pocket for the penny. This was a serious, though hardly rewarding, transaction. There was a better method. Empty bottles were redeemable for a whopping five cents each . . . if you could find them. These were depression times, and people weren't flinging five cents away so easily. I rummaged through all the trash cans in South Troy looking for empties. A nickel was such a powerful coin then. In high school, I could always tell the rich girls; they were the ones who'd call out, "Does anybody have a nickel for the phone?" My God, *lend* someone a nickel for the phone? A nickel was my lunch, a nickel was tons of newspapers, a nickel was a returned soda bottle, a nickel, for Pete's sake, was part of my admission to the movies.

Every cent I raised went to Mr. Loew and pals, and by the time I was ten I was going to the movies almost every day of the week. My schedule rarely varied. I'd leave school at three and go directly to the movie theater to see the show. And it wasn't like paying $7.50 for one lousy film, either. I'd sit down for the first show and never see the light of that day again, and all for a dime. By the time I reached high school, it cost a quarter. The theaters showed an A and B double feature, plus cartoons and newsreels and the best damn trailers for coming films you ever saw. Not the junk they throw at you now, but good swift glimpses of Barbara Stanwyck and broads like her getting into situations that you just had to go and see resolved. I'd sit through show after show watching Hollywood's idea of life, which was a far cry from what most people were living. Even if the films weren't totally escapist, you were watching someone else's troubles and could forget your own. For me, there was no such thing as a bad movie. I liked everything about them and everybody in them. No one else in my family cared so passionately about films. My mother didn't like movies, period, and she couldn't understand my obsession. I went to see a rerelease of *Camille* in the early forties, returned home completely washed out, and sat at the kitchen table and wept. Mother walked in and began putting away groceries.

"What's the matter, Maureen?"

"Oh, Mom," I sobbed, "I just saw *Camille* again."

"Are you still crying over that whore?" asked my mother. I was stunned to hear the word "whore" from my mother's lips. She just didn't use words like that and wouldn't allow cussing in her presence. Honestly, I don't know what shocked me more when mother called Garbo's Camille a whore: hearing her use that word for the first time or having it applied to the divine actress who was the furthest thing from a whore imaginable. It was extra surprising because Mother actually liked Garbo; in fact, the only movie stars she admired were Greta Garbo and Mae West. I never understood *that* combination; I still don't. I was nuts about Jean Harlow. She'd strut around those fabulous black-and-white Art Deco sets yapping away in her funny little-girl voice, and meanwhile her boobs were bobbling around, looking like they were going to jump right out of her skin-tight white satin gown and into your face. The material clung so closely to her body that you could see the crack in her behind when she turned around and wiggled out of the scene. It was watching her that gave me the idea I wanted to be an actress. It had nothing to do with inspiration or "art" or anything like that. I just figured if I became an actress, I'd have everything I wanted and automatically look like Jean Harlow.

However, while I loved Harlow, Stanwyck, Jean Arthur, and a whole bunch of other dames, I really worshiped the men. Show me something better than Robert Taylor or Joel McCrea— I dare you. The former was my first raging passion. God, I loved Robert Taylor, especially in the aforementioned *Camille.* I went crazy for Clark Gable, too. I used to tell people the real reason I left Troy was to find Clark Gable and fuck him. I've seen *Gone With the Wind* at least thirty times. (One of my favorite parlor games is to ask people to name twenty-five actors in the cast of *GWTW*—try it yourself, it's fun.) Everyone knows about my obsession. When Burt Reynolds wanted me to work with him, he gave me a *Gone With the Wind* poster. On one side, there's an actual promo picture that reads, *"Gone With the Wind,* starring Clark Gable and Vivien Leigh." Above the title is this sexy shot of Gable holding Leigh in his arms. On the other side of Burt's present is a facsimile of the same poster, only Burt had my face superimposed over Vivien Leigh's, and he doctored the script so it reads, *"Gone With the Wine,* starring Clark Gable and Maureen Stapleton." I swear to God, it looks like the real thing.

Sometimes at one of those theaters in Troy, miracle of miracles, I actually got to see a star in person. These were vaudeville days; performers traveled the circuit and Troy was part of the route. The first one I ever saw live was back in 1934. Ed Wynn came to town in some show or other, and I got his autograph. I still have it. And I have another one from Mary Dees. In case you don't remember Mary Dees—and you'd have to be as movie-sick as I am to remember—she was Jean Harlow's stand-in and actually finished *Saratoga,* the film Harlow was working on at the time of her death. All those long shots at the end are of the face-averted stand-in wearing a hat the size of a satellite saucer. Right after *Saratoga,* Ms. Dees went on a vaudeville personal appearance tour and showed up at Proctor's Theater along with the actor Monte Blue. I have his autograph, too. In 1942, a friend of my mother's went to California and got me a signed picture of Errol Flynn. As the saying goes, I thought I'd died and gone to heaven when the picture arrived in the mail. The glossy, beautiful Mr. Flynn is pinned to the wall of my present apartment, although, if the truth be known, Mr. Flynn was never in my "I want to screw him" major leagues—I don't find Irishmen sexy. Bottom line, I think the sexiest men are tall Jews—and I ought to know, I married two of them.

Getting autographed pictures was terrific; even better, though, was brushing up against the stars. One time Mother and I went to New York for a visit and were standing in front of the Dorset Hotel when Harry Carey got out of a cab. I stopped dead in my tracks and watched as he pulled his bags out of the taxi. I couldn't utter a word and stood there transfixed while my mother pulled at my sleeve. "Maureen, what are you doing? What's the matter with you?" She didn't know Harry Carey from Carrie Nation and couldn't have cared less. Mr. Carey walked by us and smiled that gorgeous smile of his; I began to tremble. Mother had to push me to get me going.

I can't help it. I guess I'll be a fan for the rest of my life, and furthermore, I'll always be most impressed with those men and women who were popular when I was young. After the opening of Tennessee Williams's *Suddenly Last Summer,* Nedda and Josh Logan threw a huge party. Everybody in the world was there, everybody: the Aga Khan, Noël Coward, Lena Horne, Robert Preston—the cream of the celebrity crop. I was chatting with Lena and Noël, both of whom I'd met before and adored. All of a sudden the door opened and in walked Barton MacLane. Now I'd seen Barton MacLane in films when I was a kid, and the minute my eyes fell on him, my mouth fell open. I went "aghaghaghagh," ran over, introduced myself, and proceeded to act like a pain-in-the-ass teenager. I was getting him drinks and doing all sorts of things to keep his attention until Lena and Noël sent Bob Preston over to retrieve me. Bob steered me across the room and said, "What the hell are you doing? Why are you hanging around that guy? What's the matter with you?" I stopped short, looked at Bob and said, "That's *Barton MacLane.*" Bob looked at me perplexedly. "Yeah, it's Barton MacLane, so what?" See, by this time, I was used to the others, the *big* guys like Lena and

Noël and Bob; they were friends. But this was Barton MacLane from millions of movies when I was in the audience and he was on the screen. I couldn't get over it. I still can't. You could put me in a room with the President of the United States, the Queen of England, and the Pope, and if Grady Sutton walked in the door, I'd dump all three of them and be chatting up Mr. Sutton faster than you can say "Jack Warner."

From the age of twelve I began preparing the family for the day of my departure, because I knew I had to go somewhere else to become an actress. All the books I read said that I'd be outnumbered in my logical choice, Hollywood, and that I could prepare myself better in New York City, where there were acting schools like the American Academy of Dramatic Art. I was just as happy to stick around the East; Hollywood seemed too far away. I kept telling Momma Walsh, my mother, and the others that I'd be leaving Troy. "Sure, sure, Maureen," was the usual response, followed by some directive like "Now will you run to the market and get some milk?" The first time I informed my mother that I was going to be an actress, she said, "Okay, okay, be an actress." She didn't get that I wasn't asking her permission, I was telling her what I was going to do. In the same way, I continued to say I was leaving, not "May I leave?" The time drew nearer and nearer, and when I actually did take off, mother couldn't make a big deal because it didn't come out of the blue; it came from years and years of my saying it was going to happen. One Monday I simply announced, "I'm going to New York on Thursday," and that was it. I didn't want to spring any surprises on my mother. Even though she had barely paid attention to my insistent declarations of intent, the message obviously had sunk in. My departure had become an accepted fact. The funny thing is, as much as I wanted to get out of town, I have very positive and good feelings about Troy and its people. While I lived there, I ached to get out; and when I did, I was just as happy to go back and visit.

No one encouraged me to go into acting, not even Vincent.

Unlike the others, however, he listened to my ideas, hopes, and plans and gave them serious consideration. My ambition came from left field. There were no actors or performers in the family, no tradition of the theater in any way: nothing to follow, just something to go after. I made up my mind to be an actress all on my own; no one had said, "Yes, you've got it, baby, go after it." Vincent had a sympathetic nature and would have encouraged me if I'd told him I wanted to become anything. He himself had shown an early initiative and left the fold at fifteen by lying about his age and enlisting in the Navy. When I said I was going to leave town and become an actress, it was a declaration of independence to which my uncle could relate.

Not only did I make up my mind to be an actress; by the time I was eight I also had decided that I never, ever, would marry. Honest to God, I knew everything there was to know at that tender age, including the fact that I should never marry. Believe me, I was as right on that score as I was about being an actress. Growing up in a matrimonial madhouse, I had no model, nothing to go by except that bitter and unsuccessful union of my mother and father. I knew so much about life when I was a little girl that sometimes I think I peaked at eight and it's been downhill ever since.

My growing-up years were filled with friends, movies, and food and lots of each. In my Freshman year in high school, I saw my first professional play. My initial encounter with the stage, and for the life of me, I can't remember what the play was, just that it was in Albany. I don't know who I went with, either. Some epiphany, huh? I must have been inspired, though, because after that I began to read all about the theater. Later, along with my girlfriends, I would go down to New York on the excursion trains and see plays. I can't remember their titles, either. I wonder if the people who saw my plays are as casual about their experiences.

I was plodding through school and all the time had my mind made up that the minute I was graduated, I would go to New York City and study acting. Mind you, I was no theatrical shining light in my childhood and youth; no one saw a Sarah Bernhardt aching to break out. Once in a while my friends and I would put on "shows" in the backyard, but that wasn't acting. In 1935 I was a tambourine-playing gypsy in a school production, and there's a picture of yours truly striking a classic gypsy pose. That was my theatrical debut and probably the last time I portrayed anyone under fifty during my school years. I wasn't in that many plays, but whatever the play, I was cast as an older woman. I was heavy, and "heavy" translates "old" on the stage whether you're twelve or twenty. So I played old dames—mothers, grandmothers, maiden aunts, stuff like that. A far cry from Jean Harlow. Still, I never wanted to do anything else but act. I'm not so sure there's anything else I could have done. My friend Zoe Caldwell says actors are sick people who only can cure themselves by acting. Sick, shmick; if you had a brain in your head, you'd do something else. I swear, you have to be young and have blinders on to ever choose acting as a profession. The condition is ever the same; there always are more actors than there are parts. That's the way it is and that's the way it will be. Acting is not like other professions. Your own "worth" doesn't necessarily come into the picture. If you're a great plumber or a doctor or a seamstress, whatever the hell, people will beat a path to your door. You can be a great actor and the best you can hope for is to get a job for a while. And no matter what job you have, you've got to accept the fact that you're going to be spending most of your time out of work. You can be in a starring role one Monday, and the next week you're sitting in your apartment doing crossword puzzles, waiting for the phone to ring. As if this crap weren't discouraging enough, you have to sell yourself, too, over and over. You have to have what they call an "office personality." Mediocre actors with an O.P. can get roles quicker than really gifted people who don't know how to put themselves across. The fact is, unless you're a superstar, you're outnumbered, so outnumbered that there never is any guarantee you're going to work again even if you have a big success. It's a constant drain. Looking back, however, I don't feel I had a choice. For a fat, struggling kid like me, the only way out was to be someone else—an actor.

A Hell of a Life

· · ·

As I got older, I fell into my movie routine. After school I'd proceed directly to the movies and stay until the theater let out. That could be from three-thirty in the afternoon till ten-thirty at night. Naturally, my mother didn't take to this and it became a running battle between us. We never stopped that fight. Every single time I walked in the door she'd greet me with, "Where have you been?" And my answer remained, "Mom, why are you acting so surprised? You know where I've been."

Often, I'd go to the movies with friends, and as much as I enjoyed the company, I actually preferred going alone. For some weird reason, my friends wanted to leave after a complete show. My idea of moviegoing was not a complete show, it was seeing as many complete shows as possible.

Some of my friends quit school early to go to work. I never could have left school, though, not while Irene Walsh Stapleton ruled the roost. My mother was so attuned to education that she started taking night courses at Siena College. In 1942, when I was graduated from Catholic Central High and my brother was graduated from grammar school, my mother became the first woman to receive a degree from Siena. Irene Walsh Stapleton wanted to better herself, and whether I liked it or not, she was going to better me, too. At the same time that I was picking bottles out of the trash, my mother enrolled me in ballet, tap dancing, and elocution classes. Ballet definitely wasn't my bag. I did, however, become a mean tap dancer. The elocution lessons were another kettle of fish. Two elderly Protestant spinster sisters named Ross, both right out of central casting, ran the school. The sisters Ross were very cultured; they traveled to Europe a lot and bowled me over with their tales of the continent. Among other accomplishments, they'd attended the Oberammergau festival. I'd never heard of Oberammergau, and I wasn't alone. Who could believe that every twenty years an entire town would get together and reenact the crucifixion of Christ? My mother must have been as dazzled by the sisters as I, and quickly popped me into their classes. I still am not quite sure what their teaching

27

method was, although I remember two things vividly. First, I was taught how to curtsey correctly before a queen, and therefore spent weeks learning how to drop to the floor gracefully. Since the probability of my being presented at the Court of St. James's was rather remote, I never figured out why the hell I needed to learn to curtsey so well. Second, the sisters didn't actually teach me how to speak; I mean, there were no phonetics or stuff like that. I was given a poem to memorize every week, and the elocution lessons consisted of a curtsey and the recitation of the poem. I'm not talking *Ode to a Nightingale* here, either. The poems I learned were a different sort. For example, one that's stuck with me all these years went like this:

> Lin Wah Sid was a Chinese kid,
>   He played on a long summer's day,
> He braided his queue like his friend used to do
>   In Chinaland far, far away.

Great. After my curtsey, I could entertain the Royals with a bit of politically incorrect light verse.

Along with her insistence on a well-rounded education, Mother felt that nothing should interfere with my schooling, so she wouldn't let me work during the week. Eventually, I did get a weekend job in a Lerner Shop. Some of the money was saved for my upcoming departure to New York City; the rest was spent on the movies.

The first job I got after graduating high school was working as a junior clerk in the Unemployment Insurance Division of the New York State Department of Labor. The ideal job during the depression had been to work for the state, and I was encouraged to do so, particularly by my grandmother. We were in the kitchen one afternoon, and she told me that I should take a requirement test. "Oh, Momma, I don't know, I don't think I'm cut out for the business world," I answered. Grandma looked at me as though I'd said I wished to become a hooker. "And who are you not to be cut out for the business world?" she said firmly. What a jerk I was. Imagine telling a woman, most of whose children were in the business world, that it wasn't for me.

I did take the test, passed, and started working in Albany. I paid a pittance to my mom for room and board and the rest went into the savings bank, the movies, and tuition for classes. I began taking night courses at Siena College. One was in Spanish. I really loved Spanish and had studied it in high school, where I barely got by; I was so bad, I didn't even know how to cheat. I was determined to learn a language, though, and put my money where my desire was. Much as I loved languages, I simply couldn't learn them. Years later, in a play called *The Emperor's Clothes,* I was supposed to be a piss-elegant little European lady, which already was a stretch, and all through the script, my character kept saying, *"Je vous en prie."* I could not get those words straight. I was so bad that they had to cut out all the *je vous en prie*s rather than risk my messing up.

The other course I took at Siena was English literature. I may have been struggling to save my money, but I was willing to take a portion of it and put it toward those classes. The Spanish was a bust. Thankfully, the English course was another story. Father Joe Van was the professor, and he knew everything there was to know about English literature and poetry. He taught me a lot, especially about poetry.

After some months of work and study, I was transferred from the Albany state office to Schenectady, and that switch eventually put an end to my affiliation with state government. The commute to Schenectady was long, and since I only made $18.75 a week I despaired of saving up the $100 for my New York venture quickly. I looked into other situations and after some searching found a position at the nearby Watervliet Arsenal—for $22 a week. Hey, that was $3.25 more than I'd been making, and every penny meant something.

The Watervliet Arsenal was a munitions factory. Since this was wartime, the factory was booming. I was hired as a "P for I" man; P for present and I for inspection. When something went wrong I had to carry around papers that had to be signed by everybody, from second lieutenant to first lieutenant, major, lieutenant colonel, colonel, and then to the general's office. Those guys couldn't take a leak unless they got permission in quadruplicate. I toted the papers around without ever knowing what the hell they were about or why they had to be signed. Who cared? I was making twenty-two dollars a week and doing my bit for the war effort, even if I didn't know exactly what the bit was.

About a year after I began work, the magic number appeared in my savings book—one hundred. Time to move on. Mom went with me to New York and helped me find an apartment on the East Side. Since the rent was a whopping forty-five dollars a month, I needed a roommate. Another girl in Troy, Cathleen Connelly, wanted to be an actress, too. She agreed to come along with me and pay half the rent. The deal was done. I kissed the relatives good-bye, took a bus down to New York, and moved into the apartment. I was seventeen years old, I weighed 180 pounds, and I had a hundred bucks in my pocket. I was invincible!

Chapter Two

When I arrived in New York City in September 1943, I looked like a bulging barn; pleasingly plump had been left way behind. When I told people I wanted to be an actress, they'd groan in dismay or grunt in disgust—obviously, neither response made me feel too good. However, I was not to be deterred. I'd deal with my weight problem in time; for the present, I was intent upon my career. World War II was being waged overseas, and, while I knew what was happening, I was also a teenager on the brink of realizing her life's ambition. Sure I was concerned about the war, but I had put on those theatrical "blinders." I had faith that my country would triumph; my energies were directed toward getting acting lessons. I was so singleminded in my efforts that I'm not sure I'd even have noticed if the United States had been invaded unless the enemy troops marched into my apartment.

But if I was bulging, then so was Broadway—with original hit shows, including *One Touch of Venus, The Voice of the Turtle, Tomorrow the World, The Patriots, Kiss and Tell, Winged Victory, Something for the Boys, Carmen Jones,* as well as major revivals of the classics.

31

The stars included performers such as Shirley Booth, Mary Martin, Betty Field, Blanche Sweet, Milton Berle, Ilona Massey, Margaret Sullavan, Billie Burke, José Ferrer, Uta Hagen, Paul Robeson, Gregory Peck, and Richard Widmark. Clearly, New York was theatrical heaven, and therefore the only place for an "aspiring" actress like me.

I loved New York then. I'm less happy with it today, a lot less. To tell the truth, it scares the pants off me. Then again, everything petrifies me nowadays. My anxieties, which include acrophobia, agoraphobia, and whatever the hell they call fear of travel—hodophobia, according to a *People* magazine article on me —have actually gotten greater even as I've grown older. Face it, I'm a phobic mess. I don't like to be on bridges and I don't like to be in tunnels. For Pete's sake, I get nervous if I'm watching a movie or television and a camera shot is taken from an airplane —and nothing could make me watch anyone parachute. What it boils down to is, I want to be *on* the earth not above or below it. Sometimes I try and figure out how this stuff started escalating; most of the time, though, I don't think about it. I just don't do the things that make me crazy, like flying. *I hate airplanes.* Nothing could get me in one again—nothing. The last time I flew was forty-one years ago, and there isn't a prayer that I'll ever be up again. You know how they say, "Face your fears"? Well, I faced mine and they won. I have been in the sky twice in my life. The first trip should have taught me a lesson.

In the summer of 1945, I was dating a guy who piloted his own plane, and one fateful afternoon he took me and a couple of my girlfriends, Janice Mars and Hope Moss, to the airport in Rahway, New Jersey, where he kept his two-seater Piper Cub. He offered to take us up for a spin, and each of my pals proceeded to take one. They had a ball. Then yours truly was strapped in, and with my friend at the wheel or whatever the hell you call it, we took off down the runway. The next thing I remember is him saying, "It's all right. Everything's going to be all right. I'm taking us right back down. Just relax." It seems that the minute that little winged contraption left the ground, I began to hyperventilate and nearly went into convulsions during what had to have been one of the fastest takeoffs and landings on record.

I never ever wanted to repeat that experience and wouldn't have had not my darling first husband, Max Allentuck, "forced" me into an airplane some half-dozen years later when he was managing *The Rose Tattoo* road company. We had just finished crossing the country and over my loud protestations were preparing to fly back to New York from Los Angeles. Weeks before, Max had public relations people from the airline come and talk to me. They'd say stuff like, "Oh, you shouldn't worry, Maureen, flying's like being in your own living room." And I'd say, "Oh no, it's not. It's like being twenty thousand feet in the air. That's not like my living room." I desperately tried to get out of it, but Max and the PR gang persisted. They said I could have anything I wanted to make me comfortable. I requested a parachute, which they advised me was not possible. "Furthermore, Maureen," I was informed, "if something happens, a parachute won't do you any good." I had to laugh; a parachute wouldn't do me any good, and they're telling me I'm in my living room.

In those days the flight across the U.S. was far from direct and definitely not nonstop. The plane went from L.A. to Dallas and from Dallas to Washington and then to New York City. I got on the plane and sat next to my *Rose Tattoo* costar, Eli Wallach. Eli was trying to jolly me up.

"Relax, honey. You'll never even know when the plane leaves the ground."

"Right, Eli," I shuddered as the earth fell away. "I can tell you we just left the ground."

At each stop I'd cry and wail and beg not to continue, but no one would let me off the hook. I completely lost my appetite on that trip; I couldn't put anything in my mouth and must have dropped about six pounds on the L.A.-to-Dallas leg alone. For the first time in my life, I understood what people meant when they said, "Thank you, I can't have any more." My perspective had always been you ate till you fell over. In fact, whatever you did, you did it till you blacked out. Well, I sat in that plane and remained incapable of eating one morsel that the stewardess offered. I couldn't believe it. Half the time I carried on a dialogue with myself, saying, "How could you not want a piece of pie or cake or ice cream? What's with you?" What was with me was total, abject fear. I sat frozen in my seat. I'd taken so many pills that they wouldn't give me any more. A bottle of brandy nestled beside me and I never touched it. All I did was pull the seat belt around and buckle in. I never undid it, either. There was an open magazine on my lap and I never turned the page. Forty-one years ago, and I'll never forget that flight. Never, never again.

Some years later I was out on the West Coast and appeared on a television talk show.

"I understand that you came all the way out here on the train," the host said.

"That's right," I answered, "I won't fly."

"You know," the host advised me, "nowadays they can cure people of the fear of flying."

"I don't want to be cured," I told him honestly.

And I don't. I just don't want to fly. I don't like anybody I know to fly, either, and what's more, I don't want to know if anybody I know is flying. *I hate planes*. Frankly, I don't much like trains anymore, either.

The one-hundred-dollar grubstake I'd left Troy with didn't have the necessary legs to keep me going in New York City; I desperately needed cash for acting lessons. The American Academy of Dramatic Arts and the Neighborhood Playhouse, the two major acting schools of the day, had steep tuition, and classes were held every day. I couldn't pay the fees or commit to a regular school curriculum. I needed money, so I began a series of part-time jobs. Those working experiences were probably as helpful to my development as an actress as any of the classes I eventually took.

I started out with night jobs that kept my days free for classes and study. I got a position at the Hotel New Yorker as a clerk, my job being to prepare the bills. I was kept plenty busy. It was wartime and you couldn't get a room for love nor money. Like all the hotels, the New Yorker was usually fully occupied. My boss was a guy named Jack; he was also my boyfriend at the time and had gotten me my job. I learned a few things at the Hotel New Yorker, such as what a "shmear" was and what constituted the fine art of "shmearing." A guy would come up to the front desk and say, "Do you have anything for tonight?" and the answer would be, "No, there isn't a room left." Next, a strange little ritual transpired. The customer would reach over and shake the hand of the front-desk person and say something like "See what you can do." Then, the prospective lodger would walk away and hang around in the lobby. Sooner or later, the front-desk man would wave the guy back and say, "Well something seems to have turned up." I watched this go on for many, many nights. For the life of me, I couldn't figure out what the hell was happening. I asked Jack why there would suddenly be an available room.

"Look, Maureen," Jack explained, "we always keep a couple of rooms empty, and when a customer shmears us, we give him one of them. It's just a way of making a few extra bucks."

The lightbulb went on. "Oh, I get it," I said, "when the guy shakes hands, he's slipping you some bills, right?"

"Right."

"Oh, so that's shmearing?"

"Right."

One night I was out front picking up the registrations when all of a sudden Howard da Silva walked into the hotel and up to the front desk. Mr. da Silva had a distinguished career on the stage and made quite a few movies, too. He was, however, a character actor, not a leading-man type, and certainly not a "big" name. Remember, though, I was the broad who went bananas when she saw any celebrity, major or minor. So when da Silva walked in, my antennae went up. I stood by while the actor asked the clerk, "Are there any rooms for tonight?"

"No," was the answer.

"Sure there's a room for you, Mr. Howard da Silva," screamed number one movie fan Maureen Stapleton at the top of her lungs, "just wait a minute." I gave the high sign to the clerk and he had to register the guest. Boy, did Jack lay me out for that one. The room was gone, and thanks to me, so was the shmear. Jack lectured me pretty good about never doing that again. But it was *Howard da Silva,* and I was eighteen years old and knocked out just by the sight of him.

The New Yorker was one of my better jobs. I toiled there for over a year and even went to an employees' reunion not so long ago. For a brief time I took another job part-time in a paint factory way the hell downtown. Too far downtown; I think it was in Baltimore. By this time I was willing to work days as well as nights. I found an ad for Bonwit Teller's department store. They were paying seventy-five bucks a week for help, which sounded okay. Bonwit's had an indoctrination program for everybody who worked there, the main point of which was to teach the employees to have smiles on their faces at all times. If you were selling, even if your customer was a sonofabitch and treated you like a dog, you had to keep that grin pasted on your lips. They called it "The Bonwit Smile." I was placed in the charge department, where I kept that special smirk on my face and ran my butt off. The phones never stopped ringing and I never stopped smiling. I'd been there about three weeks when I went into a five-and-ten to buy a lipstick. I approached a salesgirl and asked where the cosmetics were. "Over there," she grunted and pointed to a counter. It dawned on me that the salesgirl had just said, "over there" without smiling. I thought to myself, "This broad's making the same money as I am, and she doesn't have to pretend to be happy about everything." I reassessed my situation and left the department store's employ shortly thereafter. I wasn't the Bonwit type, anyway.

Fortunately, I picked up a good position at the Chrysler Exhibit of War Weapons. Of all the things I had to do to keep myself going in those early New York years, this was my favorite. Chrysler was not making or selling cars at the time; like all the major industries, the company was geared to defense and turning out military equipment. Chrysler offered its automobile showroom at the corner of Lexington and 42nd Street to the Ordnance Department and they ran this exhibition of war weapons as a kind of PR deal. They had things such as land mines, part of a B-29 bomber plane, tanks, cannons, and a hell of a lot of rifles. Even though the equipment was slightly out-of-date, the public was eager to see the exhibits and they came in droves. A lot of them had kids who were overseas flying in those B-29's or firing those cannons.

Someone must have decided to treat the whole thing like an industrial show, so naturally they wanted to get girls to demonstrate the equipment. I applied for the job and was hired. There were fourteen of us girls, and we were called the "Ordinettes." I don't know what I liked most about being an Ordinette, but high on the list was wearing a uniform—it made me feel very WAACish. The Ordinettes were trained to show people around and explain things as quickly and as simply as possible. There was a brief lecture, then we demonstrated. We crawled in and out of the B-29 turret, pointed out the dangers of the minefields, slipped in and out of the tanks, and dismantled and reassembled the M1 Garand rifle. The Ordinettes went on publicity tours and got to travel to various military bases, too. Hey, nothing wrong with a bunch of eager young ladies being thrust among United States servicemen. I even dated a two-star general for a while!

The last job worth telling about you ain't gonna believe. I was a model. Now, I'm not talking about the high-fashion kind, of course, I'm talking about being a life model for art classes. What's more, I'm talking about posing for big-time artists. I'd met another aspiring actress named Janice Mars at my acting class, and we became great pals (and still are). Janice made money by modeling at the Art Students League and urged me to do it, too. At first I was skeptical. I was so damn self-conscious about my body, so uncomfortable in my ample skin, how the hell could I parade that too, too, solid flesh in public? Between Janice's prodding and my own desire to conquer my negative feelings for my form, I decided that modeling nude might be the solution. After all, it makes you strip away all your defenses as well as your clothes. I took myself over to the League and volunteered to pose. It paid a dollar an hour and usually you worked in the mornings from nine to twelve.

The first day was some event. I trembled and gagged as I wobbled into the center of the room, where I mounted a small podium and disrobed. I probably was saying Hail Marys at a machine-gun pace, I don't remember—everything was in a fog. I do recall that I developed a really high fever that afternoon. A doctor examined me and told me I was sick. I wasn't sick, I was just nutso from sitting naked in front of a bunch of strangers. I wanted to throw up. I didn't. I went back and posed again. That first week was hell and nearly killed me, but I finally got comfortable in my skin.

Reginald Marsh taught at the League. He saw me in the classes and asked if I would work for him at his studio. I quickly accepted his offer and worked for Reggie for quite a while. He passed me on to his friend Raphael Soyer, and Raphael introduced me to his brother Moses, another painter, and I posed for them, too. I also sat for a couple of other guys whose names elude me. Eventually, I dropped everyone except for Reginald and Raphael. I was zaftig, and that's what those guys wanted: a big, blubbery young dame. As far as recognizing myself in these guys' paintings, I can't. They weren't all portraits, so the faces didn't matter. Besides, there were other models, and when you take a mess of plump ladies they can look pretty much alike. One fat ass is the same as another, I guess.

Posing in the mornings made it possible for me to take acting classes at night and, later, to make the rounds looking for acting jobs in the afternoons. I couldn't go wild on the three or four dollars a day modeling paid, but it was good, clean money and was also my brush with the world of art. Now I was ready for the serious study of my chosen career; the question was, where?

While still in Troy I'd read a magazine article about an acting teacher in New York called Frances Robinson Duff. Maybe it was the three names that did it, or the fact that Ms. Duff's classes, at five hundred bucks, were way cheaper than the American Academy, or maybe it was because the classes met twice a week rather than daily—whatever the reasons, I decided Ms. Duff's classes were for me. I was wrong.

Ms. Duff taught in her townhouse on the East Side and employed something called the Delsarte system of acting. I paid the five hundred bucks and started classes. The Delsarte technique had to do with dividing everything into three parts: the emotional, the mental, and the physical. Your whole body had to conform to this separated triumvirate—everything, including your eyeballs and your eyelids and your hands and your fingers. Right there's where my trouble started; I never understood about dividing the body parts. I naively figured that I'd get it after I studied for a long time. Now I can barely recall the crap she tried to teach us. I remember there were certain positions for emotions like ecstasy and anger and rage and things like that, and all your different body parts were supposed to be acting away. By the time you put all this stuff to use it was kind of hard just to open a door!

There were a half-dozen or so girls in the group. They were nice enough and yet I knew right away that the majority of my classmates were dilettantes, rich girls—the kind who thought nothing of borrowing five cents for a phone call. I definitely was the poorest kid in the class—and also the most serious about what I was doing. The others were just messing around with acting, keeping busy till someone popped the question. I didn't dig Delsarte, and after four months I subtracted all three parts of me right the hell out Ms. Duff's door. Delsarte or no Delsarte, those classes were too close to the elocution lessons I'd endured in Troy. I wanted to find a school with pure motives, and pure motives for me meant low tuition and no dabblers. I think people who take lessons for fun, instead of being there because they have to or want to learn, spoil a school.

What I remembered most from Ms. Duff's classes had nothing to do with the Delsarte system; it had more to do with my philosophy. Dilettantes or no, we students were eager just to act, to play roles—*any* roles. One of the girls was different, however. This kid had her heart set on playing Saint Joan and only Saint Joan. That part was her be-all and end-all and she really was driven. This look would come over her face and she'd carry on about Joan of Arc being *the* part for her and how she could bring all her own experience and understanding to her interpretation.

She wanted it *so* badly that it scared me. I remember thinking, if this broad doesn't play Saint Joan, she's going to kill herself. I also remember thinking that I didn't *ever* want to play any role that much. It's tough enough just to get a job. I made up my mind then; I'd take whatever role I could get and be goddamn happy with it. It's an attitude that has been helpful in my career. Not needing to do a specific role made it possible for me to play all sorts of parts. And it's helped me in dealing with one of the theater's biggest heartaches: You create a role on stage, you may even win an award or two for it, and then what happens when it becomes a movie? Somebody else gets the part, somebody who's box office, like Julie Andrews losing *My Fair Lady* to Audrey Hepburn or Mary Martin losing *The Sound of Music* to Julie Andrews, stuff like that. Take me, for instance. I created the role of Serafina delle Rose in Tennessee Williams's *The Rose Tattoo* and won a Tony for it, too. The movie rights were sold, and they gave the part to Anna Magnani. You wanna know something? If I'd been the movie's producer, I would have picked her, too. Who the hell wants Miss Nobody Stapleton when you can get Miss Big Box Office Magnani? See, if I'd been like that dumb broad who *had* to play Saint Joan, I'd have eaten my insides out. I loved playing Serafina, but, hell, it was only a part and I moved on to the next one.

Once I'd shaken off the effects of Ms. Duff and her Delsarte method, I concentrated on finding a class better suited to my needs. Lucky for me, Isabel Cherry, a friend of my mother's, knew about the New School for Social Research. She took me down there to check out the place and that's how I came to study with Herbert Berghof. The New School had a broad curriculum and a liberal scheduling policy. Herbert Berghof taught acting there as well as at the more expensive Neighborhood Playhouse. I auditioned and was fortunate enough to get into his classes. Thus, I had the benefit of his expertise without having to pay the higher fees. Getting to study with him was the real beginning of my life in acting.

A Hell of a Life

Herbert Berghof was a terrific guy, one of the pioneers in the teaching of acting. He was Austrian-born and in the early thirties came to New York, where he worked as both an actor and a director. In the latter capacity, he staged the first American production of *Waiting for Godot.*

Herbert taught day and evening classes at the New School and I enrolled in the latter. In my mind the days were for the rich kids and the nights were for the poor kids, those of us who had to work during the day. I always made these arbitrary divisions between rich and poor because of my own background. I assumed all struggling young actors were poor like me, a belief that persisted long after I myself left the ranks of the poor and struggling. My hypothesis, however, was shot down a couple of times.

Once I had made it financially, I made it a point to look after deserving newcomers. When I appeared in *Plaza Suite,* one of the members of the company was this kid named Bobby Balaban. He was a good actor and a wonderful guy and I kind of took him under my wing. Nothing big, a few meals where I'd pick up the tab. Years later, at one of those theatrical gatherings I used to attend regularly, we were talking about different people and Bobby's name came up. I said something about knowing him and how hard it was to be a poor, struggling young actor.

"What are you talking about, Maureen," said the informant. "Bob Balaban's not poor; he's wealthy." I couldn't believe it. I was incensed. I found out that Bob was on location in Mexico filming *Catch-22* and got right on the phone and tracked him down.

"Bobby," I blasted into the receiver, "this is Maureen Stapleton."

"Hi, Maureen. How are you?"

"Never mind," I continued. "I have one question to ask you."

"What?"

"Why didn't you tell me you were rich?" There was a bit of a pause.

"You never asked," he answered. "Anyway," he added, "it's not me, it's my father."

"You're rich," I said.

"Well . . . yes," he declared.

"You sonofabitch" I yelled into the phone and hung up.

Another "poor struggling young actor" I knew was Austin Pendleton. I was in Washington, D.C., doing *The Country Girl* when Ethel Merman showed up at a party after the performance. We got to talking and in the course of the conversation, Austin Pendleton's name came up.

"Poor struggling Austin," said I.

"Whaddya mean poor?" bellowed Ethel, "Austin's rich."

"No he isn't," I snapped back.

"Yes he is," returned Merman emphatically. The brass in her tone indicated she knew what she was talking about. Another betrayal, I thought, and I let Austin have it the next time I saw him.

In truth, neither Austin nor Bobby had ever said he was needy. Later, the two of them called and invited me out to dinner. "Only one thing," they added. "If we take you, will you promise not to tell everybody that we're rich?" I promised, and I kept that promise till now.

I think they'll forgive me. Besides, I can't help it—I still equate "struggling young actor" with "need." When I was starting out, I didn't know there was any other kind, because all the ones I'd ever known were poor. Why would rich people want to go through all that, anyway? Jesus, they could buy their own theaters and star themselves. Why struggle?

Back to Herbert Berghof. We all loved H.B., but then, he was one lovable guy. At the time he was married to Alice Hermes. Later he would marry Uta Hagen; their H B acting studio is still going strong even though Herbert died in 1990. Alice Hermes was a voice teacher and very elegant. She spoke so perfectly that it intimidated the hell out of me. I could barely communicate with her; I felt like a vocal blob in her presence. It reminded me of Dorothy Parker's crack, "Every time I talk to an Englishman I feel like I have a papoose on my back." That's the way I felt when I talked to Alice Hermes. I took speech from her and one time had to read a poem aloud. The poem contained a line about the blue sky. I was nearly tongue-tied as I stood in front of Ms. Hermes and declaimed, and when I got to the "blue sky" bit, it came out something like ". . . the bell-you sky."

"Bell-you?" queried Miss Hermes. I remember blanching and thinking, "You better get the hell out of here, Maureen." I stuck it out, though, and it was Herbert who made the difference at first. I cannot tell you what actually went on in his classes. He talked a lot, and I know that I just loved being there and soaking up the atmosphere. Janice Mars once asked me what Herbert's teaching was about and why I liked it so much. I couldn't answer.

"You've been sitting there all year and you don't know?" said Janice.

"No, I don't," I replied, "all I know is I'm happy."

While I was studying with Herbert Berghof, my mother had herself transferred from a job in the state office in Albany to one in New York City. She wanted to be with me, and when my roommate, Cathleen, returned to Troy, I needed someone to share expenses. I was happy to welcome Mother. We'd been trading visits regularly, so it seemed to make sense. We lived together for nearly a year, and actually stayed in a convent for a brief period until we found a little apartment.

Mother was a very powerful force in my life. I'd bring my friends back to our place and Mom would join us. They all liked her; she was pretty smart and kept up with most things. I, for sure, didn't tell her *every*thing that was going on. For example, while she knew I was modeling, the word "nude" was never uttered.

When it comes to recalling exactly what scenes we prepared in Berghof's classes, I find my memory faulty once again. I remember that we did two one-act plays for our final presentation. In one I played some sort of mad girl, a religious zealot, and wore a long robe and emoted. I don't remember what the other play was about; I only know that unlike the flowing gown in the first one, my second costume was extremely scanty and that bothered me a lot. I was so upset by the costume, or lack of it, I couldn't get the part right. During rehearsals Berghof said,

"What's the matter with you, Maureen? You do the first play so well, why are you so stuck on this one?" I couldn't tell Herbert, but I was so totally inhibited by having on so little clothing, I couldn't even think about acting or being bad or good. Being scantily clad on stage wasn't like modeling, where it's just between you and the artist; I was up there with this itsy-bitsy covering and it made me crazy. It did teach me one thing: I have to have a lot of clothes on or I can't act at all.

In the summer of 1945, Herbert Berghof came up with a plan for a cooperative theater project. Full of enthusiasm and certain of success, he convinced twenty-two of his students to chip in 150 bucks each to cover expenses. The money was not easily come by but the opportunity was irresistible. Herbert had located a run-down shack he dubbed a theater and a hovel he designated as a dormitory in Blauvelt, New York, about thirty miles north of New York City. I left my Ordinette job at Chrysler and with great anticipation traveled upstate for what was planned as a ten-week season. At the same time, my mother returned to Troy.

For a while, Herbert's students had the best of times in the worst of places. We lived in a dump: the plumbing was prehistoric and the roof leaked. We had to do everything, too. We cleaned the rooms, we scrubbed the toilets, we cooked the food, we did the dishes, we made the beds, we sold the tickets, and we acted in the plays. Our work was so utterly concentrated that we didn't have time to think about what we were doing. The war ended and we were so caught up with our theatrical procedures that we could barely get out and cheer!

The Blauvelt season opened with *The Warrior's Husband,* which Katharine Hepburn had done on Broadway in 1932. This was followed by *Claudia* and *Three's a Family.* The artistic group didn't want to do *Kiss and Tell* because they felt it was too commercial. This gives you a good idea of the self-destructive quality of our troupe. The final play in the repertoire was *Noah,* an esoteric piece of gobbledygook by André Auber. I truly believe that opus sank us. The money ran out and after seven and a half weeks the participants began to abandon ship. The project folded and I, too, returned to the city, along with Janice Mars, another summer stocker. We planned to get an apartment together in New York.

Undaunted by the failure of the theater cooperative, Herbert Berghof decided he wanted to start his own drama school and rented space in José Limón's studios. Limón let rooms in his building to help finance his own dance company. Herbert taught classes and also hired another teacher, Mira Rostova. As I said, Herbert was wonderful. Yet, like anything else, what you're doing in class often depends upon the teacher. When you finally click into a teacher who brings everything together and makes it all crystal clear. For me, that teacher turned out to be Mira Rostova.

Mira was a Russian émigré who'd been a successful actress on the German stage. She was a tiny thing with a large, sorrowful face, an Edith Piaf type. She didn't talk much, but when she said something you knew precisely what she meant. She could put her finger on what was wrong or right; what everyone else simply told you, she made you understand. I had no personal relationship with Mira to speak of; it was just that under her guidance everything gelled and I knew better how to work. This was true for me and for others too, like Monty Clift. He said he'd never met anyone who could dissect a role as shrewdly as Mira. She really became his acting mentor. Monty's mother, a powerhouse, opposed Mira; she thought she had cast a spell on her son. I'd say he was inspired by Mira. "Clicked" is the operative word. Some people click in to one type of teacher, while others connect with another; if you're smart you latch on to the one who's most helpful to you. Look at all the great actors who clicked with Lee Strasberg at the Actors Studio; they practically worshiped him. I was fond of Lee and his family, but I never knew what the hell he was talking about. For my taste things got too guru-ish and cultish at the Actors Studio. I wanted a teacher, not a god. Mira Rostova was just that, a teacher.

In order to finance my lessons I prevailed upon Herbert Berghof to let me work for him. Different girl students (is that sexist?) took turns being his secretary, although none of us lasted too long. Herbert was a rather flaky businessman. Felicia Montealgre worked for him for a while, followed by Janice Mars and then yours truly. As a theatrical entrepreneur Herbert tended to follow his impulses, and unless you've got a bankroll the size of Fort Knox, impulses don't necessarily pay off in the theater. I remember walking down the street with him during my secretarial stint. He stopped and whirled around to look at me.

"We're going to put on a show next week. Send cards out to every producer, director, agent, every everything, and let them know, Maureen," he ordered.

"Herbert," I said, "there's not enough time to get all those names together and send out flyers. You can't do it. There's just no way."

"Isn't there a machine that can do it?" he asked.

"No, Herbert, there isn't," I returned.

"Oh," said Mr. Berghof. "Well, there should be!"

Janice Mars and I rented an apartment at 37 West 52nd Street between Fifth and Sixth Avenues. You didn't have to say "the Avenue of the Americas" back then; Sixth Avenue was Sixth Avenue. We were right down the street from Leon and Eddie's nightclub, a popular gathering place at the time that presented terrific shows. In the afternoon the nightclub roof would be opened to let in the fresh air, and from our little kitchen you could see right into the guts of the club. I spent many a happy P.M. puttering in the kitchen and looking through the window at the rehearsals on Leon and Eddie's dance floor.

I lived at that West 52nd Street address from 1945 to 1949 and our tiny one-bedroom apartment became a pit stop for all the actors in New York—that is, all the *aspiring young actors* in New York. While Janice and I paid the rent, the rule of the house was that whoever showed up, stayed. Indeed, virtually every theatrical hopeful who needed a roof over his/her head camped out there for a while; it was like Grand Central Station. Our landlady was an elderly woman who looked somewhat askance at us even though the rent was paid on time. There was so much activity that I'm sure the old dame thought Janice and I were hookers.

One of our most frequent guests was a young actor who was making his mark in the theater and soon would answer the call of Hollywood. His nickname was "Bud" and Bud had made a splash in *I Remember Mama*. He'd go on to do *Candida* with Katharine Cornell and in 1947 would hit the jackpot playing Stanley Kowalski in *A Streetcar Named Desire*. Marlon Brando was a great actor and a charter member of the 37 West 52nd Street regulars. Marlon was an original golden boy and you knew he was going to be big time just by the way he looked. Dames chased him and more often than not he'd let himself be caught. He was always wallowing in women. He'd drop by with his girl of the moment, and then go off and leave her with us. We were supposed to pick up the pieces. I spent hours—days!—listening to those poor girls sighing over Bud. Janice and I became profession-als at doling out tea and sympathy to Marlon's exes. Believe me, they needed plenty of tea and plenty of sympathy—he was something to sigh about.

Not only did Bud hang around the apartment, he'd sleep there too. He kept his drums in the closet and would haul them out and start banging away when the mood suited him. Eventually he rented a second-floor apartment in our brownstone. Marlon often brought over his hometown chum Wally Cox, and Wally stayed with us for a while, too. He and Bud had known each other in Libertyville, Illinois, and roomed together in New York.

Wally Cox was quite an individual, really an amazing guy. When he came to New York he made jewelry, beautiful jewelry, and had no theatrical aspirations. We used to push him to do monologues and whistling acts at parties. The talent was there and everyone encouraged him. Eventually Wally created a night-club act and then went on to television and *Mr. Peepers* fame. (That show also featured Tony Randall, another habitué of 37 West 52nd. Tony mentioned my apartment in the book he wrote with Mike Mindlin. I dated Mike and kiddingly told Tony that Mike's mother "sat shivah" every time her son went out with the goy from Troy. Don't you suppose Tony wrote it down?) Wally was so brilliant and so amazingly skillful at physical things. I mean, this guy could stand on his head and juggle and stuff like that, as well as talk knowledgeably on any subject.

I used to drag him to parties as my escort. He'd go begrudgingly, and whenever we went out he pinned a little watch to his lapel with the alarm set for 11:30 P.M. The alarm would sound, Wally'd pick up the dial, peer down at the numbers, and say, "It's time for me to go." And he'd leave, with or without me. I thought he was the shyest person I'd ever met (until I worked with Woody Allen). Wally once explained to me that he wasn't bashful.

"You've got me all wrong, Maureen. You think I'm shy; I'm not shy, I'm antisocial." I couldn't believe him. I didn't know there were such people; it was so foreign to me. It was true, though. Wally really didn't like parties and didn't care about meeting new people. The friends he had were the friends he kept. Naturally, I overrode his antisocial feelings and kept dragging him around with me. To his credit, that wonderful man squired me around and only deserted me when the alarm chimed. He died way, way too young.

A year passed, uneventfully in terms of my career. I took my lessons and made the rounds like everyone else, and, of course, things were hopping constantly at the apartment. I did do some summer stock in Mt. Kisco in the summer of '46. Shortly after returning to the city, I was sitting around a luncheonette one afternoon with a bunch of actors. Everyone was moaning as usual about how there were no acting jobs around and about how even if there were, we wouldn't get them.

"Well," one of the group said, "I heard that Guthrie McClintic is casting for a production of *The Playboy of the Western World*. Burgess Meredith's got the lead."

My ears perked up. Guthrie McClintic was a well-established actor, producer, and director; Brooks Atkinson, the *New York Times* critic, called him "one of our most accomplished directors, especially for plays that depend on taste and elegance." McClintic also was married to Katharine Cornell, a "First Lady of the American Stage" and herself the epitome of taste and elegance. Now he was doing *The Playboy.* I'd been in *The Playboy* in Mt. Kisco that summer. The actress who played the lead role of Pegeen Mike was a radio star. One night when she had to make good on a previous commitment, she'd gone to a broadcast studio and I stepped on stage as her understudy. I played Pegeen Mike. I felt that I was experienced. I knew this play. I could do it. The problem was how to let the director in on my suitability and availability. As Herbert Berghof's secretary, I'd called Guthrie McClintic's office on many occasions, and as far as I was concerned having the phone number was half the battle. So on a freak thing I called McClintic's office. On an even freakier note, he himself answered the phone, something that had never happened before.

"Guthrie McClintic," came the voice over the receiver.

"Mr. McClintic," I said, immediately leaping into my pitch, "my name is Maureen Stapleton and I played Pegeen Mike in stock this summer and I wondered who was going to play her in your production?"

Pause . . . long pause.

"I don't know who's going to play it, and I see no reason why I should tell you." His reply was curt and cold and entirely understandable. However, it ticked something off in me. Before I could even think about what I was saying, I bellowed into the telephone.

"Well, I don't give a goddamn who's going to play it, so you don't have to tell me."

I had started to hang up the receiver when I heard Mr. McClintic's voice saying, "How would you like to come and see me?" I put the phone back to my ear.

"Huh?"

"How would you like to come and see me, Miss Stapleton?"

"How—would—I—like—to . . ."

"Come and see me?"

"I'd like to."

I did go to see Guthrie McClintic and was shown into his office, where I stayed for three hours. Mr. McClintic loved to talk, or so I learned later, because I never shut *my* mouth during those 180 minutes. By the time I left he knew my entire story, including my pathetic lovelife, all those tragic little romances of mine that turned into disasters. I unburdened myself to Mr. McClintic. After my melodramatic monologue he showed me to the door. "I'll call you before the end of the week," he advised me.

That was a Tuesday and I never left the phone until he rang me that Saturday. He told me to be at such and such a place at such and such a time. I hung up the receiver and jumped in the air. I'd gotten my audition and the odd thing was, in all those three hours I was with him, I don't think the subject of *The Playboy of the Western World* ever arose.

At the appointed time I showed up at the designated place eager to try out. Only it wasn't a tryout; it was a first rehearsal. I had been hired by Guthrie McClintic without reading a word for him. I couldn't believe it.

The Playboy of the Western World opened at the Booth Theater on Monday, December 30, 1946, and I made my Broadway debut in the role of Sara Tansey, one of the village girls. Mildred Natwick, J. M. Kerrigan and J. C. Nugent were also in the cast and Eithne Dunne was cast as Pegeen Mike. Julie Harris played another village girl and we became fast friends during the production—another relationship which has endured all these years. I don't think I was that good in the part. Still, wonder of wonders, when Ms. Dunne had to leave and return to Dublin's Abbey Theatre, I stepped into the role of Pegeen Mike for the last eight performances. I was terrified at the beginning of those final shows, but I have to say it was my happiest terror. This production proved to be auspicious for me. Not only had I made it to the legitimate theater, I'd made a great friend and partisan. I owe so much to dear Guthrie McClintic. He put me to work and, more important, had more faith in me than I ever had in myself;

Guthrie thought I could do anything. Katharine Cornell came to see the show and visited backstage. What a gracious and lovely woman she was, so beautiful and with such a mellifluous voice. As close as I eventually became with the McClintics, and even though I called *him* by his first name, I never could call Miss Cornell anything other than Miss Cornell. I still can't. She asked me to call her "Kit," and I said, "Sure I'll call you Kit, Miss Cornell."

I suppose if I were going to have a role model in the theater, it easily might have been Katharine Cornell, or perhaps Laurette Taylor. I remember seeing Laurette in *The Glass Menagerie,* and while I couldn't say why I knew she was *numero uno,* I sure as hell knew it. She and Miss Cornell were quite different in style; it didn't matter, I never compare actors. Whatever their abilities, women like Miss Cornell, Laurette Taylor, and Jane Cowl had a very special ingredient—presence. Ruth Gordon had it, too. I saw a production of Chekhov's *Three Sisters* with Miss Cornell, Judith Anderson, Ruth Gordon, and Gertrude Musgrove that blew my mind. Lord, I don't even remember the men, I just remember being mesmerized by the presence of those women on the stage.

While I admired Miss Cornell and others, I never consciously considered choosing any person as a role model, in part because of the lesson I learned from the Delsarte girl who wanted to be Joan of Arc. Everyone has her own way of acting, of performing, and has to develop through her own experiences. However, I do think you can learn unconsciously from someone without making her a bona fide role model. Hell, I couldn't model myself after any one person; I'd go crazy. I've never seen an actress I didn't like, just like I never saw a movie I didn't like. I'm hopeless that way. When you watch a Julie Harris or a Colleen Dewhurst or a Zoe Caldwell, you just know they've got it. There are a lot of wonderful actors and actresses around today, and don't let anybody tell you otherwise. Every so often I'll see a young actor and think, "Wow, that's it." But while there are plenty of good actors, what there isn't as much of in the theater today is the kind of integrity and kindness personified by people like Miss Cornell and Mr. McClintic. I learned theatrical behavior from them. Guthrie was a walking encyclopedia of theater lore and loved to share his knowledge. He was a brilliant storyteller and one of the most considerate men I've ever met. My God, the man was directly responsible for my first three jobs in the theater! Miss Cornell was company oriented and very kind to everyone with whom she worked, from the biggest shots to the smallest. She even took the time to come to rehearsals with the understudies, which was unbelievable. I took it for granted that everyone behaved like those two; I thought that was what the theater was like, when actually it wasn't. They were exceptional.

The Playboy of the Western World had been produced by Theater, Inc., and when the run finished, Miss Cornell prepared to go on a ten-week tour with her own production of *The Barretts of Wimpole Street,* with Guthrie directing. I got the part of Wilson, the maid. Brian Aherne played Robert Browning to Miss Cornell's Elizabeth Barrett. Among the cast members were Tony Randall and Anne Jackson, another aspiring young actress with whom I became very close and who remains a dear and faithful friend. I had met Anne Jackson previously, when she came to a play reading I was doing. In those days, young actors were either reading plays or listening to other actors read them just to keep busy. I'm sure the practice still goes on. Anne and I were introduced, and though we were about the same age, Annie told me she thought I was years older. Then when she got to know me, she decided I must be at least twenty years younger. I was that naive. And, in fact, Annie was much more street-smart than I.

We were both nuts about movies and read movie magazines all the time, a habit I had developed back in Troy. On occasion, however, I'd slip a poetry book behind the covers of *Modern Screen* and pretend to be catching up with Hollywood when I really was caught up in verse. Annie found me out and decided she had my number. "You're an incurable romantic, Maureen," she told me, "absolutely beyond help." And actually, she was right. Basically, I've never wanted to deal with reality; I want "magic."

Even at that stage of my life I was apprehensive about traveling, and here I was in a *touring* company no less! Annie and I roomed together during the tour, traveling by train the whole way. We were going across country to California when difficulties concerning one company member arose. Wilfrid Lawson had been cast as Barrett senior, and though he might not be remembered readily today, this guy was a fabulous actor. He was English and lionized in his home country; young performers like Richard Burton and Albert Finney worshiped at his throne. Unfortunately, Lawson had become a major drinker and was slowly slipping into a decline. They said he had a steel plate in his head plus a lot of physical problems and that's why he drank. Who the hell knows? I only know he was a brilliant actor and Miss Cornell and Guthrie respected his ability enough to hire him.

The tour was scheduled to end in San Francisco after ten weeks, and the closer we came to the West Coast, the more Wilfrid Lawson's elbow began to bend. Miss Cornell and Guthrie were as kind and thoughtful to him as they were to everybody else, although the further we got into the tour, the more difficult he became. In each town something else would happen and Lawson would not show up. One time we were standing in a railroad station and Miss Cornell had the train held while cast members searched for the missing actor. The train didn't budge till he was dragged into the station. I don't know how the hell she did it. Things got so bad that Guthrie assigned one of the company members, Edward Cooper, to act as Lawson's bodyguard. Wilfrid caught on and poor Mr. Cooper suffered the consequences. The two of them were standing behind the railing on the caboose, and as the train pulled out of the station, Lawson pushed his "bodyguard" over the side and onto the tracks. Fortunately the train wasn't traveling fast; still, Edward Cooper was mighty shook up. That was the end of the personal bodyguard system. After that, watching out for Wilfrid became a company enterprise. Annie and I were asked to keep an eye on him and many times had to go through alien streets searching for the errant actor. In San Francisco at the tour's end, Wilfrid Lawson finally disappeared for good; no one could find him. His understudy didn't know all the lines, so Guthrie had to play the part a few times. Since there were a couple more weeks scheduled, Miss Cornell and Guthrie were forced to hire another actor, and Cedric Hardwicke stepped in for the remaining performances. Mr. Lawson turned up eventually, in New York I think, but as far as I know, that was the end of his stage career.

While Lawson was with the company, he kept some of us on our toes *off* the stage as well as on. He liked the company of young women. At least he did when he was sober. Intoxicated, I think he'd have tried to score with Barbara Frietchie. He latched on to me early on, but I could handle him. When Annie and I went in search of him, she usually was apprehensive. Her father was a reformed drinker and she thought you could help alcoholics; I knew from *my* father that you couldn't. She wasn't too keen about dealing with our colleague, but I'd reassure her by suddenly talking very maturely: "Don't worry, I know how to handle drunks, I know all about it." It must be said that I didn't drink myself at that time and really believed I knew everything about everything. Obviously, I didn't. And I especially didn't know how to deal with men, sober or drunk. Annie swears she expected me to get into trouble because I never knew my worth, and hadn't differentiated between lust and love. The trouble came because I always felt if anyone said he needed me, then he should have me. I'd tell my stories to Annie and she'd just shake her head. I told her about an old actor who chased me around the room. I really was worried he was going to have a heart attack, so I stopped running. It was an act of mercy; I was saving his life. Annie didn't buy it. She said I should learn to deal with these situations and not just capitulate. I was a girl who couldn't say no, because I didn't want to hurt people's feelings. I also told my stories to Betty, a friend of Annie's. We young actresses always exchanged tales and dispensed advice. Betty was Irish, but wealthy and a helluva lot more sophisticated than I; her counsel was freely given and went right to the point. "Don't give it away, darling," she admonished. "Get paid for it." Oh God, if only I'd listened to her, surely I'd be living off the fat of the land instead of writing my memoirs.

Earlier in the tour, when we were in Los Angeles, Annie and I shared a room in the Hotel Figueroa in downtown L.A. As I said, the two of us got along just great. I was a pretty good companion except for my fear of travel and my disgusting eating habits. I love to have Anne tell the story about me and my breakfast ritual. She swears the only time she ever saw me act aggressively was in a food line. Come hell or high water, I had to have my breakfast in the morning—in those days it was orange juice and a bran muffin. Maybe it was a holdover from my early child-hood, but if I didn't get that meal into me pronto, I was useless. We'd be in one of those terrible touring-hotel cafeterias and I'd storm up to the counter, elbowing my way through the line right up to the front. "All your sensitivity and beauty is lost when your stomach is growling," Annie told me. I knew she was right, but it didn't change anything. Some habits just can't be broken. I still eat like a trencherman.

While we were in L.A., movie stars would come backstage to see Miss Cornell and Guthrie. I'd sit on the stairs and watch them walk by. They came so close that I could almost touch them. I was very impressed. Once, Greer Garson came back to Miss Cornell's dressing room. She was the queen of Metro-Goldwyn-Mayer at the time, a beautiful ivory-skinned redhead and a fine actress. I remember Miss Garson's visit in particular because Gertrude Macy, the company manager, ushered the MGM star backstage.

"Can you believe it?" I gushed to Gertrude when she emerged from the dressing room. "Greer Garson is in there right now!"

"Who's Greer Garson?" she asked innocently. That phrase became a byword for the rest of the company.

After the *Barrett* tour I signed on with Miss Cornell again to appear in Shakespeare's *Antony and Cleopatra*. This production was slated for Broadway. I played Iras, one of two handmaidens to the Queen of the Nile. The other handmaiden, Charmian, was played by Lenore Ulric. Miss Ulric had been a big star for, and mistress of, David Belasco in her early theater days. She'd gone to Hollywood and made films, including *Camille* with Garbo, and returned to Broadway not so much wiser as older. Nobody knew her anymore, not that she cared; she knew who she was.

Although playing handmaiden to Katharine Cornell was big stuff to me, it had to be somewhat of a comedown for Miss Ulric, who'd been a star in the 1920s. However, if it were a setback, you'd never have known from her; she played Charmian as if she were Cleopatra. Miss Cornell, that consummate lady, actually let Miss Ulric use the star dressing room on the road while the "star" herself stayed in the second dressing room. Could anyone imagine such a generous act today? Miss Ulric, as befitted a person of her temperament, was somewhat vain, and this vanity could get in the way. Her eyesight was poor, yet she refused to wear glasses even when putting on makeup. In New York, she could barely maneuver herself when she came downstairs from our second-floor dressing room to reach the stage, both because she could not see and because she wore amazingly high heels. Since Miss Ulric and I shared a dressing room in New York, I was appointed to oversee her makeup and help her down the stairs of the Martin Beck Theater.

"Shall I check your makeup?" I'd ask politely as we made ready to leave the dressing room.

"Sure, dear," said Miss Ulric, turning away from the mirror and toward me.

"Oh, it's perfect," I'd say, looking at a face that, to put it gently, had been assaulted by cosmetics. There'd be rouge on her eyelashes and eyeshadow on her cheeks and lipstick on her teeth.

"Just a bit needs to be blended, Miss Ulric, here . . . and there." So saying, I'd fiddle around and fix her up as best I could. I wasn't exactly Perc Westmore myself; they didn't teach makeup in my acting classes, and I had to learn by osmosis.

When Miss Ulric's face had been adjusted, I'd help her down the stairs and we'd stand in the wings waiting to go on. There were four women and about thirty guys in the cast, including Tony Randall. Just before our entrance a bunch of the men had a scene. They'd line up on a turntable backstage, which then would revolve around to the front of the proscenium carrying the participants. One night, Miss Ulric and I stood by, waiting as the spear carrying, kyton-clad actors took their positions on the turntable. The lights dimmed, and slowly the turntable began to move past us, bearing the bare-legged gentlemen. Miss Ulric leaned her head over and, as though we were shopping in Macy's, nodded toward the rotating tableau and inquired, "See anything you like, dear?" Up to that moment I'd called her Miss Ulric; from then on she was Lenore and we became pals.

The turntable figured in another story. Charlton Heston made his Broadway debut in *Antony and Cleopatra*. He played a lieutenant or something like that, and in his one scene was supposed to come on stage crying, "Hail Caesar, I have dispatches," at which point he handed a bunch of scrolls to Caesar. Caesar's chair was placed on the turntable, and the seated Caesar would be revolved onto the stage as Heston walked in from the wings. One night Heston stepped out and stood waiting for the stage to revolve and Caesar to appear. The stage turned and the chair came into view . . . with no occupant. Caesar had missed his cue and was nowhere to be seen. Charlton Heston stood there for a moment or two and then began looking around furtively. Seeing that nothing was happening, he waved the scrolls over his head and stalked off into the wings crying, "Ahoy, Caesar." Where he got that "ahoy" from, I'll never know.

All things considered, Lenore Ulric did pretty damn well in *Antony and Cleopatra*. Her behavior, however, could be idiosyncratic, to say the least. For one thing, she talked a lot about David Belasco. "I don't know if D.B. would approve of this," she'd say, or, "D.B. would love this." Since D.B. had been dead for fifteen years, I doubted that he'd have had an opinion one way or another. Throughout the run of the play Lenore would be in and out, sometimes in the present and sometimes back with D.B. When she was on, though, by God she was *on*. There was one line of mine that was supposed to be a big laugh for me. Iras and Charmian are consulting with a soothsayer and Iras says, "Am I not an inch of fortune better than she?" Charmian replies, "Well, if you were but an inch of fortune better than I, where would you choose it?" To which Iras answers, "Not in my husband's nose." I never got a laugh. The way Lenore Ulric read her line, *she* got the laugh. Everybody told me how to say that damn line, and I tried every suggestion and read it every way possible. *"Not* in my husband's nose. Not *in* my husband's nose. Not in *my* husband's nose. Not it my *husband's* nose. Not in my husband's *nose.*" Still, I never got the laugh. Never.

One night, Kent Smith, who was playing Enobarbas, made the mistake of saying to Guthrie, "Hey, Maureen got a titter tonight on her laugh line." Guthrie bristled and said, "She gets a laugh every night." I never did; everyone else in the company knew I didn't, but Guthrie was convinced the laugh was mine. In all those weeks of *Antony and Cleopatra,* he remained certain that I was getting the chuckles and not Lenore Ulric.

Guthrie's "Maureen can do anything" blind spot invariably clouded his judgment. The "laugh" was minor; his worst miscalculation had to do with my singing ability. We used to do a lot of warbling at parties where we'd stand around a piano and go through all the popular hits. And when we toured on the trains, we'd stay up until the wee hours singing songs. Hell, anybody can sing along with a group, and I had no illusions about my talent. I was strictly amateur. Not for Guthrie, who thought I was a combination of Jeanette MacDonald and Judy Garland. He called up one night out of the blue, and announced that he'd arranged for an audition for me to replace Ella Logan in the musical *Finian's Rainbow.*

"What are you talking about, Guthrie? I can't sing in a show!"

"You sing all the time."

"Yeah, with everybody else, at parties. I can't sing in a show! I can't. I can't. I can't."

"You will. You will. You will."

Well, I couldn't argue with him. I had to try out. My friend Janice Mars was my accompanist and we went to the audition with sheet music from some show or other. All of the muck-a-mucks were seated in the theater when I came out and announced that I would sing. I opened my mouth and sang. After the last note rang out, the muck-a-mucks rose up, came down the aisle, and stood in front of the stage.

"You could never sing this score," they said, politely but firmly.

"I know, I know," I replied and left the theater. I called

Guthrie and said, "Guthrie, I went to the audition and I was terrible. They said I could never sing the score."

"You'll practice. We'll hire a voice teacher."

"*No,*" I cried, "I'm not going to do it. You're driving me crazy."

Guthrie wouldn't take no for an answer. "Listen, you'll go back and show them." I never did go back, and Guthrie never did understand how his Irish nightingale could go unrecognized and unsung.

During the run of *Antony and Cleopatra,* I really became very fond of Lenore Ulric. Years later, when I was appearing in *The Rose Tattoo,* I found an old sepia photograph of her in a theater shop. She was wearing a frilly, feathery negligee in what was obviously a publicity shot from *Kiki* or one of those plays she did for D.B. I bought the picture, figuring I'd give it to her when next we met. A short while later, Lenore called to say she was coming to see me in the play and I told her to come backstage afterward. Tennessee Williams and his friend Frank Merlo were going to be there, too, and I alerted them that Lenore would be joining us for dinner. The three of them trooped into my dressing room and sat down while I got ready.

"Lenore," I said just before we left for Sardi's, "I have a surprise for you." I pulled open a drawer in my dressing table and took out the picture. Lenore accepted the envelope and slid out the photograph. I expected to hear a squeal of delight and something like, "Oh my God, where did you ever find that?" Nossir, not Miss Ulric. She looked at the picture and said, "Oh, that negligee was never right," and then she went on and on about the feathers and the trim and everything else in the picture. I guess she just thought everybody had a vintage photograph of Lenore Ulric tucked away.

The four of us went off to Sardi's, and Tennessee was charm itself. Lenore was very taken by him. She flirted shamelessly, furiously batting her astigmatic eyes.

"Oh, Mr. Williams, it's so wonderful being with you," she

gushed. "And you know, I would like you to write a play just for me." Tennessee smiled his sweetheart smile, leaned forward, took her hand in his and drawled, "Wah, mah de-ah Miss Ulric, all mah plays were written for you."

Frank Merlo had been watching Lenore very closely and at last said, "Tenn, look at her eyes, they're so beautiful, so amazing." Lenore's eyelashes went into overdrive as Frank continued. "Wouldn't she be wonderful as Amanda?" The fluttering lashes came to a dead halt. Wide-eyed, Lenore Ulric turned to Frank and growled, "Amanda? That's a *mother* part. There's not a maternal bone in my body." Thus Lenore Ulric dismissed one of the greatest roles in American dramatic literature and turning back to Tennessee Williams, cheerfully suggested that he rewrite *Kiki* for her and bring it up to date. What divine *chutzpah.*

After Guthrie McClintic took me under his theatrical wing, I became part of the McClintic-Cornell extended family. They often invited me to their home in Sneden's Landing, where they rented and then built a magnificent house. Sneden's Landing was a posh enclave on the Hudson, and spending a few days there was like a month in the country. Those visits were wonderful and exhilarating. Guthrie was my confidant. I told him everything and he listened intently. I complained a lot, mostly about my desire to meet Mr. Right. He took this to heart and decided the main objective was to get me a man. I made the mistake of telling him I had a crush on one of the actors in the company. Years later, that actor told me that Guthrie had gone to him and said, "Maureen Stapleton likes you. Why don't you ask her out for a date?" The object of my admiration informed Guthrie that he was gay and not interested in Maureen Stapleton. Guthrie was furious. He didn't give a damn what the guy was, he thought he should date me anyway, just to make me happy. All Guthrie wanted to do was make things nice for me and in his mind, getting me a man was the way to do it. The first time I went out to Sneden's Landing for the weekend, Guthrie was already there and I was to drive up with Miss Cornell and Gertie Macy after the Saturday-evening performance. During the show that night Lenore Ulric, Miss Cornell, and I were offstage for a long stretch when Miss Cornell turned to me and said, "Maureen, I've got to ask you something."

"Sure, Miss Cornell, ask away."

"I'm delighted that you're joining us at Sneden's, but do you really need to have a man for the weekend?"

"Huh?" I didn't know what she was talking about.

"Look dear, Guthrie is driving me crazy. He keeps saying we've got to find a man for you. It's like going shopping for the weekend—we have to get eggs, juice, milk, and a man for Maureen."

"It's okay, Miss Cornell," I stammered. "Just get the eggs, juice, and milk, don't worry about a man." Later, on the way up to Sneden's, Gertie Macy was apprised of the situation. "Well," she said, "since I'm wearing slacks and a tailored shirt, I'm in drag, so there'll be a man for Maureen."

I learned so much working with Miss Cornell and took every opportunity to watch her. During the *Antony and Cleopatra* run, she agreed to do a scene from *Saint Joan* for a benefit performance after the regular theater hours. Guthrie asked me if I wanted to watch the rehearsal. Naturally, I jumped at the chance. What I saw was interesting. Miss Cornell started out kind of cold. The more she rehearsed, the more tired she got; and no wonder, she'd just done an entire evening's worth of Shakespeare. Oddly enough, the more tired she got, the better she got. She had so much on her mind, what with being both actress and producer and having to think about the entire company, not just her own part, that she brought this baggage with her. It wasn't until she'd been exhausted by the rehearsing that she really let loose, and by the sixth run-through, she knocked me out.

Miss Cornell was a natural-born lady, and while she didn't hold herself aloof, she had an innate reticence. Marlon Brando was a member of the Cornell troupe, and I think she may have been the one person in the theater that he really respected. Probably the reason was that Miss Cornell may have been the only woman he'd ever met who didn't try to get in his pants. After the shows Guthrie and I would sit up half the night talking; she usually went home. On rare occasions she'd join us and was marvelous company. She wasn't a shmoozer, but there wasn't a more thoughtful or caring person around. One Saturday I went home between the matinee and evening performance, lay down on my sofa, and fell asleep. The next thing I knew, the stage manager, Winky Lewis, was standing by the couch saying, "Maureen, there's thirty minutes to curtain. You've got to get up." When I hadn't shown up at the theater, they thought something was wrong and Winky had come after me. For a moment I just looked dazedly at him, and then, realizing what was going on, I leaped up, grabbed my coat, and ran past him out the door, down the stairs, and into the street. I jumped into a cab, and as it drove away I began taking off my dress underneath my coat. The taxi driver looked into the rearview mirror and did a doubletake. I yelled at him, "You keep going, I'll do the acting."

We arrived at the theater and I ran inside. The understudy was about to step into my dress when I threw my coat off and grabbed the costume out of her hands. I put it on, slapped the wig on my head, and rushed onto the stage. Miss Cornell was standing there, and as we waited for the curtain to rise, she whispered, "Oh, Maureen, I was so worried about you. Winky called and told us what happened and all I could think of was how terribly upset you'd be when you woke up." I couldn't believe what I was hearing. There was no "How dare you jeopardize the performance"; nothing like that, just her concern for how awful I would feel because I nearly screwed up. That was typical of Katharine Cornell, truly a class act.

Chapter Three

For those who think the Actors Studio and Lee Strasberg are synonymous, they ain't; at least not for me and others who were with the Studio from its inception. The Actors Studio didn't spring full-blown from the head of Lee Strasberg, it was the brainchild of Robert Lewis, Elia Kazan, and Cheryl Crawford. Kazan was a member of the Group Theatre before he became a leading director for stage and screen in the forties and fifties. Bobby Lewis was an actor, director, and producer who'd worked with the Group Theatre. He's taught at Yale and Sarah Lawrence and is still involved with the theater. The late Cheryl Crawford was a producer with the Theatre Guild in the late twenties and a founder of the Group Theatre. When three people get together to start something, there are bound to be a minimum of three different versions of how the thing began. Kazan supposedly approached Bobby Lewis, then the two of them decided to bring in Cheryl as a business manager. Whatever the exact process, The Actors Studio opened in October of 1947. It really wasn't a school; it was a *workshop* for *professionals* and charged no tuition.

Right away, the Studio fit my criteria for pure motives—it was free and the students were serious.

Lewis taught the more advanced group and Kazan the beginners. I'd been in a couple of Broadway shows but technically was a beginner and should have started with the group of young actors Elia Kazan wanted to "mold." However, I was recommended directly to Bobby Lewis by my friends Kevin McCarthy and Monty Clift. I went for an interview and can't remember if I did a scene or not; knowing me, I probably went into one of those monologues from life as I had for Guthrie McClintic. Whatever I did, I leapfrogged into the advanced group. Even though I was accepted into Bobby Lewis's class, I didn't feel I belonged. Julie Harris, who'd been with me in *The Playboy,* was in Gadg Kazan's group and so were Betsy Drake, Steven Hill, Cloris Leachman, James Whitmore, and Jocey Brando, Marlon's sister. I sure as hell wasn't more practiced than any of those guys, yet my class included Herbert Berghof, Marlon Brando, Montgomery Clift, Mildred Dunnock, John Forsythe, Sidney Lumet, Karl Malden, E. G. Marshall, Pat Neal, Billy Redfield, Jerome Robbins, Beatrice Straight, Eli Wallach, and David Wayne. I may not have belonged with them, but I was very happy to be there.

Under the Actors Studio aegis, Kazan and Lewis went their individual teaching ways. In the second year, probably for artistic reasons, Bobby Lewis resigned from the Studio. He remains a good friend today, but I still don't know why he left. And I'm not about to quiz him on it some forty-odd years later, either. For a long time, there were different guest teachers in his spot, people like Josh Logan and Danny Mann. Then Lee Strasberg came, and he stayed and his name became so associated with the Actors Studio that people forget he didn't start it.

Since most actors are out of work most of the time and need to flex their dramatic muscles, the Studio filled a real need. It provided the opportunity to practice and polish your craft. What's more, you weren't stereotyped. At the same time Marlon Brando was playing Stanley Kowalski in *Streetcar* on Broadway, he was portraying the Archduke Rudolf Maximilian in *Reunion in Vienna* at the Studio. It was the kind of thing the Studio wanted, or as Cheryl Crawford put it, the aim was to offer "a sort of artistic home to the many young actors and actresses who wanted to stretch their capabilities, a sympathetic atmosphere in which they could tackle their limitations."

I tackled my limitations by playing roles like Masha in a Studio production of *The Seagull* under Bobby Lewis's direction. In 1954, when I did the same part in a production of the Chekhov classic at the Phoenix Theatre, thanks to my work with Bobby, I had a strong base upon which to build my interpretation.

When Bobby left the Studio, I continued my work with Lee Strasberg. I had my reservations. The simple fact is, I thought Lee talked too much and what he said was so convoluted, I didn't get it. It doesn't matter how fabulous a reputation a teacher may have: If someone's method doesn't work for you, then you're in the wrong place. My feeling was that if others could respond to him, okay, let them respond. All his talk drove me nuts. Moreover, Lee also exhibited a kind of rigidity that didn't appeal to me. I got along with him personally and kidded him, too. Still, I kept a working distance. I especially didn't like that "private moment and sense memory" stuff he pushed. It's okay up to a point, but that point too often was reached and then left in the dust. Who wants to see people get hysterical and start crying and moaning for real? To my way of thinking, unless you're a therapist or a doctor, you stay out of certain places in the human psyche. Frankly, I don't think Sigmund Freud was as nosey as Lee Strasberg. The whole business just didn't sit well with me; his classes could be disquieting at the very least and, in their most flagrant moments, downright intrusive. Furthermore, I think the actors often were encouraged to indulge themselves. They'd get up to do a scene and the preparation went on forever. Sometimes they wouldn't utter a line for ten or fifteen minutes! And the stuff they'd do for preparation; I mean, they'd start pouring talcum powder on each other and give each other massages to get into the right frame of mind or whatever. I remember watching this kind of idiocy and thinking, "I've got to get home. I've got a house and children to take care of. I can't hang around and watch this nonsense." All those jokes about "the Method" came from those excesses, especially when the preparation culminated in a "bedroom" scene. For a while everything had to have some sort of sexual connotation or action. I used to steel myself to walk into the Studio, because I knew that there would be a "bed" on the stage.

Once I got a call from a friend of mine who stuck it out at the Studio long after I'd stopped going. "Do you know who was in the Studio this morning?" he asked. "Prepare yourself, Maureen; Helen Hayes brought Ina Claire to observe." I'm sure Helen Hayes needs no introduction, but Ina Claire isn't as well known anymore. She was one elegant actress, let me tell you, in the old tradition where theatrical training did not include simulated intercourse or similar shenanigans.

"Don't tell me they did one of those scenes on the bed?" I cried.

"You got it!" answered my friend. The idea of Ina Claire and Helen Hayes being subjected to a clothes-tearing grappling on a broken-down bed was mind boggling. Much later, I was talking to Helen, a wonderful, down-to-earth lady, and couldn't resist asking her about that visit and what Ina Claire thought about the Studio.

"Don't ask," said Helen. "I don't know, I don't know. I've tried to forget. All I remember is, I took her to Sardi's afterward and got drunk."

People who didn't know Helen often typed her as prim and proper—maybe because she played Queen Victoria on the stage. Helen Hayes was a lady to her fingertips, but she wasn't prissy, far from it. She assured me that my language never upset her, because her husband, Charlie MacArthur, used words I never heard of. Even folks in show business put her on a pedestal. The first time I was introduced to Danny Kaye, he shook my hand and said, "Maureen Stapleton, oh yes, I've heard of you. You're the one who says 'fuck' in front of Helen Hayes."

I went to the Actors Studio steadily for about ten years and then I just stopped going. I'm still a charter member, though, and will always have a soft spot in my heart for that special working place. The truth is, if it isn't abused, the Method can help. The Method school of acting came from the theories of Konstantin Stanislavsky, director of the Moscow Art Theatre. Stanislavsky encouraged actors to "respond as much to their own inner feelings as to the requirements of the text or dramatic effectiveness." While I believe it's all well and good to give yourself over and plumb your own depths for the part, I'm afraid the Method often became a matter of self-indulgence and self-consciousness. Furthermore, I didn't think it was *the* one and only way to do things any more than I believed that the Delsarte Method was the be-all and end-all. You have to be real and alive and fresh in the part each time. That's your job, and there are many roads to good acting. I've been asked repeatedly what the "key" to acting is, and as far as I'm concerned, the main thing is to keep the audience awake.

There is one thing I've noticed about the business of acting that bears mentioning, however: I think it's a lot harder on men because of the way it's set up. If acting is your job, career, occupation, whatever, then you know you're in deep shit from the beginning, because you are most likely going to be out of work a great deal of the time. A woman can be out of work and it doesn't reflect on her womanhood. It may not be a very modern or politically correct point of view, but, basically, I believe people feel that a woman's place is in the home; that is to say, her primary role is as wife and mother and not necessarily career girl. So, if an actress is "between engagements," she's not looked upon as a total washout. For a male actor to be out of work is a double whammy. Not only isn't he working, his idleness is a reflection on his manhood. I mean, the guy is supposed to be out there earning his keep, and if he isn't, he's a failure.

In the beginning, the Studio definitely helped me keep my oars in the water. I was like an athlete going to the gym to train. It was a workout, and, in another sense, it was like attending graduate school. You got the basics at undergraduate places like the Neighborhood Playhouse, the American Academy, and the New School, and then you'd go on to the higher level. I loved being there and having the opportunity to participate in great plays and I did fine—as long as someone else chose my material. I had a positive gift for picking the wrong vehicles. Twice I chose my own scenes and both of them flopped. One was from *Liliom* and I essayed the ingenue lead. I don't remember the other play; I'm sure it was another sweet young thing. I longed to portray innocent, youthful heroines, but it wasn't in the cards. Except for Pegeen Mike and Wilson the maid, I rarely got the chance to play someone near my own age. Yes, it had to do with my weight, but even after I lost pounds and pounds, I still played ladies of descending rather than ascending summers. Now I've at last reached the point in my life where I can play women of my own (hoary) age.

The Actors Studio had everything going for it and so many brilliant and gifted people going to it. Lots of them were acquaintances and many were sleeping-bag alumni of 37 West 52nd Street. Although he was partly responsible for getting me into the Actors Studio, Montgomery Clift didn't stay there for long. Like Marlon Brando, he was sucked up by Hollywood pretty quickly. While he was at the Studio, we worked together on scenes from *Crime and Punishment.* For some reason we never actually performed them; we just rehearsed endlessly. That was fine with me; I loved working with Monty, and I loved him, too. He was bright and friendly and a brilliant actor. He also was ridiculously handsome, though for some godknowswhat reason, he hated his good looks. Truly, he seemed "happier," if that's the word, after the automobile accident that so changed his features. Monty had been at a dinner party at Elizabeth Taylor's house and while driving home in the foggy evening had crashed his car into a telephone pole. His face was smashed, but according to the doctor who operated on him, Monty had no plastic surgery done, just reconstruction, especially of his teeth, almost all of which had been knocked out. The story of the crash and of how Elizabeth Taylor crawled into the car to cradle his broken and bleeding head in her arms and comfort him till the ambulance came was well chronicled. I heard about it and remember thinking at the time that Elizabeth Taylor had to be one special broad.

A Hell of a Life

Years later, when we worked together in *The Little Foxes,* I found out that my assessment was right on the money.

Monty made the movie *The Young Lions* after the accident, and it was the only time he ever asked me to come and see him in anything. He was very proud of his work, and I couldn't help thinking that he felt that with his face disfigured, he could be judged by his performance rather than his looks. Monty Clift fought an uphill battle. Sadly, his personal difficulties invaded his professional life. God knows what demons he had torturing him.

When I first knew him, he took such good care of himself. He watched what he ate and at parties would drink very little and leave very early. I remember watching him nurse one drink through the entire evening. My God, he was practically a health nut! By the time we appeared together in *The Sea Gull* at the Phoenix Theatre, he was into serious drinking. At that time, I was drinking, too, although not like him; nobody drank like him. Monty didn't have a vodka; he'd have a triple vodka and that was to begin with. Why the hell he did it, I don't know. Some people say he was torn apart because of his sexual ambivalence. Hell, if Monty was tortured by homosexuality, he certainly didn't show it in the days when he was looking after himself. No, that's too pat. Whatever turned him on to the sauce was probably more complicated, and I'm hardly the one to say what makes someone drink. All I know is I couldn't bear watching what happened to that beautiful man. It got worse and worse.

He bought a town house in the East 60s where he gave many dinner parties. By the end of the evening, he'd be on the floor, totally out of it. One night, Roddy McDowall was there when Monty went zilch and flopped to the ground. I started crying and told Roddy, "We've got to do something. This can't go on; we've got to help him." Roddy, one of the best people in the world, said very simply and sadly, "The only thing we can do, Maureen, is hold his hand to the grave." All Monty's friends wanted to save him; Marlon really tried. He offered to do anything to help, even to going with Monty to A.A. That wonderful good-buddy quality of Marlon's is often overlooked; he could be a thoughtful, caring guy. I still have the telegram he sent when I opened in *Richard III* at City Centre: "Don't fall in the pit, don't back into any spears, lift your dress up when you go down the stairs. Be good. Thinking of you, Marlon." You could publish Marlon's cable as a classic "advice to the actor."

Once, Monty was talking to Marlon, protesting that he didn't drink that much, and the whole time he had one of those lethal triple vodkas in his hand. Through it all, he kept insisting he was okay. Sometimes in talking to me, Monty would slip a bit and mention his problem. I'd say, "Why don't we go to A.A. together?" He'd toy with the idea and pretend to be interested but never grabbed the hook. The poor bastard was like a runaway horse and nothing could stop him. I tried, Marlon tried, all his friends tried, to no avail.

But what an actor Monty Clift was. There's one scene in *The Misfits* where Monty's character is in a phone booth talking to his mother and it's so magnificently real and true. Every time I see it, I get the same kind of chill. Monty started out with more gifts than most people ever get in a lifetime. It makes me sick to think of the way his brilliance dissipated.

Fortunately, there were actors in our group who had great gifts and *didn't* squander them. Julie Harris is a perfect example. She did remarkable things both in the Studio and on the stage. There's something about that woman—always was and still is. I remember going to see her in *The Lark,* Lillian Hellman's adaptation of Anouilh's *L'Alouette.* The play was about the trial of Joan of Arc. Well, Miss Julie Harris did a number in the first act that completely knocked me out. Joan was brought out of the cellar where they'd been interrogating her for three days and nights. This elfin creature came onto the stage and while the scene went on she did something so utterly enchanting and meaningful, it centered the whole play. The poor dear girl was exhausted from her ordeal and as she stood there before the tribunal, she yawned. All she did was yawn, yet the yawn said everything about this brave little saint. I can't describe how she did it; I can only say it was magic. She yawned and I started to cry and sat through the rest of the play in tears. My God, what an actress.

A Hell of a Life

Anne Jackson and Eli Wallach were in Bobby's class and were married in the same year the Studio was founded. I swear, nobody plays irascibility better than Eli Wallach. Annie and he were very much a part of the Studio life and my life, too. They're longtime colleagues and longtime friends. E. G. Marshall, another mainstay of the theater, was a Studio participant, and so were Paul Newman and Joanne Woodward. Not long ago I visited with Joanne at Canyon Ranch in Lenox, Massachusetts, and we reminisced about the "good old days." In the early fifties, she and I appeared together in a television program called "Brillo Star Tonight." Those were the days when shows were sponsored by one company and there were programs like "The Colgate Comedy Hour," "The Texaco Star Theatre," and, of course, "Brillo Star Tonight." Today one program typically has a dozen or more sponsors. Anyway, Joanne and I laughed recalling our TV stint. The play took place in the Ozarks or something, and I played Joanne's mother—never mind that I'm only five or six years older than she. Joanne reminded me that in the play, she was an ax murderess, real typecasting, you know.

When you come right down to it, I guess Marlon Brando is the Studio's most renowned alumnus. I loved that man, and what an actor. As I said, I don't do comparisons; however, I do think Marlon was potentially our greatest actor. I remember going to see *Viva Zapata*. Early in the movie there's a scene where the Mexican army has taken people to prison. Zapata and his army come to free the prisoners, and after they've taken over the prison, they begin to talk about how they're going to keep the army at bay. The scene builds and builds and, for whatever reason, the gist of the matter is a question of cutting wires. They're going on and on and one guy says, "If you cut those wires, it means war." Then Marlon says softly, "Cut the wires." I can't describe how this was said; I know most actors would have gone for the expansive, *"Cut the wires* [exclamation point]," but not Brando. He said it in such a way that you were really terrified because you knew it was dead serious and that it meant war. I remember thinking to myself as I watched, "How the hell do you imagine to do it that way?"

71

• • •

I spent the late forties honing my art at the Studio and going from office to office trying to land parts. The process of auditioning is unbelievably wearing. You never know how it's going to be; sometimes you're good and sometimes you're not. You pray that you'll be good; still, you can't control it. I read for a Garson Kanin play called *The Rat Race*. Leland Hayward was the producer and Danny Mann was the director. I went to audition one morning and the people who were there got all excited. They lauded me to the skies and made me feel like the greatest thing since Duse. Hayward was so taken that he cast me in the damn thing.

"How do you think you'd look as a blond?" he asked.

"Blond," I replied.

The producers were so enthusiastic they called Garson Kanin and his wife, Ruth Gordon, and told them to come in and hear me, which they did. Pumped up by my morning's audition, I read for the Kanins, and whatever I had done for Leland Hayward and the others in the A.M., I didn't do for Garson and Ruth in the P.M. and was summarily dismissed. I keep meaning to ask Garson what the hell happened. I tried to picture what must have gone through Garson's mind and could imagine him turning to Leland Hayward and the others, saying, "You dragged us in from Connecticut for *this?*" I never knew what went wrong. I did the best I could in the afternoon, just as I had in the morning, and it didn't work. And that's only one example of the quixotic nature of auditioning. What it boils down to is that you simply cannot get discouraged.

In July of 1948, I was in a summer stock production of *The Beaux' Stratagem* at Westport. Brian Aherne was the star and the director. When I told Guthrie McClintic that I was working for Brian, he let out a hoot. "Oh my God, he's the most tactless man in the world." And he was. He just didn't know how to talk to us. See, if you're the boss, you're supposed to lift the company's spirits, but Brian didn't know how to do that; he had absolutely no sense of how to see the play, the characters, or the actors through any eyes but his. Consequently, he wasn't much fun to work for.

In *The Beaux' Stratagem,* I played Cherry, the landlord's daughter. Yep, Cherry, the landlord's daughter. I started out gawdawful and didn't get any better. It was just no use. While I love Restoration comedy, just like I love Noël Coward, I never could do either of them correctly. Whatever extra sense you need in order to do Restoration comedy or Coward properly, I ain't got it. There's some necessary ingredient, some special little take or part of a technique that as an actor you either have to have or have to learn, and if you don't, then these plays are not for you. Unfortunately, I never had it and never learned it. Still, I know when I'm watching somebody else do it right. In *The Beaux' Stratagem,* for example, Carmen Matthews played Mrs. Sullen and she was wonderful. Carmen is an American, yet she had that extra thing and was able to connect with the very British role.

Another memorable member of the cast was Mary Forbes, who played Lady Bountiful. She was the mother of Brenda and Ralph Forbes and had been in the movies herself. Mary was a beautiful gray-haired lady, very distinguished and very, very dear. We were staying at a hotel that summer, and one morning I came down to breakfast and found Mary seated at the table.

Now, I'd been mulling over something and at this particular moment, I gave words to my thoughts. I sat down, poured my coffee, buttered my toast, turned to Mary, and declared, "Mary, I'm so excited. I've decided that I'm going to get married."

"Oh *do,* ducky," enthused Ms. Forbes. "It's wonderful. I've done it five times."

I dropped my toast. It wasn't exactly what I had in mind. While I'd never been a girl who sat around dreaming about Prince Charming and getting hitched—quite the contrary, in fact —all of a sudden I'd come to the decision that I wanted to marry. I had no particular person in mind and no preconceived notion of a man-of-my-dreams, either. I don't know what put it in my head, but I just wanted to get married. Enter Max Allentuck.

• • •

After *The Beaux' Stratagem* I returned to the city, went back to the Actors Studio, and made the rounds of the theatrical offices. Members of the Studio told each other about the various plays that were in preparation, and between word of mouth and the newspapers, you bounced from office to office and spread yourself around. In those days, Broadway was buzzing; lots of plays were in production, so you were kept nice and busy—auditioning. One particular reading sticks out in my memory. Kermit Bloomgarden was producing Arthur Miller's *Death of a Salesman* and I tried out for the part of a hooker. Max Allentuck attended the audition and we saw each other for the first time. I didn't get the part, but later I did get Max.

There were many roles that I didn't get, and then I successfully auditioned for a new Sidney Kingsley play, *Detective Story*. The *Playbill* for the Hudson Theatre listed me in the "Who's Who in the Cast" and my *first* program biography read:

MAUREEN STAPLETON (Miss Hatch)

Miss Stapleton made her acting debut with Burgess Meredith in *Playboy of the Western World* and appeared in the road production of *The Barretts of Wimpole Street*. Last season Miss Stapleton was seen to good advantage in *Antony and Cleopatra*.

Ralph Bellamy and Meg Mundy were starred in the production and I understudied her. Ralph Bellamy was a real gentleman. Once, he actually came and played in the understudy rehearsal, which was pretty damn nice of him. Stars didn't have to do that, but the classy ones like Ralph Bellamy and Miss Cornell did.

Detective Story had a good long run, and it was during this period that I officially met Max Allentuck. Since my audition for *Death of a Salesman,* we'd seen each other at all sorts of theatrical functions like parties, dinners, and banquets, and then one night at Sardi's we were formally introduced by friends. Max was the general manager for Kermit Bloomgarden's theatrical organization. He was fourteen years older than I and had been married very briefly to Peggy Phillips. They were long divorced when Max and I met; the two of them had remained friends, however, and she and I became friendly as well. Peggy remarried and had a son; she lives out in California now and still sends me Christmas cards.

One summer, some time later, while I was in *The Crucible,* Max and I rented a house on the Sound; Peg, who had a sailboat, would visit us. Johnny Forsythe and his wife rented a house a few houses up from Max and me and there were more theater folk scattered around. We'd all get together frequently. At some point that summer, Peggy started calling me "Mo." Pretty soon, others picked it up and boom! I had a nickname. Nowadays, lots of people in the theater call me Mo, and I'm sure they think it comes from my childhood. Nossir, my ex-husband's first wife gave me that name.

It wasn't love at first sight for Max and me; we sort of drifted together. I liked him a lot; he was smart, funny, kind, caring, loving, and Jewish, a great combination. Soon, we began seeing each other. I had to perform in the evenings and Max was working, too; our dates were made around the free hours we had in common. Actually, Max and I had a lot in common: first and foremost, we were theater people.

I read for Lillian Hellman's *Montserrat,* which Kermit Bloomgarden was producing. I didn't get that part, so no one could accuse me of hanging around with Max Allentuck to get roles. Our dating game continued, and, how can I say it, we sort of naturally came together and I began staying over at his apartment. I'm sure Janice didn't miss me; I kept paying my share of the rent, and besides, our apartment was still overflowing with our friends and their sleeping bags. But while Janice may not have cared, my mother was a different story. No way could I let her know I was living with a man. When she came down from Troy to visit, I'd scoot back over to 52nd Street to receive her. Janice covered for me. Mom met Max and thought he was a nice guy but that didn't mean she wanted me to marry him. The truth is, she didn't want me to marry any man. One day, an item appeared in Walter Winchell's column stating that "wedding bells would be ringing for company manager Max Allentuck and actress Maureen Stapleton." Max and I hadn't talked about marriage, and that column was the first time the word was mentioned. "Let's not make a liar out of Winchell," Max said, and asked me to marry him. Far be it from me to make Walter Winchell look bad; I accepted. I truly loved Max and I'll always love him; we're still very close.

When I informed my mother that Max and I were going to tie the knot, she went bananas. I knew she was "loco" on the subject of men and marriage, but I had no idea just how "loco" until I wrote and told her how happy I was and how happy I knew she would be for me. The minute she got my letter, she began sending me a series of letters that were, to put it mildly, horrific. I read the first in disbelief. The contents were bloodcurdling. Happily, I've repressed most of it, though I do recall the ending, which read, "I spew you from my mouth like vomit." That's what my mom thought of me getting married. I showed the letter to Max and thank God I did, because he was a witness to this madness. He told me to tear it up, and when the subsequent letters followed, he said I shouldn't open them. A whole bunch of them did come and I followed Max's advice and burned them.

Ten years later, when Max and I were splitting, I said to my mother, a trifle sardonically, "You were so upset when I was getting married to Max, I'm sure you're thrilled now that we're getting divorced."

"I don't think that's funny, Maureen," she answered curtly. Later, while we were talking about marriage and relationships in general, I brought up the subject of the letters she'd sent me.

"What letters?" asked my mother.

"Those letters you sent just before the wedding. I only read one because it was all I could take. I burned the rest."

"What letters are you talking about?" my mother replied innocently.

"Mom, those terrible letters you wrote."

"I never wrote you any letters," protested my mother. She adamantly denied the whole business and was so certain I almost doubted myself. I got right on the phone with my ex-husband.

"Max, dear, do you remember years ago when we were getting married, my mother sent me some awful letters?"

"Of course," answered Max reassuringly. "Who could forget them?"

"Oh Max, I'm so glad you remember! Mother almost had me convinced that it hadn't happened. I thought I was crazy."

I still don't know what the hell was in my mother's mind. All I know is she was way off the deep end when it came to men and marriage. Oddly enough, despite her miserable experience with my father and her avowed hatred for him, I'm not so sure that she ever was able to write him off completely. I say that because of an odd incident which sticks in my brain. When I took my two kids to visit her in Troy, my son Danny noticed that a gift-wrapped, beribboned box always stood on a living room table. The box remained unopened. Finally, after many visits and many sightings of that box, Danny spoke to his grandmother.

"Don't you want to open your present, Grandma?" he asked.

"No," answered Mother. "A man gave it to me a long time ago. Just let it sit there." As far as I could figure out, the box contained a gift sent by my father, perhaps in an effort to patch things up. Mother kept it but never touched it. Miss Havisham had a moldering wedding cake; my mother had an unopened present.

In spite of mother's hate mail, Max and I went ahead with our plans for the wedding. Both of us were working and had no time for anything elaborate. We planned to go to the Municipal Building, have the ceremony, and then go to a nearby Longchamps restaurant for a reception and meal. Despite her misgivings, mother planned to come down from Troy along with my aunts Julie and Jeanette. Mom got to the city early, came over to my place, and said, "Well, what are you wearing?"

"I have this nice print dress, " I answered.

"Print!" My mother was as horrified by what I was wearing as she was by what I was doing.

On July 22, 1949, Max and I got married and then, along with a few friends and relatives trotted over to Longchamps for brunch. In the afternoon, we went back to the apartment and waited for other friends to drop by. We had to clear everyone out by six so we could get to our respective theaters. The party was in full swing when Jane Fortner, a friend and sometime roommate, who, by the way, dyed her hair green, came barreling into the reception and screamed across the room to me, "Well, I missed your fucking wedding!" My mother and my aunts turned the color of Jane's hair. Between hearing the f-word and seeing Jane's bizarre appearance, I thought the three of them would pass out right then and there.

That weekend Max and I spent a brief honeymoon in Asbury Park, New Jersey, and by Monday were back at work. Everything happened so fast that I don't have even one picture from the wedding or the "honeymoon." I moved into Max's small apartment on West 56th Street and life went on pretty much as it had been going on, only now I was Mrs. Max Allentuck. It still didn't get me a free ticket to any roles.

I auditioned for *The Bird Cage,* a new play by Arthur Laurents, and was cast opposite the star, Melvyn Douglas, another peachy guy. Here's the rub: I played Melvyn Douglas's alcoholic wife. I didn't drink in those days and had to use an "as if" to create my stage character. I substituted a great desire for chocolate in order to try and get a feeling for the urge to drink. Much later, in one of those sublime theatrical ironies, I played the role of Georgie, the long suffering wife of an alcoholic in Clifford Odets's *The Country Girl.* I've been on both sides of the alcoholic fence on stage, the drinkers and the nondrinkers, so I can't complain about being typecast. Harold Clurman was the director of *The Bird Cage* and I became very fond of him. Ultimately he directed me in four Broadway plays. Harold had been a founder of the Group Theatre and was an active critic, author, and teacher as well as an actor. Clurman was an enthusiastic philosopher of the theater, and his deep love of the drama was evident in everything he touched. *The Bird Cage* tried out in Philadelphia and they loved us! Full of hope, we opened in New York, but despite the drawing power of the star, the writer, and the director, we didn't last very long. I told Harold we should've stayed in Philadelphia.

I flew out of *The Bird Cage* and settled down to await the birth of my first child. While I nested in our tiny apartment, I kept up my studies at the Studio. I was in seventh heaven during my pregnancy, and when my son, Daniel Vincent, was born on July 8, 1950, I was ecstatic. Max and I both liked the name Daniel, and though I wanted to honor my uncle by naming my son after him, I hesitated about using Vincent Daniel because of the initials. D. V. Allentuck is better by a long shot than V. D. Allentuck.

I loved my role as mother and really hovered around my baby. I wanted to do things right. I kept a chart of everything that Danny did and everything I was supposed to do. Max got in the act, too, and really kept abreast of Danny's progress. He was forever questioning me. I was sitting with Annie Jackson one day and Max walked in the room.

"When did you feed the baby?" he inquired.

"An hour ago."

"Did you change the diapers?"

"Yes."

"Was there a rash?"

"No." And so on and so forth. I answered all his questions and then Max left the room. I turned to Annie and said, "Max thinks I'm trying to kill the baby."

A few months after Danny was born, my mother and Julie and Jeanette came down to New York and we all had lunch together at the Russian Tea Room. My joy at being a mother made me eager to repeat.

"I can hardly wait to have another child," I announced at lunch.

"That's disgusting!" snapped Mother. My aunts and I were stunned by her vehemence.

Although my mother loved her grandson, she could still

dredge up that depraved attitude about sex and men at the drop of a hat and conk me over the head with it. That woman could go from sane to nuts in a split second. Maybe *she* would have made a great actress.

Chapter Four

At the same time I was appearing in *The Bird Cage*, Cheryl Crawford and Daniel Mann were looking for an actress to play the lead role in Tennessee Williams's new work, *The Rose Tattoo*. Williams had already shown his spectacular stuff in plays like *The Glass Menagerie, A Streetcar Named Desire,* and *Summer and Smoke*. Although we hadn't met, I knew and admired his work. I'd been especially thrilled by *The Glass Menagerie* because I was able to see Laurette Taylor in her last stage appearance; as I've mentioned, in my opinion, that lady was the top, the very top. Tennessee Williams felt the same way and ranked her right up there with Sarah Bernhardt and Eleanora Duse.

The new play was a different kettle of fish. Williams called it his "love-play for the world." He'd vacationed in Italy and fallen in love with the country and its people. He thought the Italians were "like our Southerners, without inhibitions." He wanted to write about these "poetic people who lived without repressions," and out of this desire came *The Rose Tattoo*. Williams had Anna Magnani in mind for the part of Serafina delle Rose and in 1950 had gone to Rome to see if he could get Magnani to commit. Magnani said no. She loved the part but didn't think her English was good enough for the American stage. Consequently, the leading female role in Tennessee Williams's newest drama was up for grabs.

The play is a delicious mixture of mysticism and knock-down, drag-out realism; Serafina, who's onstage ninety-nine percent of the time, runs the gamut from rage to love. The part was a plum, all right, and all Miss Crawford, Mr. Mann, and Mr. Williams had to do was find an actress to fill Miss Magnani's shoes.

I was not in contention for the part of Serafina, and why would I be? I was acting opposite Melvyn Douglas at the time and had a decent, albeit limited, track record of theatrical experiences as well as an ongoing association with the Actors Studio. But in the big Broadway picture, Maureen Stapleton was a relative unknown; moreover, a "young" unknown. Although Miss Crawford was familiar with my work on stage and at the Studio, there was no reason why she would envision a twenty-five-year-old neophyte in the exacting role of a middle-aged woman with a teenage daughter. Opportunity might not have knocked had not Harold Clurman, the director of *The Rat Race,* recommended me to the producers. Harold didn't think I could do anything and everything the way Guthrie McClintic did, yet he had a feeling I might be right for Serafina. When he was told they were looking for a Magnani, he said, "Why don't you get Maureen Stapleton?" Later, when I was cast, he admitted, "To my surprise they took her." That sonofabitch Harold had my number; he once wrote, "Maureen must have been a victim in her early life of some nameless wound; to bear it she requires the escape of acting and the solace of close embrace." I could have saved myself a lot of dough if I'd consulted with Harold Clurman instead of all those shrinks. Because of his suggestion, Miss Crawford, Mr. Mann, and Mr. Williams decided to give me the opportunity to audition. Cheryl Crawford's secretary telephoned and told me to come over and read for her boss and the others.

I went to the audition with my Actors Studio pal Eli Wallach, who read for the part of Mangiacavallo. We began what turned out to be a World Series of readings. The auditions had been going on for a while, and though I can't name them, I'm sure everybody in the world had tried out for the part of Serafina delle Rose. Apparently, the leading contender before I came on the scene was Eleanora Mendelssohn, a German-Italian actress whose German accent bothered Miss Crawford; lucky for me that she didn't have an Italian accent. Eli and I did a scene for Crawford, Mann, and Williams; I knew Crawford and Mann from the Actors Studio, but this was my first meeting with Tennessee Williams. I later learned that Tennessee had heard of me and actually wrote a letter to Paul Bigelow, Miss Crawford's assistant, and Jordan Massee, asking them who I was. "I hear," he wrote, "she's an American Anna Magnani." I know this for a fact because Jordan made a xerox copy of that letter and gave it to me. Tennessee Williams was nearing forty at the time I met him and was a short, youthful-looking guy with blue eyes and a full mustache over a generous mouth which usually was clamped on a cigarette holder. Tennessee always used a holder when he smoked, and he smoked often. After we became friends, we spent an evening together and I realized that Tenn hadn't had a cigarette all night.

"How come you're not smoking?" I asked.

"Oh yeah," sighed Tennessee, "I forgot." That floored me.

"You forgot?" I howled. "You know people bust their balls trying to give up smoking and you just forgot?" I couldn't get over it. I've never forgotten to smoke in my life.

Tennessee had a wonderful warm smile which he generously bestowed on Eli Wallach and me as we began *The Rose Tattoo* reading. After we finished, they thanked us and we left. We were called back to do another reading. We did a scene; they thanked us and we left. We got called back and did another scene. Again, they thanked us and we left—and were called back. This happened a few more times, and by then Eli started going insane.

"I won't read it any more," he swore to me following the fifth or sixth audition, "I won't!"

"Oh yes you will, Eli," I advised him in my calmest, most

measured tone. "We'll read it again. We'll read as many times as they ask us." I figured if they were calling us back, they were interested. I knew damn well the competition was tough, but as long as there was a glimmer of hope, I'd read. After a while, I got the feeling that they actually *wanted* me but were too scared to act on it. There was a lot of pressure because this was a major production by a major playwright, really big-time stuff, and they wanted to make absolutely positively certain that they were doing the right thing.

Following an inordinate number of readings, Eli and I were called into Miss Crawford's office. Tenn was there, along with Miss Crawford and Danny Mann. Tenn's literary agent, Audrey Wood, and her husband, Bill Leibling, were also in attendance. I kind of knew we were down to the wire. Something was in the air—fear, probably—and you could sense how jittery they were about giving the two leading parts to relative unknowns, especially the bravura female role. They kept asking questions about how I felt about doing Serafina, and, in particular, they wanted to know if I could positively, absolutely, honestly say that I could do it. Obviously they'd been impressed by my reading, but they seemed to want me to *promise* them I could succeed. First Crawford, then Mann, then Miss Wood asked for some sort of guarantee. What could I guarantee? I'd done all I could; I figured the ball was in their court.

"Look," I finally said, "I don't know about this. I can't promise you that I *can* do this part, 'cause I don't know. I'd like to play it; I hope I can play it; but I can't promise."

I finished talking and Tennessee Williams jumped up from his chair, declaring, "I don't care if she turns into a dead mule on opening night. I want her for the part!"

That did it. I got the part.

From the beginning Tenn had been different from the others; he couldn't be bothered with all the worrying and fussing about my age and/or experience. He'd been rooting for me all along and had insisted that I do the readings to overcome the others' concerns about my youth. For the last audition he even counseled me to get into character makeup and suggested I mess up my hair and wear an old robe and dirty up my face so I'd look right. Later he wrote about the reading in his autobiography:

> There was great trouble casting Serafina. It was I who found Maureen Stapleton for the part. Her reading convinced us all that, despite her youth, she could do it; she was a very young girl at the time but nevertheless I thought she was so brilliant in characterization that the obstacle of her youth could be overcome. So I kept insisting that she read again and again.

The mystery of the multiple readings was solved; that darling Tennessee set them up to insure my being cast. P.S.: I could dine out for the rest of my life on his statement, "It was I who found Maureen Stapleton for the part." I'm delighted to have been discovered by Tennessee Williams, courtesy of Harold Clurman, by way of Guthrie McClintic. Whoever actually was responsible for my being there, it was pretty heady stuff for a twenty-five-year-old to be chosen by Tennessee Williams to create the leading female role in one of his plays.

Rehearsals began, though to tell you the truth, Eli and I read so goddamn many times it felt like we'd been running in the play for a while. We rehearsed in New York for about four weeks and then went to Chicago, where we opened at the Erlanger Theatre on December 29, 1950, for a pre-Broadway tryout. In Chicago you performed every night of the week including Sunday and did two matinees as well. Nowadays that may be standard practice; in 1950 you didn't work Sundays except in Chicago. During the tryout we rehearsed in the daytime and did the shows at night. Changes were made, though not a lot of them. Sometimes you can go crazy with the pre-Broadway alterations because there are so many. Over the years I've learned that it's a helluva lot easier to work with a dead playwright; live ones usually mess around with the script and keep changing things on you. God forbid *you* try and change a line, however;

do it and they go ballistic. Fortunately *The Rose Tattoo* had a minimal amount of fixing with Tenn making the necessary additions and corrections.

He and I became very friendly and eventually wound up calling each other "Maw" and "Paw" like the Kettles. I liked him a lot and was crazy about his companion-*cum*-majordomo, Frank Merlo. Frank and Tenn were together for fourteen years. When they broke up it was very hard for me because I couldn't take sides; as much as I loved Tenn, I also adored Frank. Frank was smart, kind, and wickedly funny and acted as Tenn's liaison officer to the world. When Tennessee went to Hollywood and met with one of those studio muck-a-mucks—I think Darryl Zanuck in this instance—he brought Frank right into the meeting. The studio head never even looked at Frank Merlo during the entire discussion. After the business had been transacted, he finally deigned to address him. "And what do you do?" asked the mogul. Frank smiled and said, "I sleep with Mr. Williams." Frank was my dear buddy, a wonderful guy; what great times the three of us had.

Tennessee Williams really was a piece of work. His conversations could be so off the wall that I always felt as if I was playing George Burns to his Gracie Allen. One day he showed up at my door and came in for a chat. "Mah cousin Stella's son is visitin' with me," Tenn announced.

"That nice," I said. "What does he do?"

"He's come to New York to study dancin'," answered Tenn. "He wants to be a ballet dancer."

"How old is he?"

"Twenty-eight."

"Twenty-eight? Tenn, that's too old. I think people start in their teens if they want to be ballet dancers."

"Ah know, ah know," sighed Tenn. "Ah told him he was a little old, but he is bound and determined and ah feel, well, maybe if he does that, it'll help his weight problem."

"Weight problem?"

"Yes, well, he is obese. And he is stocking my house like it was a restaurant. I can't open the refrigerator or the cupboard but that food doesn't come tumblin' out."

I decided to move in another conversational direction. "How is Cousin Stella?"

"Oh, her unemployment insurance has run out."

"Yeah? What does she do?"

"She's a fortune teller."

Tenn just loved to go on about his relatives, and I honestly never knew if he was telling the truth or saying the first thing that came into his head. I was the perfect audience because I believed everything.

One day he called and excitedly told me that we had been invited to dinner at the home of Brooks Atkinson. I thought he was pulling my leg. Mr. Atkinson was the drama critic for *The New York Times* and a powerful and influential man. Ordinarily drama critics don't consort with playwrights and actors; however, Atkinson was an early champion of Tenn's work, and had indeed invited us to dine with him. Tenn was thrilled at the invitation and so was I. The night of the dinner, Tenn, resplendent in black tie, called for me. I had on a smashing cocktail dress and looked pretty swell myself. In fact, the two of us looked like something out of *Vogue*. We arrived at the Atkinsons' apartment and after being announced went to his door. Tenn rang the bell and in a few seconds the door opened and there stood Mr. and Mrs. Atkinson. He was wearing a pullover and khakis and she had on a simple housedress. Good old Tenn wrongly assumed we were going to a formal dinner. After the initial embarrassment, we became as informal as black tie and lots of drinks would allow. Brooks Atkinson was an exceptional person who cared for the theater and didn't try to make points through barbs and wisecracks. Tenn admired him but was a bit guarded about many other reviewers. I've kept a note from him that reads, "Dearest Maureen, I do not say fuck the drama critics because fucking is too good for them. Love, Paw."

Tenn had a calm Southern-gentleman way which was absolutely captivating, and being around him was like being around drama history in the making. History, I have to add, sometimes was made in the nuttiest ways. After the main roles had been assigned in *The Rose Tattoo,* auditions were held for the children in the cast. I sat with Tenn as the kids were brought up on stage and put through their paces. One half-pint pranced on and said, "My name is Judy Ratner and I don't go to school."

"You don't?" inquired Danny Mann. "How come?"

"I have a tutor," announced the little miss.

"Oh," said the director, "so you have a tutor."

"Yeah," she answered.

"And what does he do?" asked the director.

"He toots," snapped the kid.

Tennessee went crazy laughing. She knocked him out with her sassy attitude, which was totally wrong for the role. The part called for an angelic child, but Tenn was so enthralled with this kid's cheekiness he cast her anyway.

"Did you see that divine child?" he said to me after she flounced off the stage. "Did you see? She has no neck! That child has no neck!" And he began cackling like a hen. Tenn was always laughing and giggling. A few years later, Tenn created the "no-neck monster" children in *Cat on a Hot Tin Roof,* and I'm here to tell you they came right out of Judy Ratner's audition. When *Cat* went into rehearsal, Tennessee invited me to sit in on the first run-through. I took Janice along and we went to the rooftop theater at the New Amsterdam on 42nd Street. Tenn also invited his friend Carson McCullers, another Southern writer, who'd adapted her novel *The Member of the Wedding* into the memorable play in which Julie Harris lit up the stage. McCullers brought along a friend of hers, a lady who hung around the writer all the time. To this day I don't know who she was; that broad never uttered a single word.

After the rehearsal, Janice, Carson, the silent woman, and I were to join Tenn and Frank for a bite to eat. Frank came over and suggested that the rest of us should go on and wait for Tenn in the restaurant.

"Tenn's busy with Bill Leibling," explained Frank as the five of us stepped into the elevator. "Bill thinks the elephant joke is too dirty and is insisting that it be taken out. Did you all think it was too dirty?"

Carson reflected for a moment, shook her head, and said, "Too dirty? Wah, Frank, ah didn't he-ah anythin' even spicy in that play!"

Nothing spicy? I gotta tell ya, the original *Cat* was all about fornication, which was discussed in no uncertain terms and was plenty spicy in those days. For the rest of the ride down in the elevator, everyone but Carson's friend, who stood grimly regarding the door for the entire descent, argued about whether the elephant joke was too much and should be cut. By the time we reached ground level, the consensus of opinion, save for that of Carson's silent chum, was that the joke wasn't too much and should stay. We stepped out of the elevator and Janice gave the final word.

"Yeah," she said very seriously, "the elephant joke should stay, but," she continued, looking at each of us individually, "maybe we're not exactly a cross section of public opinion."

Carson McCullers and I became pretty close. Much later, after I'd become an established actor, she declared she was going to write a play for me. I was very flattered and spent a lot of time working with her, one of the few times I've actually been involved in the creation of a drama. The play was called *The Square Root of Wonderful* and it opened on Broadway with Anne Baxter in the lead. Somewhere between the declaration that the play was written for me and its opening, I got lost in the shuffle.

The Rose Tattoo opened at the Martin Beck Theatre on February 3, 1951. Before the premiere, Max called me in Chicago and announced that the marquee had been set up.

"Yeah? So what does it say?" I asked in my most nonchalant manner.

"Well," said Max, "it reads, 'Eli Wallach and Maureen Stapleton in *The Rose Tattoo*."

". . . Eli Wallach? and Maureen Stapleton . . . ? You mean Eli's name is first?"

"Ha," laughed Max, who'd gotten me. "Hambone, know thy name."

The Martin Beck marquee actually read:

THE ROSE TATTOO
A New Play by Tennessee Williams
with
MAUREEN STAPLETON AND ELI WALLACH

Not long after *The Rose Tattoo* opened, Joan Crawford came to the show and after the curtain fell went backstage to congratulate the cast. She walked into Eli's dressing room and my costar was beside himself. "Miss Crawford, just wait till I tell my children I met Joan Crawford." She answered, "And, Mr. Wallach, just wait until I tell the world I met Eli Wallach." Joan Crawford was one hundred percent right: Eli Wallach was absolutely sensational. But I swear I don't know whether I was good or bad. My reviews were good, and it pleased me when reviewers commented on how authentically Italian I seemed to be. Imagine, the Irish girl from Troy gets praised for being convincingly Mediterranean. When I got the part they told me to go out and mix with Italians to get the flavor of the language. I didn't have time to "mix." I learned all the words at rehearsals and the foreign rhythms of my speeches were there because Tennessee wrote them that way; it was his genius. He didn't use anything as ordinary as dialect, either, none of that sappy "I'm-a gonna do-a thees-a an' that-a." He simply put a lilt in the lines, and the minute you said them you sounded Italian. There was no trick to it; everything had to do with the script. It's always special to appear in a great writer's play; having Tennessee as the author was like a gift. He gives the actor so much, and yet it's hard to describe any of it. A line in *The Rose Tattoo* provides a good example. In the first scene of act 3, Serafina and Mangiacavallo are out on the porch. She walks into the house, and he follows her inside and asks what's the matter. She answers, "I got a feeling like I have—forgotten something." Now that line has absolutely no connection with anything else in the play; there's nothing that subsequently happens from it and there's nothing leading up to it. You can't later put your finger on whether she forgot to do this or do that. What it boils down to is, the line is a gift. You can do whatever you want with it. I don't mean the actor should go into a big number or anything like that; it simply provides the actress with something utterly attractive, a beautiful pocket of space in which to move.

There's another point in *The Rose Tattoo* that is similarly beneficent. In act 1, scene 3, a priest and a couple of Serafina's friends come to tell her that Rosario has been killed. They walk into the house; she spots them and says, "Don't speak." They haven't said a word and yet she knows instinctively what they're going to say. I sure as hell don't remember doing it, but people who were in the audience told me the scene was electrifying. Apparently I just looked at the guys and waved my arms in front of me as I stepped back and shook my head back and forth in a silent "no." The way it was done told you that Serafina knew her husband was dead, but as long as no one spoke, it hadn't happened. She didn't want to hear it. "Don't speak" are her only words; the rest is pantomime. Such are the potentials for acting behind the exact words, and they are the actors' extras. You don't want to overdo and kill the poetry; still, you want to seize the opportunity. Consequently, whenever these "presents" appear, you simply must use them. On the other hand, as terrific as the actor may believe he or she is handling the moment, it's not always totally successful. There have been a few times when I erroneously thought I'd found acting nirvana; one of the earliest occasions was in my first starring vehicle.

The play had been going on for months and Tenn and Frank went off on a European trip. After many weeks they wrote and told me they were returning and would come to the show and then take me out for dinner. It would be the first time Tenn had seen the production in quite a while. I was excited about him being in the audience because I'd "improved" upon one of the scenes and was eager to get his take. Specifically, Serafina set up a prie-dieu in her living room for her husband's ashes and the urn is nestled at the feet of the statue of the Virgin. A vigil candle is kept lit in front of the statue and Serafina spends a lot of time praying and talking to the Virgin. At the moment in the play when Serafina finds out that her husband was unfaithful, she goes berserk-o. She takes the urn and heaves it, screams at the Virgin, blows out the candle, and runs out of the house. That's the way the scene was written and directed, and that's the way I did it night after night. Then, while Tenn was away, I was doing my number one evening and something happened. After I yelled at the Virgin and blew out the light, I was overcome with a desire to do "more" and suddenly found myself hugging the statue and kissing it before I ran off. I liked what I'd done and in subsequent performances kept it in. It was one of those deals where other actors would mention the scene and say how spectacular it was, and their comments along with my own "good" feeling convinced me I'd found real acting heaven. All this occurred while the playwright was out of town.

The night of Tennessee's return, I did my statue shtick and after the performance returned to my dressing room to change and wait for him and Frank to pick me up. I was getting out of my makeup when the two of them came into the room. I finished washing my face and continued getting dressed. Tenn and Frank waited as I changed into my street clothes. I kept expecting Tenn to say something about the grand scene he'd just witnessed, but all he did was chatter about everything else under the sun. He told me how much fun they'd had in Europe and how terrific it was to see old friends and stuff like that. Not one word about the play. Nothing. I finished changing, and as we walked out the door, Tenn helped me on with my coat, stepped back to let me pass, and said casually, "Oh, by the way, dahlin, what are you doin' slobberin' all over the Virgin?"

"Slobbering?" I protested. "But Tenn, I thought it was such a terrific thing to do. I mean, Serafina's so overcome and so emotional and so religious and so, you know, so I decided to hug and kiss the statue. You don't like it?"

"No, no, dahlin," advised the playwright ever so gently and ever so firmly, "just blow out the candle and get out of there." So much for my magic moment. I dropped it; though I must

92

admit that when we went on the road, I slipped the hug in twice more. I couldn't resist because it felt great. That's what I mean about working with a living playwright as opposed to a dead one. I couldn't buck Tennessee's wishes; however, if I decided to do a kazatski in the middle of *The Sea Gull,* Anton Chekhov couldn't touch me. As firm as he was about his plays, in other situations Tenn could be pushed around. His good friend Maria Britneva was about as bossy as you can get, and Tenn lapped it up. She really looked after him over the years. Even after she married an English lord and became Lady St. Just, she still ordered Tenn around. At Tenn's memorial service, Maria came over to me and started giving orders. I forget what the hell exactly she told me to do; I only know I put the kibosh on it. "You know, Maria, you could do that kind of stuff with Tenn, but I ain't Tenn and you ain't pushin' me around," I told her, and by gum, she stopped. Maria died recently. I'll miss her and those occasional phone calls from England. I loved them because the operator would say, "Please hold the line, Lady St. Just is calling." It made me feel pretty fancy to get phone calls from a bona fide lady.

Serafina was an exhausting role. For one thing, she's on stage for the entire first act. Mangiacavallo doesn't come on until the second act, so Eli could take it easy while I was busting a gut. I'd get through the act thinking, "Hold on, kid; Eli'll be out here soon and you'll get some rest." We were on tour and one night I was so exhausted that as Eli stepped out from the wings, I turned upstage and yawned. Actually, I did that in a few performances. Then one evening Eli came offstage and let me have it. He was *so* mad.

"What the hell are you doing, Maureen? I walk out and you yawn; that's great!"

"Jeez, Eli, it doesn't mean anything. It's just that by the time you get on the scene, I'm so tired. I was just taking a little rest. I mean, nobody sees me yawn except you." Eli really was pissed. I told him I'd stop. I didn't, but I tried to make sure he never saw me do it again.

Acting in a Tennessee Williams play is a treat, but you do pay your emotional dues. Serafina is a volcanic character; all the stops have to be pulled out and quickly jammed back in again. Her roller-coaster temperament began to affect me; I lived under great tension and pressure and after six months I got a little nutty. I felt anxious all the time and it was due to what was happening on stage every night. Screaming at the Virgin's statue regularly was a strain, and so, indeed, was the scene in which I had to shriek and carry on and physically claw at the priest. That's tough to do once, but to keep doing it over and over again takes a hell of a lot out of you even if the priest is just an actor in costume and you're a lapsed Catholic. It forces you to keep yourself on an emotional track full-time. I was unbelievably stressed out and whether or not it was a consequence of my anxiety, the fact remains that it was during the run of *The Rose Tattoo* that I began to drink.

I'd never been a boozer before. Sure, I'd have a snort with my pals if someone brought a bottle of Southern Comfort over to the apartment, but I never went out and bought liquor. That wasn't my thing. Smoking, however, was a different story; I always smoked. I began at eleven or twelve years of age and am still at it. When I started, nobody worried about what the surgeon general had to say, and, no offense, the surgeon general could march into my apartment today and I'd smoke in his—or even her—face. Smoking was a part of my life from early on; drinking was an acquired skill. Tennessee was a drinker, although I swear I never saw that man act drunk. He could have been nine sheets to the wind; he remained the gentleman. Alas, my sails have not remained as unsullied. As a result, there have been instances in my life I do not remember. Fortunately—or unfortunately—others *have* remembered and dutifully have reported on these times. Today there are enough alleged tales about my adventures with alcohol to keep a contemporary Scheherazade in business with a bushel of sultans. Those will have to appear in another book: I can only relate the stories that I recall, and surely there are enough of those.

Why did I begin drinking? Sheer luck. That, plus the struggle of serving up Serafina every night and, later, situations in my personal life which became increasingly difficult to face. When I started, the idea never crossed my brain that because my father was an alcoholic I might have had a propensity toward liquor. I simply didn't think about my family's drinking habits except that I was aware that my father guzzled anything he could get his mitts on. My mother, on the other hand, didn't drink except maybe at parties or when she dined out, and none of the Walshes were heavy drinkers. My brother drank, though not as much as my father—no one did—and I don't know about the other Stapletons because they weren't in the picture. Why do I drink? I guess being Irish doesn't hurt.

I've had my drinking bouts off and on since *The Rose Tattoo,* and one or two of those sessions knocked me for a loop. One thing I want to get straight, though; I never drank—I never drink —when performing. That is a major no-no and qualifies as unprofessional behavior. Whatever else I may be, I'm first and foremost a professional. I was never inebriated during a performance. However, once the curtain was down and my obligations had been fulfilled, I could do as I pleased, and it pleased me to drink. As long as I was in control during my working hours, my drinking was my business. And so, over the years, the drinking began to escalate almost without my realizing it. Because I functioned perfectly well at my job, I never had to face the fact that I was drinking much too much—well, almost never. Come to think of it, I *did* get into a patch of trouble on one occasion.

After a Saturday matinee someone threw a party that I attended. I usually went home for a nap after matinees; this day I went to the party and had a few drinks. Somewhere in my subconscious lurked the realization that I had an evening performance to deal with, and while I didn't drink much at this gathering, I did drink. That night as I stood in the wings waiting for my entrance, I felt woozy. I wasn't drunk, but when I went on stage, I had a bit of difficulty in getting around or at least in remembering where I was supposed to be. Ordinarily, I'm so at home that everything's on automatic pilot; I don't even think about such things. Now I had to think. I had committed a cardinal acting sin; I had stepped onto the proscenium with my faculties dimmed by liquor. For a moment I panicked and was terrified that I wouldn't be able to get through the evening. I sobered up pretty quickly.

This kind of liquor-induced situation is far removed from the simple lapses that most actors experience, like going up on your lines. That's a whole other kettle of fish. Fortunately, if you lose track, there's usually another member of the cast who'll bring you back. I remember a fluff in *Detective Story.* I had a small part and during my scene I was supposed to pick out somebody in the police lineup. I said half the line and stopped; everything went blank and I stood there, dumb. Ralph Bellamy looked at me and just by my expression knew I was gone. He quickly covered the gap and rescued me. Another time, I'd been playing for nearly nine months in *Toys in the Attic* and had a line in which I was supposed to address another character by name. One evening, the line was coming up but not her name. That goddamn name was absolutely out of my memory bank; I couldn't have come up with it for a million bucks, and I'd been saying it every single night for months. I stood there silently praying some other cast member would identify her before it was my turn to speak. None of the other actors had an identifying line. My cue came and I had to call her something! "Well, *honey, . . .*" I said. I don't think the audience noticed, although it bothered me plenty. In character, I'd never have been that familiar quite so soon. In a long run your brain gets kind of fractured and you can fall victim to your own sense of "ease," which is what I did in *Detective Story* and *Toys in the Attic.* Those are examples of ordinary gaffes and are vastly different from being intoxicated on stage. Jesus, much as I loved the sauce, I couldn't do it. Sure, there have been actors who've performed while under the influence, and they've done damn well, too. Not me, though; I wouldn't feel right. I made a vow after that Saturday matinee party/evening event that I'd never touch a drop of liquor before a performance. Translated into my everyday living, this meant that the moment the curtain fell, I began drinking and continued till I went to bed—or passed out. Whatever time I awoke on the following day, I would have nothing to drink until after that day's performance. My pal Carol

Matthau tells the story about recommending me to some producer for a play; he brushed me off, saying I was a drinker, and
she went at him hammer and tongs. "Maureen never drinks
during a performance," she declared. To prove it, she told him
to go and visit me in my dressing room immediately after the
show. "You'll see," swore Carol, "Maureen is as sober as a judge
on stage." That night the curtain fell, I grabbed my vodka on the
way to the dressing room, and when the guy showed up a few
minutes later, I was feeling no pain. He went back to Carol and
told her I was drunk as a skunk and nothing would make him
believe I hadn't been that way the whole night.

So yes, I drink. I've never tried to hide it, either. Everything's
been out in the open, and everybody's been free to take it or
leave it.

The Rose Tattoo ran for almost a year on Broadway and then we
toured. Despite all the pressures of doing Serafina, there were
real pluses. The play kind of set me up as a Broadway entity,
and I did get a Tony. Hell, the way that part was written, a dead
mule could have played Serafina and gotten an award. Tennessee
Williams created great characters and great acting parts, and
there's an infinite number of things you can do with them because no matter how many times you perform these parts,
there's always something more to find. (Not many people know
it, but Tennessee wrote an original television drama for me called
Stop Rocking. Unfortunately, it was never produced.) No doubt
about it, I was lucky to be given the opportunity to impersonate
the luminous creatures of Tenn's fabulous mind.

That's the part of acting I love most, the challenge and the
opportunity to leave reality behind and become someone else,
often someone completely different from myself. Difficulties do
arise. Acting can be all-consuming, but you can't allow yourself
to be consumed. You shouldn't continue acting when the curtain
comes down. Sounds easy, but it's hard to extricate yourself
from inside that person after being in character for an evening.
As I grew older and more experienced, I tried to close the door a

bit tighter and not drag my impersonation into my real life. Coming back to reality is tough, though, and when you're in a long-running play, it becomes even tougher. I had a strange notion about long-running plays for a good part of my career. Years ago, when you signed a contract it was for the "run of the play," whether that turned out to be two weeks or two years. That's how I always did it, and until I appeared in *Plaza Suite* with George C. Scott in the late sixties, I thought it was the only way. George told me he'd signed for eight months, and this was long before we knew how the play was going to do. I'd never heard of such a thing and asked him what he meant. "Maureen, after eight months I get squirrely," replied my colleague. "My brain goes berserk-o. I can't do it anymore, so I only sign for eight months." My mouth must have fallen open. Who knew you didn't have to stick around until the last line? Who knew there was an option? Anyway, I didn't think any actress, except maybe for Ethel Merman, had a problem with long runs; it just wasn't something that came up a helluva lot.

I've been asked so damn many times to expound on the "art" of acting and how you do it and all that crap, and I'm still at a loss as to how to describe it. Listen, acting is acting. Your task is to keep the audience awake and interested, and make no mistake, keeping them awake is *numero uno*. You get your skills going, the technical stuff like movement and voice projection—although with all the goddamn miking going on today, who the hell needs to project?—and after that, you have to center your energies. Concentration is a pretty big number in show business; hell, at a certain level, it's pretty big in any business. You have to be totally focused when you're on stage. I consider myself a fairly diligent performer, and yet there have been times when my concentration was challenged. I've always been terrified by loud noises, and you'd be surprised how many big bangs can occur even in a closed theater. Something as dumb as an exploding lightbulb can send me up the wall. Loud noises kill me, and yet I'm not especially thrown by the natural sounds of an audience, things like coughing and sneezing or talking. Lots of actors do react, however. When I was appearing with Jason Robards in *Toys in the Attic,* he'd go bananas when people coughed. You know what he'd do? He'd start to cough right back at them! Apropos of coughing, I remember a wonderful line of Vladimir Horowitz's. After a concert during which someone in the audience had a fit of coughing, Horowitz complained about the disturbance. "But, maestro," he was advised, "it's winter, people have colds; and besides, you played for a long time. People naturally have to cough, even during a performance." "I don't cough during a performance," answered Horowitz. "Why should they?" I'm not Horowitz; I'm not Jason, either. I don't care about coughing and I don't even care if people chatter during the performance; those are "familiar" noises and they bounce right off me. I can take any human sound, but let there be a popping lightbulb or a thunderclap or a jet plane roaring overhead or a balloon break and you'll see me buckle.

When we did *The Rose Tattoo* in Philadelphia, at one matinee the screech of fire trucks and the squeal of tires came right up to the front of the theater. The audience began to buzz and I stood transfixed on the stage. A fire had broken out next door, but we didn't know where it was, and from the sound of things it sure as hell seemed to be right in the theater. I turned pale as a ghost and kept standing there like a dummy while some members of the audience started heading for the exits. Thank God, one guy out front got to his feet and yelled, "Sit down." The audience settled back and the play continued. Boy, did I feel like an ass. Some fearless leader I was.

Please, just because I'm relating stories of my qualms, don't, for heaven's sake, assume that I was a total scaredy-cat. Everyone has things that spook them; mine happen to be loud noises and certain (aka basically "all") forms of travel, although you'd be surprised how courageous I could be in circumstances that made strong men tremble. Years ago, when I lived in a brownstone on West 70th Street, I used to let people who needed a bed stay in what had been my son's room. I had this young actor, Michael, living there for a while. Michael had been on the Harvard football team and was one big mother. We'd been in a show together and he was staying with me while he looked for a permanent residence. I was a nervous nellie and one of the reasons I had this kid staying with me was for protection. I'd come home alone at night and make Michael go through the apartment with me to make sure no one was there. One day I asked him to accompany me down to the cellar; I wanted to get a little table that was stored there and bring it up to the living room. It was about nine at night, the perfect hour for redecorating. Michael followed me down from his room to the basement door. I opened it and turned on the light. Mike was right behind me, and when the light went on we saw at the bottom of the rickety staircase these two rather large furry animals gnawing away, or whatever they do, at the wooden steps. I started down the stairs and then turned back to my protector, who had not budged since the rat sighting.

"Mike, go into the first floor apartment and get me a bottle of ammonia," I ordered.

He ran off and came back and handed me the bottle. I started down the stairs and began throwing the ammonia on the rats. They scurried off, but I continued chasing and sprinkling, madly "ammoniating" them. Finally the little bastards flipped over onto their backs and just lay there, feet up, quivering. I walked back to the stairs and called to Mike.

"Get me some more ammonia."

"There isn't any more," cried my hero, not moving.

"Come on down here," I yelled, "and take a look."

"No thanks," answered Mike. "I'll stay here."

I went back to check the rats. They didn't look too good. They were still belly-up and I figured they'd be out long enough for me to call an exterminator. I started back up the stairs, reached the top, turned off the light, and shut the door. Big Mike was standing there with his mouth open, shaking his head.

"You're no goddamn help," I said, "where the hell were you? All you could do was get me the ammonia."

"Jesus," he replied, "I don't believe it. You're afraid of everything, yet you went after those rats." Admiration shone from his eyes. Miss Fraidy-Cat had shown her mettle.

A Hell of a Life

Mike was flabbergasted. He'd never seen anyone, especially a woman, stand up to rats before. Most women don't, even the most courageous. My dear friend Phyllis Seaton, the director George's wife, wasn't afraid of anything; she was so fearless that she once served as mayor of Beverly Hills. Phyllis lived through politics and earthquakes and was as tough a broad as you can imagine—except when it came to mice. If a mouse appeared, she became catatonic. Once, she was visiting friends, caught sight of a little four-footed creature and froze. She became stiff as a board and had to be carried out of the house.

As for me, when it comes to mice, rats, or cockroaches and creatures like that, you bet your knickers I'll go after them. I never poked fun at Phyllis Seaton because she was so terrified of mice; however, I don't knock anybody's fears or phobias. I have so many of my own that if someone tells me he's afraid of moths, I say fine, keep away from them. About fifteen years ago, my fear of getting in elevators really went into gear. My lawyer was on the eleventh floor in a New York building and I reached the point where I'd go to his building and have him meet me in the lobby to transact our business. If I drank enough, I could go on elevators. However, if I drank enough, by the time I got to the floor, I didn't know where the hell I was anyway, so it was no use. The last elevator ride I remember was a journey up to the Rainbow Room at Rockefeller Center. Someone who was with me said that when the doors opened on the top floor, I fell out and lay there. Bottom line? I don't like any large thing that moves with me in it. But a rodent? No problem. I lived off that slaying-the-rats-with-ammonia story for years. Anytime anyone started in about what a coward I was, I'd drag it out. I was so proud to find something I wasn't scared of. It was my finest hour.

Another important task the actor has is to keep "fresh," which after a long run ain't the easiest thing in the world to do. You have to, though, because each night is a different audience and you owe them your best. You can't just let down one night and say, "Gee, too bad you guys didn't catch me yesterday, I was in tippytop shape." When you're performing you have to be in peak condition; you've got to get lots of sleep and you've got to keep the level of your performance up. Again, it's part of the territory. I could keep my performances up okay, but there's one thing I could never do; I couldn't simply end a performance and then go home. Some people, though not many that I've known, can; they do their thing and when the curtain comes down, they go to bed. Miss Cornell was like that. She'd go home and retire while Guthrie and I sat up half the night talking. I could never just go home; I still can't. I have to go somewhere, sit down, and have some drinks and conversation. This is the only way I can wind down—and in those Broadway years, I needed to unwind.

When you're acting in a play your aim is to be the character and while you're working you can't be outside yourself and looking in. You plunge in. You cannot help but be involved, because your full attention and concentration is on the problems of whomever you're pretending to be. And you have to pretend anew at each performance. The key word is "pretend." I enjoy pretending. I've never been a big fan of reality. Give me magic any day; magic is what you get in acting. I love the pretense and I love being part of a theatrical "family." Some of the enchantment comes from being with a group of people with whom you bond so intensely. It's not that your own family doesn't mean everything to you, but for me, being in a play or a movie is made infinitely more marvelous because of the relationship among the members of the company. You're united in one purpose and come together to do your business the best way possible. The hardest thing for me, always, has been the finish, the end of the run of a play or the end of the shooting of a movie. The family breaks up and although you often do form lasting attachments and keep up with each other, the special intimacy is lost. I don't like to give up that "bonding;" I need to feel it. It's like an extra added something you didn't know about but which comes with the territory. Again, it's hard to describe. It isn't "real" family, it's a created family. I suppose it's like being in the army or maybe in a sport where everybody's after the same goal. The feeling is totally compelling and the sublime sense of belonging is overwhelming.

When you're working and part of the family, no matter how long or short the run, you try not to think of "The End." If the play is a sinking proposition, you can't allow yourself to give up until the final curtain. "Even in a turkey that you know will fold," you go out there and give it everything you've got. No matter if the audience is only a handful of people, you've got to play. Hell, you never know, a little audience might go out and spread the good word and keep you in business a bit longer. Early in my theatrical career, in every part I got I became very attached to the company and was hit hard when the play closed. I would cry for days; not just because I didn't have a job—reason enough for a good bawl—but because the family was gone. Max did his best to comfort me, but I would be inconsolable, at least for a time. After a while, and it always takes me awhile, I realized this was the nature of the beast, like knowing you're not going to be working all the time. The coming together signaled the coming apart; it was going to be over the moment it began and I'd goddamn well better get used to it and get on with the next order of business. In the final analysis, the show ain't over till its over—but, sure as hell, it is going to be over and the players are going to break up. I suppose one of my ways of dealing with the impending and inevitable loss was to drink it away.

A few things went amiss during *The Rose Tattoo*'s run. I remember a performance where I tried to open the screen door to the little house that was on stage. I pulled and pulled, but the damn thing was stuck and wouldn't open. I cursed under my breath and just walked around and went in the back door. A few minutes later, Eli Wallach came on stage and opened the door, easy as you please, and walked right in. It almost broke up the house. Then, something really weird happened during the post-Broadway tour of *The Rose Tattoo*. Early on, though I forget what city we were in, I was on stage doing my Serafina bit when all of a sudden I was overcome with this terrible fear that someone was going to shoot me, and I couldn't shake it. I got through the performance and didn't mention anything to anyone. How stupid can you get? was my feeling and I didn't want to let my colleagues in on my off-the-wall concern. Unfortunately, the fear didn't go away and in subsequent performances it became even stronger. In order to avoid being a perfect "target," I began to move around more. I never focused on what was going on, either, but darted my eyes this way and that in order to catch sight of my assassin before the trigger was pulled. I had no vision of who my executioner might be, I only felt that someone was out there gunning for me. This went on for weeks and I was slowly driving Eli Wallach crazy because he had to keep up with all my sudden changes in direction and inability to look him straight in the eye. I couldn't tell him the reason I was behaving this way because it was so ridiculous. Eli, understandably, got more and more frustrated with my behavior. "What the hell is the matter with you?" he asked justifiably. I hemmed and hawed and didn't come up with any reasonable explanation. Eli shook his head, and looking at me with total exasperation, said, "If we were the last man and woman on earth, we'd *be* the last man and woman on earth." Finally, one evening before the curtain went up, he announced, "Maureen, I'm going to show you what it's like working with you." During the performance, he tried to approximate my herky-jerky moves by darting his eyes and quickly moving from one place to another. I had to laugh because in his zeal to show me up, Eli outdid himself and wound up tripping over his own feet and lines.

I returned to New York and decided to go to a psychiatrist and see if therapy would help. At that time everybody was going to shrinks and I figured it was worth a try. My internist recommended an analyst and I trotted off to his office and told him what had happened.

"Boy, I'd give a button to know what's the matter with me," I said at the end of my story.

"I'm afraid it's going to cost a great deal more than a button," replied the analyst.

Many years—and many, many dollars—later, I realized that doctor's estimate was right on the "button." (I only went to him for that particular problem, but eventually I went into therapy with a female analyst for fourteen years.) While I can't say for sure that the doctor made my anxiety about being shot go away, it did go away. Part of the doctor's explanation went something like, if you don't face what's really bothering you and deal with it, it's liable to take some other form. In my case, my subconscious created an unknown hitman. With hindsight, I believe what was really bothering me was my marriage. On the surface everything seemed fine, especially to me; underneath I must have sensed that things were not kosher, and I desperately did not want to lose what I had. Hence, an armed bogeyman took the pressure off the actual problem and my everyday life continued.

Aside from this incident, being in *The Rose Tattoo* established my "way of life," if you want to call it that, for the next dozen years or so. I worked in the theater, studied at the studio, and in between jobs tried to raise my family. Danny was six months old when *The Rose Tattoo* opened, and we hired someone to look after him while I was at the theater. He was little enough to be "portable," and you can do plenty with portable kids. I took him along with me on tour. As kids get older, it gets more difficult, especially if you're the kind of performer who's always on the road. Maybe it wasn't as hard on me because I wasn't that kind of performer; I didn't want to travel and did so only when it was absolutely required of me.

Touring after a Broadway triumph isn't so hard; you know you've been successful and now you're out to strut your stuff. Pre-Broadway out-of-town tryouts are a different story. Everybody's under such a strain and, in most instances, the pressure is pretty agonizing, especially for the playwright. As far as I'm concerned, the writer is the most vulnerable member of the company and it's up to the other participants to try and help the poor bastard get through the rewrites. I've never been too keen on actors actually collaborating with writers, though. I'm neither a playwright nor a director; I'm an actor. Give me the lines and I'll say them. If I have a good and close relationship with a writer, then I'll give an opinion—if I'm asked. You have to be careful not to step on toes. During tryouts, the author is definitely facing the firing squad and the actors and director scurry around trying to help the playwright and serve the project at the same time. Artistically speaking, actor, director, and especially writer are anxiety-ridden in the pre-Broadway stages; although, as far as anxiety goes, the most worried person on the tryout trail has to be the producer. He or she has the greatest responsibility, those big bucks that may be going down the drain. I have a devout appreciation for the dollar. From day one I've never separated my art from my pocketbook. I left Troy, New York, nearly fifty years ago to seek fame and fortune and have managed to achieve some success in the former and fallen far short in the latter. I'm not complaining, just relating the facts. I think I instinctively knew from the beginning that no one should go into acting to make money. I earned my keep working in the theater, but for me the first law of being an actress is to survive, and good hard cash makes it possible to survive in style. The more money I have, the finer artist I feel I am, and while I think I was an okay actress, it's too damn bad I never got really rich at it.

After *The Rose Tattoo* tour ended, I began auditioning once more, only this time I had a certain recognition factor. I was now Maureen Stapleton the "Tony award-winning actress." As befitted my august position, I began thinking about getting an agent. Up to that point, I'd been working without one and there were difficulties. It's the old familiar story: some producers wouldn't see you unless an agent sent you and an agent wouldn't send you if he or she didn't know your work. Chicken or egg? Egg or chicken? The Actors Studio was a terrific source of information; we kept one another informed and when I signed for a show, I did my own negotiating, which is to say I took what was offered. I needed someone to negotiate for me. Tennessee was satisfied with Audrey Wood and suggested I use her agency. Bill Leibling managed the actors end of the business there, and so he became my agent for the next twelve years.

Okay, I was an award-winning star with an agent. Did that mean everyone was rushing to my door throwing parts at my feet? Hardly. Anyway, how many parts like Serafina come along? I had arrived but, in a sense, so what? Someone once asked me in an interview if it helped to know that I was a good actress. My answer was an unequivocal "Not at all." I learned about this from Mildred Natwick, a terrific actress who was in the cast of my first show, *The Playboy of the Western World*. I'd seen Millie as Madame Arcati in Noël Coward's *Blithe Spirit* and she was simply marvelous; she was great in *The Playboy*, too, and got excellent reviews. I thought it must be heaven to be an actress whom everyone acknowledged as terrific. Millie and I were waiting for a train in Westport one afternoon and I blurted out my feelings.

"Gee, Millie, it must be wonderful to know you're a good actress."

She looked at me like I was crazy and said, "What do you mean?"

"Well," I continued blabbing in absolute ignorance, "to be like you, you know. To know it."

"I don't know it," she answered.

"You don't?"

"No."

"But . . . but you are," I stammered, "everybody knows you are."

She kept saying no and I kept saying yes and finally she said, "Face it, Maureen, till the day you die you'll never know whether you're a good actress or not."

Honestly, I think I should have left the theater right then and there.

Was I a good actress? I don't know. All I know is that instead of starring in my next Broadway show, I appeared opposite Lee J. Cobb in *The Emperor's Clothes*. Lee was billed above the title; I played his wife, the one whose *je vous en prie*s were jettisoned. I played the role of *wife* better on the stage than I ever did off, where there was no script to follow and no director to lead me. I didn't know how to play the wife in life; I learned everything at the movies and in the movies boy met girl, boy got girl, they married, and then fadeout, the end. So what happened afterward? I could handle things up to the fadeout, but I didn't know what to do beyond that. I had no guidelines to portray Mrs. Max Allentuck and poor Max suffered the consequences.

The Emperor's Clothes did not set the theatrical world on fire. I couldn't relate to the part; moreover, although I couldn't say it then, I didn't know what the hell I was doing in it! One critic correctly sized up the situation by writing that "Maureen Stapleton played her part as if she hadn't yet signed the contract with the producers." If nothing else, *The Emperor's Clothes,* which opened in February 1953, started me on a "run" of engagements. Mercifully, the emperor was deposed and in July I replaced Beatrice Straight in Arthur Miller's *The Crucible,* which had been playing at the Martin Beck for six months. I negotiated my contract with the company manager and told him I thought I should receive the same salary as Beatrice Straight. The company manager said that was too much money and I wasn't worth it. So, I took less. The company manager was Max Allentuck. I bring up these stories only to show how little awards can mean in terms of recognition—and remuneration! If I had a choice of a medal to put on my mantel or good old cash to put in my pocket, there's no question as to what I'd pick.

I enjoyed my stay with *The Crucible;* it was my one and only stage association with Arthur Miller and afforded me the opportunity to play opposite a good friend and gifted colleague, E. G. Marshall. In December I rounded out this year of incredibly steady employment by appearing in my second and last Shakespearean play on Broadway, as Anne in the New York Theatre Company's production of *Richard III,* along with Vincent Price, Florence Reed, Jessie Royce Landis and the star, José Ferrer. *Richard III* was my first-ever appearance under a woman director, Margaret Webster. Miss Webster, the daughter of Dame Mae Whitty, started out as an actress and in the mid-thirties began to direct. She, Cheryl Crawford, and Eva Le Gallienne founded the American Repertory Theatre in 1946; later Miss Webster became the first woman to direct an opera at the Metropolitan Opera House. Woman or no, Margaret Webster was a real pro. I wouldn't dream of separating directors by their sex. Actually, I haven't really worked with that many women, simply because there just aren't that many around. I can tell you there was no difference in the way Margaret Webster did her stuff. She was damn good at what she did and extremely efficient. We had only two weeks in which to rehearse and she really pulled the thing together. I found her easy to be with and thought her work first-rate.

My next New York appearance was in an off-Broadway presentation of Chekhov's *The Sea Gull.* The play opened at the Phoenix Theatre and reunited me with a number of old friends. Mira Rostova, Kevin McCarthy, and Montgomery Clift were responsible for the adaptation of Chekhov and all three appeared in it as well. Because they'd done the research and produced the script, they became the "authorities," and when rehearsals began, everyone followed their leads. Neither Mira nor Kevin nor Monty spoke up, but mumbled their lines into their "beards." The Phoenix Theatre didn't have the best acoustics in the world and there was great difficulty in hearing what was being said by the triumvirate. We let it go because the rest of us figured if those guys were doing it, that was the way it had to be done. Max came to a rehearsal and afterward rushed backstage and as he climbed the stairs called out to me, "Maureen, you can't hear anybody." I thought I'd been speaking okay, but my energy must have flagged; so from then on, I began to belt my lines. I didn't care if it was good or bad; I just wanted to be loud.

The whispering routines continued and toward the end of the rehearsals Thornton Wilder and Arthur Miller were invited to come in and view the proceedings. Thornton came to follow the text and make sure there was no sin against Chekhov. He found no transgressions nor did he say anything about the low level of sound. Arthur Miller, on the other hand, got up at the end and announced, "I don't know what the hell happened because I couldn't hear a thing. I couldn't hear a word anybody said." This was music to the ears of one of the stars of the play, Judith Evelyn. Miss Evelyn played Madame Arkadina and was from a very different school of acting from most of the members of the cast; for starters, she spoke up and projected her lines to the back of the theater. Now, I'd been playing peacemaker during the rehearsals and running between both camps, the speak-ups and the mumblers. It was tough because I liked and respected the members of each side. Judith was incensed because she couldn't hear the dialogue and had bitterly complained to me. I tried to allay her fears by explaining that things would pick up once the actual performances began. I told her an old joke about a bunch of animals who went on a picnic late in the afternoon. First came the eating, and they all gobbled up the goodies except for one who absented himself from the proceedings and sat under a tree while his cohorts gorged themselves. Spying him on the sidelines, the other animals went over and began exhorting him to keep up with them. "You've got to join us and do what we do," they exclaimed. The lone animal listened to their pleas, and when they'd finished he smiled and answered, "Don't worry about me joining you, fellas; in the cool of the evening when the fucking begins, I'll be there . . ."

"Have patience, Judith," I told the actress at the end of my cautionary tale. "Everything will work out in the end."

At the first preview performance exactly what I'd predicted occurred. Monty, Kevin, and Mira raised the decibels and, at last, Chekhov was heard in the land. At one point we were all on stage together and Judith Evelyn was about to leave for the wings. She had this huge ostrich fan and as she made her exit, she walked by me, wafted the feathers in front of her face and mine, and in a triumphant aside announced, "It's the cool of the evening, Maureen."

It occurs to me that while I've discussed most of my "vices," the drinking, the smoking, et cetera, I have not touched upon one particular aspect of my persona—my mouth. My language can get pretty rough and this, too, was an acquired skill. I didn't talk dirty when I was a kid; no way was Irene Stapleton going to allow a foul tongue in her nest. In fact, when I arrived in New York, my language was as pure as the driven snow and for quite some time rarely did I curse. I'd been in the city for about six months and had started acting classes. I made friends with Janice Mars and Jane Fortner and neither of them cursed. We were anomalies in our theater crowd, most of whose members could curl your toes with expletives. And because the three of us "nice" girls wanted to fit into the inner circle, using foul language seemed to be the most "in" thing possible. Janice, Jane, and I decided that we'd give ourselves a crash course in offensive language. For one week the three of us practiced cursing and literally forced ourselves to use all the terrible and forbidden words we could think of in every conceivable setting. We'd sit at the table and say simple things like, "Pass the fucking bread, you cunt." Seven days of this and now I can't *not* say those words. We did it so well that it became second nature to curse. It was so stupid, and yet I've never been able to unlearn it.

When I appeared in *The Bird Cage* there was a lot of foul language being used by the ladies in the cast, and, though you may not believe it, I wasn't the big offender. Eleanor Lynn, Jean Carson, Kate Harkin (Zero Mostel's wife), and Rita Duncan were the culprits; they struck fire with each other's tongues. The talk was so vile that Melvyn Douglas went to the director, Harold Clurman, and said, "I've been in the army and I've been in show business all my life, and I've never heard such language." At one point, we were going to do a run-through for the backers and Harold gathered us together for a pep talk. He told us what the stage would look like and what would be expected of us and ended by saying, "Now, we'll read this for the backers, and ladies, please, watch your language; there'll be gentlemen present."

Wally Fried, the producer of *The Bird Cage,* ran into a little financial trouble when we were in New Haven. He needed more backing and brought in a guy named Lars Nordenson as co-producer. Between the acts of a performance, Wally escorted Lars to our dressing rooms to introduce him. Rita Duncan promptly forgot his name and from then on introduced him as Hans Christian Anderson. Lars went to Wally and complained.

"After all," said Lars, "I'm a coproducer of this play and no one's got my name straight. They call me Hans. You've got to do something about it."

"I'm not saying anything," answered Wally. "With these girls you take your chances."

Once, the cast got together for a party and played charades. I'm an avid player and got so carried away that I banged my hand on the coffee table so hard that my finger was swollen. I thought it was broken. Harold went and got a pan of warm water and I soaked my finger. While this was going on, Jean Carson said, "What's the big deal? It's just a little finger. Look at this gash I got the other day." Jean lifted her skirt and revealed a cut on her thigh. "See," she continued. "Look how big it is, and I never said a word."

"That's because you're a peasant," said Ellie.

"Peasant," screamed Jeannie. "How dare you call me a peasant, you fucking cunt!" and she immediately lunged for Ellie. The two of them went berserk-o and were battling it out until Rita separated them. Meanwhile, the guys were laughing their heads off because Jeannie was offended at being called a "peasant," probably the mildest epithet Ellie ever used. Max bumped into the stage manager for *The Bird Cage,* who told my husband about the way the women in the cast were talking. "I'll bet my wife is right in there," sighed Max. Was he ever surprised to learn that I was the Emily Post of that production. For some reason I didn't join in, maybe because I was pregnant with Danny.

Fortunately, my friends today know what to expect, and at this stage of my life, I don't think my language would surprise anybody. There was a time, though, when being outspoken wasn't condoned. My pal Pete Semonian was an eye (ear?) witness to my many adventures with the mother tongue. Pete's been my escort on lots of occasions and every time he'd come with me I'd introduce him by saying, "This is my friend Pete. We don't fuck." That's crude, sure, but what I was trying to do was make it clear that Pete and I weren't a couple. I didn't want to cramp his style. Fade-in to the White House and a Kennedy

A Hell of a Life

Awards gathering. Pete and I are moving along in the reception line and ahead of us are the President and First Lady. Pete breaks into a sweat, leans over, and whispers, "For God's sake, Maureen, when you introduce me don't say, 'We don't . . .' "

Chapter Five

I was pregnant during the run of *The Sea Gull,* and on October 16, 1954, gave birth to a daughter, Katharine. Now we had a son and a daughter. Max and I both had looked forward eagerly to having children. I never thought that my having an acting career would interfere with my being a mother. There were those long stretches where I wasn't working and could give full attention, and even when I was working, it was at night. Now our family was complete.

During my pregnancy, Max and I decided to move into larger quarters. Our apartment was nice but inadequate—there were only two bedrooms, not enough for an expanding family. We found a terrific place on West 70th Street, a four-story brownstone that had been divided up for two families, the Browns and the Meltsoffs. Blanche and Milton Brown lived on the first two floors. They're art historians; she worked at the Metropolitan Museum of Art and he taught art at NYU. They're retired now and still living at the old homestead. The Meltsoffs, who owned the top two floors, wanted to move to the country and Max and I were shown their place; we bought it just after Kathy was born. Now each kid had a bedroom and there was plenty of space to spread out. When I moved to Massachusetts, my son, Danny, and his wife, Nina, took over the place, so it's still in the family. Max and I settled into West 70th and "between theatrical engagements" I took on the role of wife, mother, and home-maker while continuing to flex those dramatic muscles at the Actors Studio.

On April 19, 1955, at the Playhouse Theatre, I appeared in a Tennessee Williams one-acter, *27 Wagons Full of Cotton,* which was on a triple bill called *All in One.* This was my second venture into the world of Tennessee Williams, and what I remember best about the production is Tennessee's reaction to the set when we opened in New Orleans. *27 Wagons* takes place on a plantation in the South. After the builders had done their stuff, Tennessee walked into the theater one afternoon to view the backdrop for the first time. He stopped dead in his tracks when he beheld a magnificent plantation on the stage. The antebellum mansion definitely wasn't what Tenn had in mind; he wanted a run-down facade with a little porch and what he got was a full-blown Tara. It seems that the producer's husband was a builder and she'd assigned the sets to him. This guy was used to building real houses so he *built* a set. Jesus, did he build a set; I mean, you could have moved in and raised cotton on that plantation. I actually crawled under the porch to look around and I'm telling you that house was made to last forever. Obviously, no one had spoken to the builder about theatrical "illusion." Really, it was ridiculous.

"What's that?" asked Tenn from the audience.

"Why, that's the set, Mr. Williams," someone answered.

"The set for what?"

"*27 Wagons Full of Cotton,* Mr. Williams."

Tenn paused, drew in his breath, and said, "Well, who is responsible for this disaster?" Tenn wanted it pulled down immediately, which was an impossibility because of the solidity of the construction and the nearness of the opening date. Undaunted, Tenn got hold of the builder and tried to work his wiles on him.

"My dear sir, this is an extraordinary accomplishment; alas, it is uncalled for in this play. Surely a man of your resources can get this out of here?"

"Well, truth is, Mr. Williams, that set's been built to last. I'm afraid there's nothing we can do about it."

Poor Tenn tried everything; he even volunteered to pay for independent wreckers to come and remove it. It was no use; that set couldn't be budged. You couldn't move it; you couldn't dismantle it; and you couldn't hide it. Short of dynamiting the theater, the plantation was there to stay. All Tenn could do was have them put a swing in front of the house, and that's where the action took place.

One momentous day after *27 Wagons* had rolled off into the sunset, I walked into the West 44th Street headquarters of the Actors Studio and noticed a newcomer in the crowd, a really pretty blonde seated way off in the corner. She slouched in her chair and did everything imaginable to keep from calling attention to herself. Fat chance; this broad was immediately recognizable. Let's face it, Marilyn Monroe could *not* not be noticed. The papers were full of stories about Hollywood's megastar. She'd come to live in New York for a while and was dating Arthur Miller and observing classes at the Studio. That day was the first time I ever saw her. After the session someone introduced us. We shook hands and Marilyn spoke.

"I saw you in *27 Wagons Full of Cotton* and I really liked it."

"Why didn't you come backstage and say hello?"

"Oh," she answered in her whispery voice, "I couldn't. I didn't know you."

"Jesus Christ," I said, "you don't have to know anybody to come backstage, you just go back!" I couldn't believe it; the biggest star in Hollywood, for crying out loud, the biggest star in the *world,* was too shy to come backstage and see me.

Marilyn observed classes for a time and then joined in. Lee Strasberg paired her with me and gave us a scene from Noël Coward's *Fallen Angels,* which Nancy Walker and Margaret Phillips had just done on Broadway. Marilyn and I began rehearsing two or three times a week, dividing our meetings between my slightly run-down brownstone and her sleekly handsome rental on Sutton Place. The initial sessions went okay; still, I was troubled by my old bugaboo, acting in a Noël Coward play. Marilyn was fine; I was very uncomfortable. I knew it was stupid for me to try and bulldoze myself into Coward's drawing rooms. I was gawdawful; something had to be done. Marilyn came over to my place and was ready to rehearse, when I voiced my misgivings.

"Look," I said, "I really love working with you, but I'm having a terrible time. I simply cannot do Noël Coward. I don't want to mess things up. I think we should find another scene."

Marilyn's face fell to the floor. "Gee, I'm sorry, Maureen," she apologized, "I've really been trying to get things right and I thought I was doing okay."

"You're doing great," I protested; "I'm the one who's not with it." Much as I argued, Marilyn wouldn't buy my explanation. She thought I was being polite and trying to spare her feelings by blaming myself. The truth was, she was damn good; I was lousy. She was so incredibly sensitive, though, that I couldn't convince the woman that the problem was mine, not hers. Happily, she did agree to use another play. I looked around and picked out the barroom scene from Eugene O'Neill's *Anna Christie* where Anna makes her entrance and talks with the old prostitute, Marthy. I brought it to Marilyn and we read together. I felt a helluva lot easier with O'Neill than with Coward, and Marilyn was simply terrific. Truthfully, I think she probably was more convincing than Greta Garbo had been in the movie. No disrespect to Garbo: I adored her, but I always thought she was wrong for the part of a hooker; I never could picture her as that. I'm not saying Marilyn Monroe was perfect for the part of a hooker, either; it's just that she was more believable as a vulnerable fallen woman.

"Oh, Marilyn," I exclaimed at the end of the first reading, "this is so much better than the *Fallen Angels*. How do you feel about it? Do you notice a difference?"

"No," said Miss Monroe.

"You don't? You don't feel any different from what we've been doing?"

"Nope," she answered. "I didn't think I was very good in either one."

"Jesus Christ," I said, "can't you get it through your head that we've switched because *I* wasn't good?" I'm telling you, that woman never got it straight. Actually, *Fallen Angels* would have been a better deal for her because she had a natural light-comedy bent. Marilyn was plenty brave to do the *Anna Christie* scene. The part was serious and so well known it set her up for comparison to all the others who'd played Anna. Those comparisons could also fuel harsher criticisms.

Marilyn and I worked hard on the O'Neill scene and in the process formed a nice relationship. She was a sweet kid and very easy to take—and desperately insecure. The sweetness was mixed with a funny kind of naïveté. One time we were to meet at my place before going to the studio to rehearse, and Marilyn was way overdue. She telephoned and apologetically explained that she was unavoidably delayed.

"I'm on my way right now, Maureen. Go downstairs in ten minutes and I'll be by to get you in a cab."

I went down to the street and waited and waited and waited. Forty minutes later, the cab drove up and I got in.

"I'm so sorry we're late, Maureen, but the poor driver doesn't speak English too well and got a bit lost." The driver nodded his head in agreement as we drove off to the studio. When we arrived, the cabby stopped the meter and looked back with a big grin. He had every right to smile, because the fare on the meter was astronomical. We got out and Marilyn paid the cabby and told him not to worry about getting confused. "You've got such an adorable accent," she said. He drove off, and as Marilyn and I headed into the studio, I couldn't resist saying, "You know Marilyn, a couple of businessmen will get in that cab now, and if that guy takes *them* on a joy ride, he'll be in big trouble."

After our rehearsals, we girls would sit down together, have our wine and tell each other sad stories. Marilyn was open and friendly and willing to share her thoughts and feelings; me, too. I think I had more pathetic love affairs to talk about than Miss

Hollywood Sex Goddess. Whenever we met at my place, Marilyn would take time to play with my kids. She loved children. Danny was about six then, and I remember one particular evening when he walked into the living room where Marilyn and I had been rehearsing. My son was in his pajamas and barefooted. He had a big blister on his foot and had been paddling around in his stocking feet most of the day. He and Marilyn began horsing around, and then Danny turned and ran out of the room toward the stairs. Marilyn took after him, and as he ran up the steps, she grabbed him by the foot and broke the blister. It hurt. Crying and wailing, Danny ran into his room. Marilyn followed and tried to comfort him, but Danny would have none of it; sex goddess or no sex goddess, in his mind, she was responsible for his pain.

"Get out of my room!" he ordered. "Get out of here." Marilyn was smart enough to beat a retreat and came back downstairs. I told her not to give it a second thought, Danny would forget the whole incident. My son has to have been the only guy in the world to throw Marilyn Monroe out of his bedroom. Years later, people were over at the house and I called Danny downstairs.

"Tell my friends about the time you kicked Marilyn Monroe out of your bedroom," I told him.

"Nope," said my son. "I'm saving that story for my book."

Danny never wrote that book and is possibly the one person who said hello to Marilyn Monroe and didn't try to make a buck off it in print. I want to say something right here about Marilyn and all the crap that's been heaped on her. I *knew* this woman and am amazed at the number of people who never even met her and feel qualified to tell the world how she thought, what she did, and who she fucked. I can't say anything about her alleged affair with Jack Kennedy, but I'm telling you right here on this page that to my knowledge, she never had an affair with Bobby Kennedy, no matter what those books and television miniseries would have you believe. What a field day those mamsers had, and continue to have, with the Kennedy family. For a time, everyone came out of the woodwork claiming to have had an affair with Jack Kennedy. That's why I love Bette Midler. She did this concert with her girls, the Harlettes, and at one point she stopped and said to the audience, "I want to tell you something. I want you to know that I had an affair with Jack Kennedy. Not only did I have an affair with Jack Kennedy, they"—pointing to the Harlettes she continued—"all had affairs with him. Talk about your Bay of Pigs."

All this bullshit about Marilyn Monroe and the Kennedys makes me sick, especially the bit about her being pregnant by Bobby and having an abortion. Marilyn couldn't have a baby. She'd had an operation to try and have one when she was married to Arthur. She wanted a baby always! She got pregnant and miscarried in the third month. She was devastated. I'm telling you, if Marilyn Monroe had been pregnant, she never ever would have had an abortion even if the father had been King Kong.

I'm sure people will be dismissive of me and even irritated if I say she didn't have an affair with Bobby. They've heard all the stories. Well, don't kid yourself, stories like that are manufactured all the time, and invariably someone will believe them. I knew a really rich woman married to a famous man who gave extravagant dinner parties in her New York City apartment. In the middle of these feasts her butler would walk in and say, "Mr. Robert Kennedy is on the phone from Washington." She'd get up, go to the telephone, and have an intimate conversation with "Mr. Robert Kennedy." She wanted everyone to think she was making it with Bobby; she wasn't. She had friends in Washington call and pretend to be him. Talk about *sicko.*

As for Marilyn and Bobby, there's one person around who really knows the score; his name is Ralph Roberts. He was Marilyn's masseur and friend, and she confided in him. Ralph and I were swapping stories not long ago, and he told me that he and Marilyn had discussed the rumors about her and Bobby Kennedy. She said she'd met him a few times and thought he was very brilliant and a nice guy but not her type. She laughed about the stories of them having an affair. Ralph said he'd thought of writing a book on Marilyn just to set things straight. "You *should*," I urged Ralph. "People are doing books about her right and left, and they hardly knew her. Jesus, some of them didn't even know her at all." I really wish Ralph would do it; he knows the truth—Marilyn's truth, anyway. Everything's been dragged into the act except the facts, and all that hearsay has become dogma. I'm sick of these people dancing on that poor girl's grave.

I forget exactly how long Marilyn and I worked together on *Anna Christie.* I do recall that she was seeing a psychoanalyst at the time, and she told me some of the stuff they were going over in their sessions. She described one hour when she and the analyst were looking at photographs of Marilyn and Joe Di-Maggio.

"Look at this picture," said the analyst. "You and Joe DiMaggio are kissing. Look at your hands, though; they're flat against his shoulders. You see, you really didn't want to marry Joe, because you're kissing him and at the same time you're pushing him away with your hands." Marilyn finished the story and then, furrowing her brow, said earnestly to me, "See, Maureen, deep down I didn't want to marry Joe DiMaggio." I listened and answered, "Marilyn, you must have wanted to marry Joe DiMaggio more than you *didn't* want to marry him because, flat hands or no, you married him, honey." Poor Marilyn; as if she didn't have enough problems, she had to deal with the doctors. With everyone telling her this and that and the other thing, it's amazing that she survived as long as she did and that she was as pleasant as she was. Throughout our association she was as nice as pie to me. I found her really easy to get along with both professionally and personally.

During the rehearsals, Marilyn talked on the phone a lot, mostly to her beau, Arthur Miller—lots of billing and cooing and giggling, as far as I could hear. One evening we were at her place. After going over the lines, she expressed concern that her voice wouldn't project into the audience. See, she was a film actress, and in movies you don't have to worry about projecting, because the microphone can make a Caruso out of a canary. Don't forget, way back then we didn't use electronic amplification in the theater; we relied on our own lung power.

"Don't worry, your voice will carry fine," I assured her, "just talk louder; that's all you have to do. It's not a big deal."

I kept reassuring her and she kept going on about how her voice was too thin. Then the telephone rang. Marilyn's agent was on the other end of the line. From what she was saying, I gathered there'd been some sort of mix-up in a contract. Marilyn wanted to know what went wrong. She was pissed off and spoke in no uncertain terms. She started to talk in a loud voice and kept getting louder and louder. She demanded to know exactly what had happened, and apparently her agent didn't give her a satisfactory answer. This was a side of Miss Monroe I hadn't seen; a really determined business woman. She kept pressuring the agent, and finally I went into the kitchen to get away from the noise. I could still hear her, so I went into the bedroom and closed the door. I could still hear her. After the phone call was finished Marilyn knocked on the bedroom door and in the old familiar breathy voice, called, "Maureen?"

"Yeah," I answered, "I'll be right out." I left the bedroom and rejoined her in the living room. "Listen, Marilyn, I want to tell you something," I said, my ears still ringing. "Don't you worry your pretty little head about your voice carrying. I was trying not to hear you because I didn't want to eavesdrop, but, baby, they could hear you in Canarsie. When you want them to hear you, trust me, they'll hear you."

Marilyn was also worried about appearing in front of an audience. She knew the lines perfectly yet had no confidence and was terrified that she wouldn't be able to remember. The night before we were to perform she called me on the telephone and practically cried because she was so sure that she'd lose it.

"Look, honey," I counseled, "you know those lines, but if you're really that scared, why don't you do what a lot of us do from time to time? Just take the script and leave it on the table we're sitting at, and if you need to, you can glance at it during the scene. It's no big deal, I've done it."

"I can't do it, Maureen," answered Marilyn, "if I do it that way now, I'll do it like that for the rest of my life."

"Okay," I said, "okay, forget that method. Try this: Write your part out in longhand tonight, and I'll meet you early tomorrow morning and we'll go over it once more."

As a rule, Marilyn Monroe was not what you'd call punctual. Her tardiness was justifiably legendary. Put it this way: We'd been rehearsing for eight weeks or so, and on a couple of occasions she'd been on time. But that morning, she was at my house early.

When we were ready to do our scene, I put up a notice on the Actors Studio board. We didn't use our names; none of us did. I just wrote down the title of the play in a time slot. A week before we were to appear, Marilyn called me.

"Maureen," she said, all excited, "we've got to get to the studio on time next week; there's some scene everyone's talking about and the place is going to be mobbed!"

"Some scene?," I answered. "Don't you get it, Marilyn, that's *our* scene they're talking about." She had no idea; she never realized it was we, I should say, she, who had everybody panting to watch. Nope, she just figured it was somebody really important.

On the appointed day we got there early to set up the props and stuff. I knew (know) *bupkis* about the technical aspects of the theater and/or the silver screen; Miss Marilyn Monroe knew plenty. She walked into the arena and right off the bat went about getting the lights correctly positioned. She knew exactly how to present herself in the best possible light. Make no mistake, that lady was smart. She sure as hell knew everything there was to know about lighting.

You wouldn't believe the number of people crammed into the Actors Studio on the day of our *Anna Christie* presentation, none there, I somehow think, just to see Maureen Stapleton as Marthy. From the minute Marilyn walked on and said, "Gimme a whiskey—ginger ale on the side. And don't be stingy, baby," you could have heard a pin drop in that place; everyone was riveted by her performance. She did the scene beautifully and, boy, was the audience ever surprised. See, they expected her to fall on her face. We finished and the viewers burst into applause. Kim Stanley said it was the first applause she'd ever heard in the Actors Studio. We weren't supposed to clap, you know; we were supposed to feel like we were in church or something. Afterward, we went over to a bar on Tenth Avenue and had a few. Marilyn was riding high; it was quite a breakthrough for her, and I'm proud to have been associated with that big moment.

Later she may have done scenes with others, I don't remember. All I know is that she didn't have a chance to grow. Poor kid, she really was serious about learning her craft and they wouldn't let it happen. Among other cheap shots, the press had a field day when she announced she wanted to do Grushenka in *The Brothers Karamazov.*

Shortly after her New York stay, Marilyn made the movie of *Bus Stop,* with Josh Logan directing. I knew him slightly, and he called and asked me for a rundown on his star. "Don't worry about Marilyn Monroe," I told him; "she'll be great." She sure was great in that movie, and in a helluva lot of other films, too.

There were many facets to Marilyn Monroe's knowledge, not all of them related to acting. One time Eli Wallach came over; the three of us were sitting around talking and Eli began expounding on financial matters. He was going on about capital gains when Marilyn entered the conversation and talked with real authority about the subject. She knocked Eli's socks off. Who'd ever suspect there were such goings on in her brain?

Marilyn and I stayed in touch over the years, though we never again were able to connect for any length of time. After she married Arthur Miller, I went to dinner with them, and later, when she was doing *Some Like It Hot* and I was filming *Lonely-hearts,* we exchanged a couple of visits on our respective sets. Our friendship continued via the telephone rather than in-person visits. One of the last times I spoke to her, we had a phone conversation about Janice Mars. I'd heard through the grapevine that Marilyn was looking for a secretary, and I knew Janice wanted a job. I called Marilyn and told her that Janice was looking for work and that I thought she'd be wonderful for her.

"Oh dear," said Marilyn with genuine concern, "I'm so sorry. I'd love to have had Janice with me, but I've already hired someone else."

"Well, that's the way it goes," I said.

"But listen, Maureen, thanks so much for thinking of both of us." I thought it wonderfully thoughtful of her to put things in terms of helping "her" as well as Janice, a pretty nifty response if you ask me. Then again, Marilyn Monroe was a pretty nifty lady. Too bad the world wanted her to be a ditzy blonde. I just don't believe people ever would have bought her as an actress, least of all a serious one. See how lucky I was? I never had that problem. People looked at me onstage and said, "Jesus, that broad better be able to act."

While Marilyn was a real part of my life for a little while, at about the same time another lady came along who was with me for nearly three decades. Eloise White appeared on the scene a short while after my daughter, Kathy, was born. What a piece o' work that lady was! And how much I miss her. Eloise died a couple of years ago and there'll never be anyone like her. She was a wondrous character; her zest for life was contagious. She enjoyed herself and had a good time no matter where she was. You could take her to the Black Hole of Calcutta and she'd make a picnic, and if you were lucky enough to be with her, you had a ball, too. I've been fortunate to know a few people with that special quality: Eloise; my agent, Milton Goldman; and Pete Semonian, my old friend from Troy. Each of those three had the ability to make you happy just by being in their presence. Eloise and Milton are gone now, but Pete's still around and still making life that much more delightful.

Someone had recommended Eloise as a cleaning lady and that's how she started out with me. She stayed as a domestic for a spell and then gave me notice: She didn't want to do household work anymore; she wanted to be a theatrical maid. I was just about to go into *Orpheus Descending,* my third Tennessee Williams production on Broadway, and when Eloise made her request, I went to the producer to ask if she could come on board. Let me tell you about the producer: His name is Robert

Whitehead and he is a prince among men and I love him. I love his wife, Zoe Caldwell, too, so don't get any ideas. Bob Whitehead is almost the last of the theatrical producers who can justifiably be called a "gentleman of the theater." We met back in 1947; Terry Fay, whose brother was married to my friend Ginny Beyer, worked in Bob's office, and she brought him backstage one night while I was in *Antony and Cleopatra.* That was the beginning of a cherished friendship as well as a professional alliance. I didn't work for Bob until he produced that fabulous *je vous en prie* epic, *The Emperor's Clothes. Orpheus Descending* reunited Bob and me professionally, although it was by an old familiar fluke that I got to play the role of Lady Torrance. Tennessee Williams once again had written a part for Anna Magnani. Magnani had become a lot more comfortable with the English language and agreed to appear on Broadway. However, she announced to the producers that she'd only stay for two months. This was too short a time for the Whitehead organization and, lo and behold, they turned to little old me. Filling in for Anna Magnani wasn't sloppy seconds by any means; I was thrilled to have another opportunity to work with Tenn and Bob Whitehead. Rehearsals had already begun when Eloise expressed her desire to work in the theater. I had no qualms about asking Bob and he agreed to hire her. Eloise's employment marked the first time I would have my own dresser; up to then, someone from each production had been assigned to help me if needed with quick changes and stuff like that. Now I had a personal assistant. Eloise White was with me right through my last Broadway appearance, in *The Little Foxes.* If I weren't working, she'd help someone else and did time with Lauren Bacall and Kaye Ballard, among others.

Eloise's first duty was to have my vodka waiting for me in the wings at the final curtain, and, bless her, at that task she never faltered. She was my caretaker and unofficial caregiver. She'd greet the people who came back to see me and had the knack of making everyone feel welcome. Life with Eloise was marvelously wacky; she shared some traits with my own mother, one of the most obvious of which was a tendency to filch. I guess everyone's snatched an ashtray or towel or two, but Mom and Eloise raised this kind of petty thievery to a fine art. Both of them had a habit of taking things when they stayed at hotels or traveled or went out. I'll admit I've done a bit of "taking" myself; I don't grab *things,* however—I take food. Once, Ross Hunter gave a big blast at a Broadway restaurant to celebrate the opening of his show *Shangri-la,* and I went with my huge handbag at the ready. I always grab tidbits and stuff my purse. Not this time. In keeping with the theme of the show, the food was of an Indian bent. Everything "floated" and had been brought in bottles. There was no way I could fill up my purse without soaking it. Another time my pals gave me a birthday party at a dance hall/restaurant in upstate New York. There was a band playing and the place was decorated with big balloons. Toward the end of the evening, I spotted this hunk of meatloaf sitting on the table and quickly picked it up, wrapped it in a napkin, and dumped it in my handbag. The damn thing weighed a ton. I was excited because that meatloaf would make a couple of meals, at least. I proudly showed my goods to one of my friends.

"Look what I got," I said, opening my bag and pulling out the napkin-wrapped chunk to expose the contents.

"What's that?" I was asked.

"Meatloaf; can't you see? Don't tell anybody I took it."

"I can see," replied my chum; "but that's no meatloaf, Maureen, that's a brick." I looked closer, and, sure enough, I'd picked up one of the bricks that had been anchoring the balloons. Mom and Eloise never would make such an error. They were professionals.

I was doing a movie in Hollywood and brought out my mother for a visit; she was to stay with me at the Beverly Hills Hotel. I sent a limo to pick her up at the airport and was in the room to greet her when she arrived. As we hugged, I knew something was peculiar. She felt different, heavier or something like that. She was wearing a coat, which for California was a bit odd to begin with, and then, when she removed it, the "difference" became evident. Carefully wrapped around her body was a blanket from the plane. Believe me, she didn't need it; she could have bought a million little blankets but she had to have it. Right away I tried to protect myself.

"Mom, you gotta do me one favor."

"What's that, dear?"

"People know me in this hotel. Please, if you want something, just tell me and I'll arrange to buy it for you. Please, Mom, don't take things; it doesn't look good."

"Pshh, Maureen," answered my mother as she folded her stolen blanket, "don't you worry about me taking things. I don't need to take things."

Here's the inventory from that trip, at least the stuff I learned about, none of which was purchased. Mother gave one of my cousins a set of a dozen wine glasses suitably inscribed with the Beverly Hills Hotel logo. Other relatives and friends, about a half dozen of them, were presented with little pewter coffee pots also engraved as the property of the Beverly Hills Hotel. How the hell my mother managed to scarf those items, fragile glasses and cumbersome pots, is beyond me. She had to do it, though; she just couldn't resist.

Eloise White was the same way; she had to take her "souvenirs" and everyone knew about her singular behavior. During one tryout we were staying at the Ritz Hotel in Boston, and, naturally, there was heavy liquid traffic going up to my room. The Ritz had lovely champagne buckets engraved with its emblem, and Eloise White wound up as the proud possessor of *four* of these inscribed buckets. How on earth she got them out of the hotel, I don't know; I think she put them under her coat. Ice buckets, yet. Eloise's apartment was just like my mom's house, full of purloined crap. Honestly, my mother could have cornered the market on swizzle sticks alone and Eloise had enough kitchen supplies to go into the catering business.

Since Eloise's penchant for pinching was well known, she'd occasionally be twitted about it. One night after the first act of *The Little Foxes,* an announcement came over the loudspeaker.

"Ladies and gentlemen, may we have your attention. There are two missing props from the last act, an umbrella and a flowerpot." Pause. *"Put them back, Eloise."* Eloise didn't think it was funny; in fact, she was genuinely upset about the missing props. "To tell you the truth," she confided, "when something's missing and *I* didn't take it, it bugs me."

Eloise and I shared many adventures together and whatever the situation, she always got the better of me. I relied on her for things outside of theater, for which I should have had my head examined. Eloise drove a car and I no longer did. Believe it or not, I once had a driver's license. I got it during a summer vacation when David Rayfiel and I were staying in Connecticut. I went to driving school, scared the daylights out of the quivering instructor, and then managed to pass the test. In the beginning I did pretty well. People told me I was a good driver and I think I was. Then things started to get worse and worse. I don't know what happened; I know I began to feel a lot less sure about being behind the wheel. After a few years I reached the point where I felt like I'd become a hazard to everyone else on the road. One afternoon I was driving with David and something came over me. I pulled over to the side of the road and said, "That's it; I'm not driving anymore," and turned the car over to him. I told David I'd return to driving when I felt I could do it again; I never did feel confident enough to get back behind the wheel. One problem was my drinking, which had accelerated. I was hung over most of the time, and no one should drive in that condition.

Eloise became the official "chauffeur," and we tooled around the city together. Her driving was fine, although there was a slight hitch: She had absolutely, positively no sense of direction. It's odd, really, because in all other respects, Eloise was a terrific driver; it's just that she could never reach her destination by a direct route. When you traveled with her, you were at risk of never getting anywhere on time, and perhaps of not getting there at all.

I was appearing in *Toys in the Attic,* and there was a cute looking guy named Percy Rodgriguez in the cast. One night early in the run, Eloise offered to give Percy a lift to his home in Harlem and he happily accepted the ride. The next evening, Percy walked into the theater with a glazed look in his eyes, and while Eloise was busy elsewhere, related the misadventures of the previous night's journey.

"I don't know what happened," said Percy, shaking his head. "We went all the way through Central Park three times and kept coming out at 57th Street. I couldn't figure out whether Eloise was trying to put the make on me or what."

"No, no," I reassured Percy, "Eloise isn't after you. You just gotta remember never to set foot in a car with that woman without a detailed map in your hands. It's that simple."

In 1969 we were doing S. N. Behrman's *The Cold Wind and the Warm*. Bob Whitehead was the producer and the tryouts were in Boston. The company had already gone up to Massachusetts, and I was joining them after finishing some business at home. Eloise insisted that we drive, and though I thought it would be easier than taking the train, I was concerned about actually getting there. I'd never been on a long trip with her before and didn't know what to expect. I expressed my doubts to her.

"Stop worrying," Eloise urged, "I can do it fine. Why bother with the train? This way we'll have a car up there." What the hell, I figured to myself, Boston is due north—how far off can we get if we follow the signs. We loaded the car, got in and began driving . . . and driving . . . and driving. I thought Eloise might have had a new route mapped out, so I didn't say anything for a while. We reached the Tappan Zee Bridge and Eloise turned left. Left, I had a suspicion, led to Arizona.

"El, are you sure this is the way to Boston? I don't think this is the right direction. We're going west; Boston is due east."

"Don't worry," answered Eloise, "I come this way all the time to see my cousin."

"El, I don't know that much about directions myself but we're supposed to go northeast. I'm telling you, this isn't the way to Boston."

"It isn't?"

"Nope."

"Okay," said Eloise. She took a quick look around and then made a U turn—in the middle of the Tappan Zee Bridge. Within seconds sirens started going off and assorted policemen on motorcycles began bearing down on us.

"You just shut-up," Eloise ordered me as the police motioned us to pull over. "Keep your mouth zipped; I'll handle this."

Eloise stopped the car, and as the policemen approached us, she began to cry hysterically. I'm telling you, this was an Academy Award–winning performance of Barbara Stanwyck proportions.

"Oh, officer, officer; oh, officer," she sobbed and kept on sobbing until the cop said, "Lady, stop your crying. Just stop."

"Oh," wailed Eloise, "oh, officer, I got so confused. I'm just a poor old colored woman and I got confused."

My blood ran cold. I cringed in my seat. I couldn't believe my ears. I wanted to strangle her. Meanwhile, she went on crying and lamenting until those poor cops had to let her go. How long could they hang around that act?

"Bless you, officer, God bless you, thank you, thank you," cried Miss Butterfly McQueen to the officers, who beat a quick retreat to the safety of their motorcycles and got the hell out of there. Eloise was chuckling as she pulled the car back onto the roadway and headed, maybe, toward Boston.

"You're a poor old colored woman?" I said with venom dripping. "A poor old colored woman? Eloise White, you are shameless. That's disgusting. If you ever, ever, say that kind of thing again, I'll kill you."

"Shut up," said Eloise. "We didn't get a ticket, did we?"

We didn't get a ticket and we didn't arrive in Boston until ten o'clock that evening. Listen, it's hard enough to get into that city under the best of circumstances, but with Eloise at the wheel, it was an impossibility. We must have gone through every damned suburb surrounding the Hub. A miracle got us to the Ritz, and while Eloise made the arrangements I ran to the theater. The rehearsal was over and everyone was sitting around.

"What happened?" asked Bob Whitehead. "You left New York early this morning. Where have you been?"

"Don't ask," I answered. "I don't know; we made a lot of wrong turns."

"Turns, what turns? Weren't you on the train?"

"No," I said, "Eloise and I decided to drive up."

"You and Eloise alone?"

"Yes."

"That shouldn't be," exclaimed Bob. "You and Eloise should never be allowed in a car together."

Eloise White became well known in theatrical circles as a "character." I myself enjoyed a similar reputation, so, in the final analysis, Eloise White was what you call a "character's character." If there's such a thing as heaven and if that dear lady managed to get there without too many detours, I'll bet a dollar to a donut that she's waiting for me up there in the wings with a filled glass in her hand.

Characters. The theater overflows with them and I've been lucky to have been associated with some of the most outrageously remarkable people in the world, including geniuses like Noël Coward. I bemoaned my inability to perform Noël's works, and why not? He was an early admirer of mine, and it hurt not to be able to return the compliment by doing something wonderful in one of his plays. We met when I was doing *My Fiddle Has Two* (or is it *Three?*) *Strings,* or something like that, in summer stock in Westport. Lee Strasberg was the director. John Wilson was one of the directors of the Westport company and a good friend of Noël's. Noël had come down to visit his pal and catch the show. He came backstage and was so charming and warm that I immediately fell madly in love with him. Every time he came to America he'd come and see me if I were performing, and he wrote lovely things about me that you can read in his diaries. I've kept the telegram he sent on the opening night of *The Rose Tattoo* among my souvenirs. Noël was such a gracious man, I never felt like I had "a papoose on my back" when I spoke to him. One time he was staying in New York and went to observe classes at the Actors Studio. That evening he came to the theater to see me perform. After the show he slipped backstage, closed the door to my dressing room behind him, and began jabbing his finger in my face.

"Maureen, I went to the Actors Studio today."

"Yeah."

"Maureen, what are you doing in that place?"

"Oh," I answered nonchalantly, "it keeps me off the streets."

"Maureen, you belong in the streets. Get out of there."

Noël didn't have a high opinion of the goings-on at the Actors Studio. We discussed the different styles of instruction and occasionally I'd tell him about my least favorite aspects of the Strasberg method. One specific approach drove me batty. When you finished a scene Lee would nod his head and clear his throat and after an interminable interval would say in Moses-like tones, "What were you working for?"

"Please, darling," Noël begged me, "the next time he asks you what you were working for, promise me you'll say, 'Money, Mr. Strasberg, money.' "

We were at a party one night and a woman kept zoning in on Noël. She wore a voluminous white satin gown. Noël and I were talking and boom! the woman in white barged in and began chattering. Every time Noël moved off to another group, she'd circle, and then, in a flash of gleaming white, she'd strike. I watched as she tried over and over to corner him, Noël all the while desperately attempting to give her the slip. He came running back to me a couple of times, and I'm afraid I didn't protect him too well, because I'm not good at that kind of stuff. Realizing the poor man was under a blitzkrieg, I went into another room and got one of Noël's friends to come to his aid. "Listen," I advised him, "Noël is being besieged by a nutty lady in a white dress. You better check it out; she's driving him crazy." The friend took off and succeeded in getting the woman away. I returned to the main room and found Noël alone. We went to the buffet table together, got some food, and sat down on a sofa. We were sitting there eating and drinking and talking dirty when Noël turned pale, arched his back, and cried, "Oh my God, no."

"What is it?" I asked.

"Here comes Moby Dick again," groaned Noël.

In July 1955 Chuck Bowden and Richard Barr planned a revival of Noël's *Fallen Angels,* and they wanted to cast me and Nancy Walker. Noël gave them his permission: "They're both good actresses," he wrote in his diary, "so I have said yes. It's an old play and if it's a flop it doesn't much matter and if it's a success, which it might be, so much the better." Or course, I never did do it on Broadway, nor could I bring myself to do it with Marilyn at the Studio. I have to say, at this point in my life it looks like I ain't ever going to appear in a Noël Coward play. Even so, he remains one of the significant characters I have known.

Characters? High on the list has to be that beautiful lady Colleen Dewhurst. We met the way people in New York meet, at parties and shows, and sort of knew each other but really didn't get to be good buddies until her husband George C. Scott and I were appearing together in *Plaza Suite.* My daughter, Kathy, was about fourteen then and would come to the Plymouth Theater on Saturday nights. After the show we'd go up to the country to George and Colleen's place. This was their second marriage; they'd been divorced and then got back together again. They had two boys, Campbell and Alex, who were quite young and adorable.

Colleen completely bamboozled me at first. She struck me as one of the most powerful women I'd ever come across. She looked like an Inca princess, tall and regal and with a resounding low voice. This was some strong broad, I thought, a real *shtarker* as they say in Yiddish. Funny, both Colleen and George looked like warriors, yet both were pussycats. I'm slow, so I didn't find out until five years after we met that Colleen was a marshmallow, a pushover who shouldn't have been let out in public alone. I've never known a more giving person than Colleen Dewhurst. And what a sense of fun. My friends gave me a surprise fiftieth birthday party and, naturally, I didn't have a clue as to what was going on. I only knew I was going over to my friend Billy McIntyre's apartment for a few drinks. A pack of my pals hid out in Jordan Massee's apartment across the hall. When I arrived at Billy's, they spilled out and enveloped me with hugs and wishes and gifts. Colleen's present knocked me for a loop. She bought me this soft sculpture of the Statue of Liberty. The damn thing was seven feet tall. I looked at it and said, "Colleen, that's what

I've always wanted." I hope she believed me. I kept it on the stairway at 70th Street for years.

Colleen and George had this place, a so-called farm, in South Salem, New York, and, as at my old joint on West 52nd Street, people were always there. They'd come for a visit and stay for months. Colleen collected strays, human and otherwise, and there was a revolving roster of residents at the New Salem farm. I went there for a couple of summers along with my pal Elizabeth Wilson. Elizabeth worked with me in a few plays and is a wonderful actress and a good friend; we shared a house together for a summer or two. You'd arrive at Colleen's, go in the house, and suddenly men, women, and children started coming out of the woodwork, or so it seemed. We had such fun, eating, drinking, playing parlor games. My favorite was something called the Hollywood Fucking Game. Two people were declared "terminals" and the players tried to get from one terminal to the other through screwings that were or were not sanctioned by marriage. Of all the stars that shone on the screen, I'm here to tell you that the preferred "terminals," by a long shot, were Paulette Goddard and Margaret Sullavan. Those two ladies could lead you on an amorous path through all of Hollywood, bless their hearts.

Life at the farm had all the coherence of a circus with three rings going at full tilt, and Colleen presided regally over the activities. The Earth Mother, though a fabulous hostess, knew nothing about running a household. Colleen was clean as a whistle about her person, but the house? Forget it. She had a lot of help, too; the trouble was, nobody did anything. For example, Colleen had hired a woman to prepare the meals. The cook would make a fantastic dinner and Colleen would go crazy. "Oh, this is so fabulous; it's so delicious. Oh, this meal is wonderful." The cook would accept the praise with a big smile and then disappear for weeks. Honestly, this broad would come in once a month, cook dinner, Colleen would wax ecstatic, and then zilch.

"You know, Colleen," I told her after we enjoyed one of the chef's rare culinary presentations, "you have a cook who does cameo appearances."

There wasn't a person or a cause that Colleen Dewhurst wouldn't champion. One night she told me that a lady named Nancy would be joining us for dinner. Nancy came from London and had been George's secretary when he filmed the movie *Patton,* in Spain. Nancy arrived that evening. The cook, naturally, was AWOL and Colleen really hadn't planned a menu; I don't think she'd even given it a thought, at least not enough to go food shopping. There were some staples in the house and Nancy volunteered to make a potato omelet. We dined on the omelet, which was fine with me; I don't worry about food when there's enough wine and beer.

The next day, Colleen and I were sitting by the pool and Colleen started talking.

"You know, Maureen, Nancy wants to stay in this country."

"That's nice," I said.

"Yeah, but she needs to have a job so she can earn money. You can't stay here without means of support."

"Right," I answered.

"Wasn't that a fabulous omelet Nancy made last night?"

"Yeah, it was pretty good."

"Listen, Maureen." Colleen leaned forward and looked me right in the eyes. "I've been thinking. Nancy needs to have a job and she's such a terrific cook, I'd like to set her up in a catering service, and until she gets on her feet, I thought that she could marry my friend Stuart. If she's married to an American citizen, then she can stay and work here without any problems." Colleen continued to bombard me with her ideas. At the point where she mentioned the sum of around $65,000 she would be giving to Nancy to start her catering business in a house equipped with many ovens and stoves, all of which would be bought and paid for by Colleen Dewhurst, I interrupted.

"Colleen . . ."

"Yes, Maureen."

"Are you nuts? What the hell are you talking about?"

"What do you mean?" asked the Inca princess.

"I mean the following: This broad made one potato omelet, and you're already marrying her off to that nice homosexual friend of yours and giving her $65,000 to start a catering business. That's what I mean. What the hell is the matter with you?"

"Listen, Maureen, you're the one who's always said that actors should have a sideline, a business that they can count on."

"Yes, yes," I agreed, "a business they can count on and a business they know something about. What the hell do you know about catering?"

"Well, people around here complain all the time about having to do their own cooking."

"What people? We're in the middle of the goddamn country. There's no people here. There's us! Period. Anyway, if you are serious about this, you've got to do research. Do whatever the hell you do before you plunk down big money. Stand with a stopwatch and see how many people call up looking for a catering service."

"Oh, Maureen," groaned Colleen, "don't be so fussy."

That's what Colleen Dewhurst was like. She would literally give you the shirt off her back; Christ, she'd give you her back. She had to take care of everybody. After I got her number, I watched her like a hawk. Whenever she was planning to do something for no money or too much of her own money, she'd tell people, "Don't mention this to Maureen." They'd usually tell me and I'd call her and scream—to no avail.

Colleen cared so much about other people's creature comforts but was pretty casual when it came to her own. Like me, she didn't give two hoots about her wardrobe. Lillian Hellman occasionally acted as my clothing counselor, and Zoe Caldwell similarly guided Colleen. Remember how Eric von Stroheim got called down because he spent so much money outfitting all the extras in silk underwear while filming *The Merry Widow*? "Why do you need to have them wearing such expensive stuff? No one's going to see it." von Stroheim was asked. "Ah, but *they* will know they're wearing it. It will make them feel like aristocrats." Zoe was from the von Stroheim school of dress, and when she was directing Colleen, she insisted that her star be reoutfitted in underwear. Colleen favored the utilitarian over the fancy in her underclothing, but Zoe said the "scratchy cotton" had to go. This was in Chicago, and the two of them hit the lingerie department of Marshall Fields, where Zoe started picking up dainty things and dangling them in front of Colleen.

"How do you like this? Or"—putting down the item, she'd pick up another equally frilly number and hold it up—"how do you like that?"

"Panties are panties and bras are bras," Colleen protested.

"No," exclaimed Zoe, "it's important to have good underwear so you feel good all the way down to your body." Zoe didn't just talk, she acted the procedure and used her hands to run up and down her body to illustrate the concept of delicate underwear making you feel better. Colleen went into the dressing room and tried the stuff on while Zoe stood outside the curtain and encouraged her protégée.

"Doesn't it feel good on your body? Don't you love the touch of that silken material next to your flesh? Doesn't it make you tingle, darling?" Zoe oozed enthusiasm as she continued to run her hands over her own body to get her point across. The saleswomen stood around watching and listening to this ardent dialogue about underwear. Colleen bought the underwear and wore it, because it made Zoe happy. So much of what Colleen Dewhurst did was done to make others happy.

As generous as she was with humans, she was absolutely gonzo when it came to her pets. Three huge German shepherds, about six cats, and a bunch of turtledoves were in residence on the farm. For a while there were horses, too. Thank God she had to get rid of them, because they started coming in the house. None of her animals knew they belonged outside, which was okay for the turtledoves; they were in birdcages and the bottoms were lined with newspaper. The dogs and cats were a different story. They had plenty of space in which to roam, at least thirty acres of woods and meadows, and they'd go out and run and jump and play and do whatever animals do. Then, after running wild on the property, they'd turn around and come back into the farmhouse where they'd pee and shit all over the floor.

"I'm just curious Colleen," I said one afternoon. "You've got thirty acres out there; how did you manage to train the dogs and cats to crap in the house?"

Colleen decided to redecorate the farm. She went to a fabric store and got swatches of material and wallpapers and brought them home to make a selection. She wanted me to help her choose. I have no taste whatsoever and was reluctant to advise. Colleen brushed aside my demurrers and sat me down in the living room to display the array of merchandise. She picked up a leafy print and said, "How do you like this for the living room?"

"It's nice," I answered.

She grabbed another swatch, this time one with flowers. "How about this, Maureen?"

"It's nice, too."

Then she lifted out a solid light blue–colored patch from the pile and again asked my opinion.

"That looks nice, too," I told her. Everything did look nice to me.

"Oh, Maureen, what do you think of this one?" Colleen pulled out a square of embossed gold paper.

"That's nice."

"Yeah, it's nice," said Colleen thoughtfully, "but don't you think the gold is a bit too elegant for a farmhouse?"

"Colleen," I answered, "we are sitting in here up to our elbows in dog and cat shit. Way down on your list of worries is how elegant this paper is going to look. You can put anything you want on the wall and this joint ain't ever going to look elegant."

I'm a cleaner by nature. I'll grab a dustcloth or a vacuum and go right to work. Colleen couldn't have cared less—as precise and as exacting as she was on the stage, she was that careless in her offstage life. We were in the kitchen one night, and when it became evident that the cook wasn't going to cook, Colleen decided to make dinner. I poured myself a glass of wine and looked on as Colleen got her ingredients together. It was painful to watch. Every two seconds she would drop something on the floor, like a tomato or a piece of bread or a lettuce leaf or a chicken wing; whatever the hell she was using, every item bit the dust. She'd stoop down, swoop it up, and fling it back in the pot. I got dizzy watching her drop and pick up, drop and pick up.

"Colleen," I sighed as she pried up a smashed potato from the floor, "I just wonder, what the hell would you have done if you hadn't found acting?"

How fortunate we all were that she did find her profession. She may not have been a great housekeeper but what an actress Colleen Dewhurst was! When I saw her in *A Moon for the Misbegotten* I nearly passed out from the sheer force of her portrayal. I really regret that we never did a Broadway show together. We did appear in a television adaptation of *Alice in Wonderland* for PBS; Colleen was the Red Queen and I was the White Queen. Tons of interesting people were in that production, actors like Eve Arden and Jimmy Coco and Austin Pendleton. Kate Burton played Alice and her dad, Richard, was the knight. We had a blast. Oh God, how I loved that Colleen Dewhurst. Her generosity of spirit was as overwhelming as her generosity in material things. I tried to pull in the reins on her but most of the time I gave in. That smile of hers was dazzling; one look and you were gone. She didn't take care of herself, though; she was too busy looking out for everyone else. You want to talk smoke? That woman smoked. Oh boy. I'm an amateur compared to her. I remember being on a television show with Colleen and Zoe Caldwell; Mariette Hartley was the moderator. Colleen smoked through the entire program. Zoe and I had been talking pretty frankly about the state of Colleen's household. I told the story of the animals using the farmhouse for a toilet and the camera panned in to get Colleen's reaction.

"I'm disregarding what has just been said here," she smilingly announced in her smoky tones. "Let's just say my house has its personality."

That gallant woman shouldn't have died, she really shouldn't have, and it kills me that she allowed it to happen. Colleen was doing her cameos as Murphy Brown's mother on the popular television series when it was discovered that she had cancer of the cervix. The doctors told her that if she had a hysterectomy, she'd be fine. She walked away from the doctors' office and said, "I'm not going to do that." Colleen's mother had been a Christian Scientist and something unfolded in Colleen's mind. She was a long way from Christian Science herself—she smoked, she drank, you name it—yet when she heard the news, she reverted to her mother's belief.

Colleen continued working as the cancer gradually got worse until finally she couldn't work anymore. Then she sat at home and wouldn't take drugs even when the pain was excruciating. She suffered terribly and still held on to the notion that God would look after her and it would all go away. Bob Whitehead tried to get through to her. He told me he was going crazy because Colleen wouldn't do anything for herself. By then it was too late to save her life, but something could have been done to ease her suffering. Bob and Zoe took me to see her a couple of times. I'd get there and start cleaning the house. I couldn't bear to look at Colleen. It was the kind of nightmare with which I simply cannot deal. This was the *real world* forcing its way onto center stage, and, goddamn it, there always should have been magic for Colleen Dewhurst.

After she died, I was asked to speak at her memorial service. I was in such anguish, and the way I deal with distress is to drink. I went to the memorial with a bottle in my handbag. Jason Robards was sitting next to me; Zoe had told him to keep an eye on me. Everyone made their speeches and I was taking my nips when Jason wasn't looking. I got up to speak. I was loaded. I don't think I knew what I was going to say. I started talking about the evening of the Tony Awards the year that Colleen, George C. Scott, Zoe, and I all were nominated.

"George hired a limousine to take us," I told the audience, "and since we were certain that one of us was bound to win, we each had written acknowledgments of the others in our acceptance speeches. We sat there smiling and ready. When they announced the nominees for best actress, Colleen and I turned and nodded to each other and got our speeches ready. And, whaddya know, they gave the Tony to that cunt from Australia." The minute I said it, everyone looked at Zoe. She was roaring with laughter. Reassured, the audience joined in.

Ron Silver was sitting next to Helen Hayes, and after the reaction to my bombshell pronouncement, she turned to him.

"What did Maureen say?"

"I'm not quite sure, Miss Hayes," Ron answered.

"Well, you were laughing," insisted Helen. "You must have heard. What did she say?"

Ron gulped. "I think she said that Australian cunt got the Tony."

"What did she say?" asked Miss Hayes again.

Helen Hayes couldn't accept what I said. I don't even know if I accept what I said. I realize now that I can never speak at a memorial service for someone I love and I *never* will again.

Chapter Six

I went to my first old-fashioned Hollywood wingding during the Los Angeles leg of *The Rose Tattoo* tour in 1951. Max and I received an invitation to a gathering at the home of Kurt Frings, the agent, and his screenwriter wife, Ketti. I knew I'd be seeing plenty of movie stars, yet nothing prepared me for the actual experience. I walked into the Fringses' home, took a look around, and came close to dropping dead. *Everyone* was there—all the screen personalities I'd been worshiping my whole life. I thought I'd died and gone to heaven. Dizzy with recognitions, I nearly pulled off Max's arm as I alerted him with yanks to one after another of my idols.

Bette Davis came late, and her entrance was as dramatic as any she'd done on the screen. She was mad as hell and ranted and raved to anyone who'd listen. Ruth Roman, with whom I'd been chatting, smilingly filled me in on the details. Davis had just had a lover's quarrel with her latest boyfriend and was dishing him to death. I didn't get near enough to hear, although from her agitated movements and the fury in her Bette Davis eyes, I knew she was ready to kill. Seeing her acting out in person what I'd previously witnessed only on the screen was awesome. Indeed, I was so thunderstruck, I had no recourse but to drink.

Betty Bacall and Humphrey Bogart were among the circulating couples, and Max and I found ourselves conversing with them. Every so often I'd pinch myself just to make sure I wasn't dreaming. Max and I and Lauren Bacall and Humphrey Bogart. Chatting together. Jesus! Bacall was pregnant; we swapped a few mother and mother-to-be stories and then she wandered off. Bogey was a guzzler, a veteran of many scenes and brawls, and immediately spotted me as a fellow drinker. Actually, you didn't have to be Sherlock Holmes to realize I was fast getting into my cups. Bogey also recognized that I was starstruck and understood that my excitement at being there was activating my drinking.

I got more and more carried away and was really plastered by the time Burt Lancaster arrived. He wore dark glasses and I kept looking over at him. "What the hell is Burt Lancaster wearing sunglasses for?" I shouted to no one in particular. "We're in a house, for god's sake; he doesn't need 'em." I began to build up a case against the actor, and when he wandered over to our group and was formally introduced, I said exactly what I'd been saying to the others: "What the hell are you wearing dark glasses for?" Burt Lancaster looked quizzically at me and offered no answer, so I took a swing at him. Fortunately, my powerhouse right missed by a mile. Immediately Bogey came to my rescue. I was wearing a stole, and Mr. Bogart gently wrapped it around my neck and dragged me off to the kitchen. He sat me down at the counter and poured some coffee. "Take this," said Bogey, handing me the cup, "and drink it all." I swallowed the hot brew, and all the time my brain was reeling. I was drunk, and Humphrey Bogart was taking care of me. Just thinking about it made me drunker. Oh, and there was that little matter of my trying to deck Burt Lancaster. Years later, I had a small part in the movie *Airport*—can you beat it, me in a movie about airplanes?— and one of the stars was my potential sparring partner from the Fringes' party.

On the first day of shooting, I chatted with a production assistant.

"Wanna know something funny?" I asked him confidentially. "About twenty years ago I took a swing at Burt Lancaster at a Hollywood party. I'm sure he doesn't remember."

"Oh yes, he does," said the assistant. "He told me all about it."

Burt may have recalled the incident but didn't bear any grudge; we got on fine together. I couldn't get over the fact that he did remember what I'd done; and yet, why wouldn't he? It's not every woman you meet who tries to knock you out.

Humphrey Bogart was definitely my hero and savior at the Fringses' party. He took it upon himself to look after me. Sometimes, if you're a pretty good drinker and somebody else is getting drunker than you, it's your job to look after the less sober one, and that's what Bogey did for me. Was it the damned leading the damned? I don't know. I only know we came together and because he helped me, he made himself accessible. After that experience, I didn't think of him as Humphrey Bogart the movie star; he was Bogey, my friend.

My theory is, if you have lunch or dinner with any big star or celebrity, they're no longer formidable creatures. I had many opportunities to meet and dine with my idols, first, because I was an actor, and second, because of people like Harvey Orkin. Harvey was an agent by profession and a social catalyst by inclination. He knew everybody in the whole entire world, and what's more, he wanted all his friends to meet each other and love each other. Harvey introduced me to some of my greatest idols. A few eventually became friends; others touched my life briefly but meaningfully.

An example of the brief but oh, so meaningful occurred when I was doing some screen tests for 20th Century-Fox. Harvey threw a big party the night before I was to report to the studio. I had a ball at the party and struck up a long and amiable conversation with a guy who knew a lot about movies, a theatrical agent whose name unfortunately eludes me now. The next day I reported to 20th Century-Fox for my tests—and little Danny Allentuck came with me. His nurse had gotten sick, and since I had no place to put him, I brought my son along for the ride. We were waiting in the reception room when the door opened and in marched a whole bunch of people among whom was the agent I'd met at Harvey's party the night before. The agent spotted me and came over.

"Hey, Maureen, what are you doing here?" he asked.

"Oh, nothing much, just a couple of camera tests."

"No kidding. Gee, my client's got some interviews here. Let me introduce you to him." He waved his client over.

"Maureen, this is Elvis Presley; Elvis, this is Maureen Stapleton."

"How do you do, ma'am," said Elvis. "It's a pleasure to meet you."

We shook hands and Danny began tugging at my skirt.

"This is my son, Danny Allentuck," I told the singer.

"How're you doing?" said Elvis as he bent down and shook Danny's hand.

I was pretty calm during this interchange because Elvis Presley wasn't yet "The King," and for me he wasn't Barton MacLane, either! He was, however, damn good looking and about the most polite young man I'd ever met. As a matter of fact, the guy practically "ma'am'd" me to death. Elvis took a shine to little Danny and started playing with him as we talked together. My name was called by the receptionist and I stood up.

"Well, it's been great meeting you, Elvis," I said as I prepared to go into the studio.

"Same here, ma'am. Say, ma'am, what are you going to do with Danny while you're doing the tests?" asked the singer.

"Hell, I'll just take him in with me."

"Why ma'am, I'd be proud to look after him for you. You just leave the boy with me."

Elvis insisted and convinced me that his offer was sincere. So I left Danny in his care and went to do the tests. When I returned, I found Elvis and Danny sitting together on the couch. Elvis had taken his guitar out of its case and was showing Danny how to finger the strings.

146

"How were the tests, ma'am?" asked Elvis as he put away the guitar.

"Okay, I guess."

"How do you feel, ma'am?"

"Frankly, I feel like throwing up," I confessed.

Elvis snapped shut the guitar case, looked at me and said softly, "You know something, ma'am, I feel that way all the time."

Harvey Orkin once showed up at a performance of *The Rose Tattoo* accompanied by Gary Cooper and brought the movie star backstage to meet me. We exchanged pleasantries. Coop said something like "How wonderful to meet you, and what a marvelous performance." I answered, "Aaahaahaah," or something similarly inarticulate. Wonder of wonders, Coop invited me to join him at Sardi's for dinner. The invitation wasn't out of his lips before I accepted. Not content with a solo appearance, I asked permission to invite some friends to join us. "Sure," said Coop, "how many?" "Oh, just a few," I answered. He and Harvey left, and I got on the phone and called every girlfriend whose name popped into my head. "It's Maureen," I blurted again and again into the telephone, "get over to Sardi's, pronto." I must have extended the invitation more times than I realized, because that evening, Mr. Gary Cooper presided over a sizeable banquet—and was as gracious and charming as could be. True to my theory, we had dinner together and became friends. While we were dining, somebody came by and said to me, "We're going to a party, come along." I never turned down an opportunity to party in those days. "Okay," I said and turning to Coop, I asked, "Would you like to go?" "You bet," he enthused. I was struck by his eagerness. The guy was lonely. Coop was going through a tough time. All Hollywood knew that he'd fallen in love with Pat Neal, his young co-star on the film *The Fountainhead,* and their affair nearly ended his marriage. Finally his wife put it to him, and he'd decided to return to the fold. At the time I met him, he'd broken up with Pat and was kind of at loose ends. The reentry into marriage wasn't easy. He needed friends and people to shmooze with and, God knows, I'm a shmoozer.

Not long after my introduction to Gary Cooper, *The Rose Tattoo* hit the road. We were in Detroit, and Max, Danny, his nurse, and I were staying at the Hotel Barham. Early one afternoon the theater manager called me at the hotel and said that someone claiming to be Gary Cooper had contacted him and requested a ticket for the performance. "It's okay," I said. "I don't know what the hell he's doing in Detroit, but it's probably Coop, so let him have the ticket." Coop himself called me shortly thereafter and again invited me to dinner. One of the kids in the show, a fourteen-year-old named Salvatore Taormina, was in our suite when the doorbell rang. "Will you answer the door, Sal?" I asked. "Sure," said the kid, and he goes tripping over to the entrance. He opened the door, took one look at all of Gary Cooper standing there, and after a moment's pause just shook his head and sighed. It was exactly the reaction I would have had—if Coop hadn't been my friend. After we greeted each other, I asked Coop what he was doing in Detroit. "I came to see my old Dusenberg," he said. "The man who bought it lives here." I knew he was looking for things to do, but boy, he must have loved that old car plenty to schlepp to Detroit for a peek. While he was in the city, Coop also visited Henry Ford and had spent the previous night at his home. No question, movie stars get around. We went to dinner and I was shocked to hear Coop order a scotch and soda. He'd been operated on for a duodenal ulcer a couple of months before and had been in the hospital for weeks.

"Coop, how come you're having a scotch?" I asked. "Did the doctor say it was okay?"

Coop sipped his drink and answered, "I kept going till I found one who said it *was* okay."

I learned something from Coop's remark that I later used to my (dis)advantage. After being dry for a few years, I started to drink again—just wine and beer, though; I haven't had hard liquor in almost thirty years. The kids were so upset about my drinking anything that I told them I'd found a doctor who said it would be okay to have one glass of wine a day. Danny and Kathy were livid and blamed my drinking on the "doctor" who said it would be okay. There was no such doctor, of course; but I gave that excuse so often that I almost believe the story myself.

Gary Cooper sure could drink, but he wasn't alone. I soon discovered that Hollywood was full of boozers. Spencer Tracy had been a big drinker and then went dry thanks to the urging of friends like Katharine Hepburn. I came into contact with Tracy when he was about to star in *The Mountain,* a movie in which he played Robert Wagner's big brother. I'd been sent a script for the film, but I hadn't had a chance to read it when I came down from the country to have lunch with Spence, R. J. Wagner, and the director, Edward Dmytryk, to discuss the possibility of my joining the cast. R.J. had to leave right after lunch, but Tracy, Dmytryk, and I continued to talk about *The Mountain.* Even though I hadn't read the script, I was eager to do it because I wanted to get into movies.

I hadn't been overwhelmed with offers from Hollywood, despite my success on Broadway; actually, I'd been sent maybe five scripts in all since receiving the Tony. One of them was for a movie based on Ruth Gordon's autobiography, *Years Ago,* called *The Actress.* Jean Simmons had been cast as the young Ruth, and Spencer Tracy was to play her father. I was up for the part of the mother. I read the script, and though it was delightful, I decided the mother role was a nonpart—you know, sweet and loving and caring and all that crap but nothing to do. I was so full of myself that I wanted to do something flashy on the screen. Furthermore, unlike my old pal Lenore Ulric, who thumbed her nose at maternal parts, I had a legitimate reason not to do "mother" roles; I wasn't even thirty! I was young enough and dumb enough to turn down *The Actress.* Teresa Wright, who was in her mid-thirties, wasn't old enough, either, but was quite smart enough to take the part. The movie was a little gem. I never wanted to make the mistake of turning down a role again. Consequently, I was keen on doing *The Mountain.*

Dmytryk, Spence, and I sat in the hotel dining room swapping stories and shooting the breeze until five in the afternoon. I drank lots and lots of wine, while Spencer Tracy sipped club soda. I don't remember whether Dmytryk drank or not. Even though I was having lunch with Spencer Tracy, I still had vestiges of fan worship clinging to me and hung on his every word. Spence was something! He was graduated from the American Academy of Dramatic Arts, appeared briefly on the legitimate stage, and was gobbled up by Hollywood. He made a big splash in pictures and then returned to Broadway to appear in a Robert Sherwood play. He told me that on opening night of the Sherwood drama, he received a note from Laurette Taylor. It was trimmed in black like a condolence card and read, "Welcome back to Calvary." Ms. Taylor knew that the surest way to be crucified is to return to the theater. Spence continued to tell delicious theater stories and I continued to drink while working up the courage to question him about my part in *The Mountain*.

"Let me ask you something," I finally blurted out. "If I take this part, do I get to do anything?"

"No," said Spence.

"Well, is there like a scene where I—"

"Nope," repeated Spence.

"Wait a minute," interrupted Edward Dmytryk, "it's a great part."

Tracy waved the director off, turned, and faced me. "Look, Maureen, you haven't read the screenplay yet, but I'm telling you the part is nothing."

"Well," I argued, "suppose I did it in a special way; like I could—" Again Spencer Tracy interrupted.

"This movie is a setup. All you do is go off into the sunset with me. My part's the only one with anything to it, and if you think that's something," he continued, "in my next film, there are *no* other people, just me and a fish. Forget *The Mountain*, Maureen. Trust me, you could drop your pants and nobody would notice you in this film."

Tracy really talked me out of that movie, though, if the truth be known, I really was so eager to appear on the screen that I'd have been willing to play the mountain. Apparently Claire Trevor didn't mind merely going off into the sunset with Spence; she took the role.

So, though I talked about it and thought about it a lot, I didn't make a movie until 1957. I was appearing in *Orpheus Descending* when Dore Schary sent me the screenplay for *Lonelyhearts,* his adaptation of Nathanael West's book *Miss Lonelyhearts.* Monty Clift had the title role of the newspaper columnist who gets too involved with his readers' problems. I read the script and thought it was incredible—except for a ridiculous "happy" ending. I was shocked because this ending was exactly opposite from the book's. I called Monty on the telephone to talk things over.

"Gee, Monty, everything else is terrific, but that ending is so inappropriate. It's like taking Christ off the cross before he dies. I'm really disappointed."

"Ha," laughed Monty. "This is Hollywood; I'm used to being disappointed."

Deciding to be pragmatic about it as well, I took the part. Hollywood never disappointed me. I liked working in films; I still do. I don't think there's any disgrace in a theater person doing movies, and I felt that way back when it was considered a sellout if you left Broadway for Hollywood. I have always liked to make money, and Hollywood was a better place for doing that than the stage. You'd go out to the West Coast, do your stuff, get the dough, and come home. I still make movies today, although I don't haul my ass across the country anymore to do them. My recent films have been shot in places like Richmond, Pittsburgh, Toronto, and New York City, cities I can get to by car or train. Honestly, I think I like doing movies better than performing on the stage. It's far easier physically, though it can be a drag when you have to sit and wait hours while they redo the lights or whatever. Doing part of a scene on one day and the rest on another wreaks havoc on your sense of continuity. You can learn how to do it, though. Bottom line, it's just a matter of acquiring a different technique, and the more you work in films the better able you are to adapt; you figure out how to channel things rather than letting them spill out as you do on the stage.

There were some real pros working in *Lonelyhearts:* besides Monty, Bob Ryan and Myrna Loy were featured. Myrna Loy—oy, I was knocked out to be working with her. This was our first meeting and she was just as lovely a lady in person as she was on the screen. A great, classy dame. One day, early in the rehearsing stage, we took a break in order to participate in a PR luncheon. A bunch of reporters had been invited and the *Lonelyhearts* cast was going to answer their questions. Myrna and I were walking into the dining room when she turned to me and said, "Maureen, I think you could use some lipstick."

"Jeez," I said, "I don't have any with me."

"Here," said Myrna Loy, "take mine." She handed me a tube, which I quickly opened and dabbed on my lips. Meanwhile I'm thinking in my brain, "Oh my God, this lipstick has touched the lips that have kissed Robert Taylor, Clark Gable, and Spencer Tracy." I nearly swooned.

I had taken the part in *Lonelyhearts* for two reasons: one, I thought it was good; and two, not that many offers were coming my way. I was relatively young but had been playing "old" for so long on Broadway that Hollywood didn't know how to cast me. I didn't have the luxury of turning down roles, and, consequently, wasn't so artsy-craftsy anymore. I was willing to go off into the sunset with anyone, let alone Spencer Tracy, and was more of a mind to take what I could get and not hang around waiting for the *Saint Joan*s to begin materializing. I was green when I did my first film and learned through experience how to organize and conserve my strength. My character wasn't a particularly admirable person, but I was able to find something in her to which I could relate. I had to find it, or else I don't know if I could have played the role.

I don't think I've ever actually disliked a character I portrayed, and, frankly, I don't think I could play anyone I detested, even though an actor is supposed to be able to do that. The idea is that since you're capable of anything, you should be able to play all kinds of parts. Supposedly we are all capable of doing anything, but you don't have to walk in the snow if you're supposed to come in with frozen feet, and you don't have to commit murder to play a murderer. If you don't like the person you have to portray, then you're meant to find something in the role that's "you" and run with it. You have to use a certain amount of common sense. You "pretend." I turned down a role once because I simply could not relate to the person—Lee Harvey Oswald's mother. I had seen her on television and formed an opinion of her, and you cannot play an opinion. I'm pretty sure that was the only time I ever refused to play someone because of my personal feelings. If the truth be told, even though I won an Academy Award for Best Supporting Actress, I wasn't that crazy about Emma Goldman, the woman I played in the movie *Reds*. Like all fanatics, Emma had no life of her own, no humor—just a cause. She was one of those "I'm-going-to-help-you-if-it-kills-me" types. And although I was not terribly fond of the woman I played in *Lonelyhearts*, I could understand the reasons why she did what she did, and if I didn't totally empathize, I did sympathize.

Lonelyhearts was my introduction to the Hollywood technique. After eleven years on Broadway, you'd think I'd have been able to waltz into films. Not so. Movies weren't easy. For some weird reason, I had trouble learning my dialogue . . . dialogue?—I couldn't remember my own name for a time. I struggled to get the text right and kept telling myself "You learn three acts in plays, why the hell can't you remember one little passage?" The knack finally came, however, and once I'd mastered the art of memorizing, I faced that other intrinsic movie hurdle. I'd be tuned up, ready to do the whole thing, and we'd start shooting and the director would yell, "Cut!" Everything would come to a halt while a technical glitch or some such was fixed. Much later they'd pick up the scene, do another section, and ten times out of ten, stop again.

Obviously, this method is the exact opposite of performing on the stage. In the theater you're primed to shoot the works from eight to eleven, and your energy has got to be—well, put it this way, you have to have enough gas to get to Pittsburgh. You have to go from A to Z without pause except for the scheduled intermissions. On a film set, you shoot, cut; shoot, cut. I learned how to shift my acting gears in Hollywood and, equally important, how to "idle," without losing the character. The skill didn't come in one fell swoop on the first film, either; it took a few of them. Stage or screen, acting is still acting, only you route it a different way. The person who drives in the Indianapolis 500 also has to know how to maneuver through New York traffic, a whole other ball game, probably even scarier than the Indy race. The point is, wherever you're going, you still have to know how to drive the car, and wherever you're acting, you still have to know how to act. For years people have been trying to pin me down and get me to describe what it is I do. In the beginning of my career I was very frank in answering questions about my life. At the end of one session the reporter actually said, "Miss Stapleton, this is an interview, not a sociological study." Candid as I can be about most personal aspects of my life, I've never been able to go on about my "art." Once, a young journalist kept questioning me about the psychological aspects of acting, not my favorite subject.

"What do you do to achieve the level of truthfulness you exhibit on the stage?" he asked.

I shrugged.

"Well," persisted my questioner, "what do you seek when you begin to study a part?"

Again I shrugged my shoulders.

"What qualities do you want, Miss Stapleton?"

"Look," I said to the kid, "I like to act *fast.*"

"Of course, of course," he smiled, "but what is it that you are looking for; what psychological underpinnings do you hope to uncover and reveal?"

"Honey, I think if you're a good actor, you'll be a fast actor. What's more, you'll be a better actor if you're a faster actor."

The kid looked at me without answering. He was thinking and I could see the wheels turning.

"Oh, Miss Stapleton," he said, "that can't be true. I mean, you can't say, for instance, that Henry Fonda is a fast actor!"

"Henry Fonda may look like a slow actor," I replied, "but he's really a fast actor."

In the final analysis, that was my best definition of acting and, as far as I'm concerned, it still stands—fast is good, faster is better.

I like working with fast actors and fast directors whether it's on Broadway or in Hollywood, and I don't see any difference between the people in those places. I've always found the California folks terrific to work with; they know what they're doing. Actually, I loved the old Hollywood and wasn't in the least disillusioned when I arrived there. Critics can say anything they want about guys like Louis B. Mayer, Jack Warner, Harry Cohn, or Darryl Zanuck; whatever their shortcomings, those gents knew how to run the "railroad." The old moguls knew how to make movies and how to manage the studios, and I'm here to say that I liked the way those guys ran the business. People didn't get to go thirty million dollars over budget like they do today, because back then someone was in charge. Nobody seems to be responsible anymore, or, as is often the case, the person who's responsible on Monday is out on his ear on Tuesday.

In the past, many stage actors were snooty about appearing in films; they don't get on their high horses about it today. Similarly, you don't find many movie actors unwilling to appear on television because it's "beneath" them. Beneath? There's no "beneath" in acting. My God, I'd act on a beer barrel if you paid enough . . . make that paid, period. I have utmost respect for the Hollywood professionals, the crews, the costumers, the set designers; the members of the whole shebang are crackerjack. You can always learn something, too. I'd been in a few movies when I made *Airport,* and by that time figured I'd gotten the technique down pat. We did the filming at the Minneapolis airport, and in my first scene I came in, frantically looking for my husband. I walked on and began rotating my head from side to side. George Seaton, the director, shot the scene and then after the cut, took me aside.

"Maureen, this film is in Cinemascope and the image projected on the screen is huge. If you jerk your head around that quickly, it doesn't look as though you're trying to find your husband, it looks like you're crazy. Instead of twisting around, just take a little time to see if he's there. Think about it and then slowly turn your head in the other direction." I followed George's advice and cut my speed, and it made a big difference.

Television filming usually goes faster than the movies, but the same statements I've made about the latter hold true for the former. The crews are fantastic and they really know their stuff. Movies are easier to do, mostly because you have a lot of rest time and unlike performing live, when you're working on a film, somewhere deep inside you have to be aware that if anything goes wrong, you can do it again. Since television in the present day relies on filming or taping, you get the same feeling as you do in movies, which wasn't true in the early days.

My first TV appearance was in 1945 in a play called "The Story of a Lost Boy" on the *Armstrong Circle Theater,* and I've done quite a few bits and pieces on the small screen since then. In the early fifties I appeared in a weekly half-hour show that was broadcast from the Actors Studio, and I did stints on dramatic shows like *Curtain Call Theater, Goodyear Playhouse, Philco Television Playhouse,* and *Studio One.* Remember, all these shows were live! You took your chances whenever you went on because anything could happen and often did, and it was terrifying. On TV, if you did something wrong, your mistake was splattered all over the airwaves and not confined to the four walls of a twenty-five-hundred-seat theater.

To be sure, I made my share of boo-boos. At the beginning of my TV career, I played a character named Mrs. Marr on one of those drama programs. I had a scene with another woman whose name was Mrs. Jones. I began the scene by calling out, "Would you come in here, Mrs. Marr." I had addressed the other woman by my character's name and kept right on doing it for the entire act. It must have been awfully confusing for the audience. Errors weren't confined to individual actors, either. Mistakes could be made by the entire crew. George Roy Hill directed a big production based on a then-recent Illinois mine disaster, "Blast in Centralia No. 5," for CBS's *Seven Lively Arts* program. I played the wife of one of the trapped miners. I've never seen so many sets for any one show in my life. It was unbelievable; there were sets behind sets behind sets. It was like looking in the mirrors in the fun house. There were so many goddamn sets that in the final production, a scene between two miners actually got lost in the shuffle. No one gave the cue or, if it was given, no one picked it up, and the cameras glided by the waiting actors. After the broadcast someone said, "What happened to the scene between the two guys in the shaft?" As I said, anything could happen on live television.

In 1959 I played Pilar in the television version of Ernest Hemingway's *For Whom the Bell Tolls* on *Playhouse 90*. That production of two 90-minute segments was a killer. It doesn't sound like such a big deal in an era when there are miniseries of six, eight, and ten hours, but in those days it was unusual and cost a whopping $300,000—which probably wouldn't be enough to cover a thirty-second commercial in today's market. The cast was as big as the production and was headed by Maria Schell and Jason Robards, Jr., as the lovers. It was like old home week because Eli Wallach, Nehemiah Persoff, and Steven Hill were also in the company. A. E. Hotchner did the adaptation and John Frankenheimer directed. *For Whom the Bell Tolls* was a blue-ribbon presentation, all right, and a madhouse to work in. Most of the cast, including me, were appearing on Broadway at the same time. We had to be at the TV studio at eight in the morning and rehearse until it was time to leave to make our theater curtains. Between performing and rehearsing, the actors were exhausted. Many of us lay down on the floor and went to sleep. Maria Schell was an angel lady and the Florence Nightingale of the studio. She'd tiptoe through the resting troops administering TLC and aspirin. A wonderful woman.

Playhouse 90 had bought the rights to do a television film, or kinescope version, of the Hemingway book. The property had been purchased and paid for when an ugly little clause reared its head—the adaptation could be shown once and never again. Furthermore, ten minutes of the broadcast had to be done "live," probably to make sure the show couldn't be rerun.

The story takes place in Spain, where partisans battle the fascist oppressors. The partisans live in the mountains and ride horses. So now we have a studio full of tired-to-death actors, of which I am one, and rarin'-to-go horses. The animals were tethered in a corner of the working space and would snort and rear and do horsy things. While Pilar, my character, was fearless, I was petrified.

"I'm nervous about those horses," I confided to a colleague.

"Oh, stop worrying, Maureen, those horses have been trained for TV."

"Yeah? How do they know?"

We began rehearsing the scene and Maria Schell and I took our places. We were standing and talking to each other, and two guys were supposed to come galloping across the set and stop in front of us. Maria and I exchanged our lines, and on cue the horsemen dug in their heels and came galloping across the set. They were halfway to us when I turned and ran behind the camera. Hey, how did I know those horses would stop? I had visions of them plowing through me and Maria and the walls of the studio. The director coaxed me out from my hiding place and we did the scene again. Once more, the horses took off, and once again, I bolted behind the cameras. This happened over and over. Those animals were finicky and acting up. They may have been trained, but in my opinion, they hadn't counted on working for long hours and under hot lights. Maria took me aside.

"Are you afraid of horses?" she asked me.

"In a television studio when they're galloping toward me, yes," I answered.

"Don't worry, Maureen," said Maria. "I'm not scared. I'll get in front of you and protect you." That darling woman did exactly that. She stood right between me and the oncoming animals and we finally did the scene.

At the end of the third week of rehearsing, something snapped; I just couldn't pull myself together to go to the studio. I was in bed hiding under the covers when the call came from CBS asking what the hell had happened to me.

"I quit," I said. "I don't care if I ever work in television again. I don't care about anything. I cannot move out of this bed. Get someone else, throw a wig on her, and nobody'll know the difference." I hung up the phone, pulled the covers back over my head, rolled over and went back to sleep.

A half-hour later I heard sounds in my bedroom. I pulled down the covers, opened my eyes, and saw Johnny Franken-heimer and Arthur the assistant director standing over my bed.

"You've got to come to the studio," said Johnny. "Please, you've got to come."

"No," I insisted, "I can't do this anymore. It's impossible. I'm falling apart. I can't be doing a play on Broadway and rehearse all day for television. I'm exhausted."

"Please," begged the director.

"I'm not going to do it. There's no way I can prepare. You think people can work twenty-four-hours a day. It's impossible for me to continue. You don't get it. What do you know any-way? You're from California, you sonofabitch, and you're full of shit." I continued my verbal rampage, insulting Johnny Franken-heimer right and left. I finally ended my tirade, and Johnny said adamantly, "I am *not* from California!" I had to laugh. I'd called him every name in the book and that was the only thing that offended him.

Of course I gave in. They threw a bathrobe over me, dragged me down the stairs and out the door into a waiting taxi. I did the damn telecast. All that work and God knows what's become of those 170 filmed minutes.

You may have caught on to the fact that there might have been more to my exhaustion than just the amount of working hours. While I was worn out from all the work, my tiredness was exacerbated by heavy, heavy drinking. And why wouldn't I be drinking—my marriage had failed. Even as I cowered before those charging horses on the television stage, Max and I were in the middle of divorce proceedings.

Almost from the first I'd had a sense that things weren't the way they should have been in my marriage. The "someone's going to shoot me" episode brought those feelings a lot closer to the surface. I couldn't put my finger on the problem then and I don't think I can now. I believe I became a heavy drinker when I sensed that my marriage was not giving me whatever it was I wanted. I still attribute my failure as a wife to my inability to *be* a wife. It wasn't my table; I didn't know the rules. The searing memories of my parents' unhappy marriage were baked into my soul; I wouldn't face up to anything or, if I did, I tried to drink it away rather than deal with it. While I adhered to my regimen of not drinking until after a performance, I wasn't always performing. I was too frightened to drink before a show, but after the curtain fell, forget it. Max once said, "If only you could scare yourself after eleven-thirty at night, that'd be good." I couldn't do it. The curtain came down and I went into the vodka. I wasn't a closet drinker, either; I never attempted to hide my indulgence from anyone. Although I did try not to flaunt my drinking in front of my children, they knew early on that their mother had a problem. Little Danny would get very upset. I'd be in my cups and slurring my words, and he'd cry out, "Stop talking German, Mom. I hate it when you talk German." I'm not proud of this.

There's no question that my children were raised in an often unconventional fashion, due in part to my profession, but more to the point, due to my drinking. Still, Max was a good father and I gave my all to being a good mother, which in lots of ways I was. Kathy's told me that despite the idiosyncrasies of her upbringing, she always knew she had my unconditional love; and because I was able to dish it out in abundance, she felt she could overcome any obstacles. Danny may have had a harder time with me because he was older, but he knows, as Kathy knows, that I'd give up my life for them. I thought Dan and I had a great relationship when he was young. We talked and laughed and then one day—he was about fourteen—he went to school in the morning, came home at three in the afternoon, and loathed me. I guess he arrived at the age when kids start to look at parents as human beings and not just as mom and dad, and Dan must have seen that I didn't exactly fit into the everyday world around him. Most of the other mothers were normal and that became very important to my son. Well, I wasn't "normal" —never had been, never could be—and while I would gladly have done anything to spare him and me the pain of that time, it just

The Walsh family: Grandma and Grandpa in the back, presiding over the front stoop. On the left, my beloved Uncle Vincent, with his sisters Julie, Jeanette, Annamae, and my mother, Irene. No, I hadn't passed out—the sun was just in my eyes.

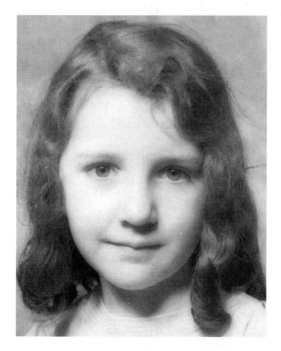

2

I was five or six years old here, although it's hard to be sure since all the women in my family lied about their age.

3

My theatrical debut, on June 25, 1935, at Troy's Harmony Hall. According to the program, I was either a Twinkling Star or a Gypsy Tambourine.

4

The Ordinettes and, in civilian clothes, our Commander-in-Chief, Major Bowes of the Original Amateur Hour. I'm the one toward the middle of the back row who is not flashing her teeth.

5

Rafael Soyer painted my portrait a number of times; this one he gave to me. It was one of the few I could show my mother.

6

An early head-shot, 1949.

7

ABOVE: Me on Broadway circa 1947. With Katharine Cornell, no less, as Cleopatra and me as her handmaid Iras in *Antony and Cleopatra.* To the left, Godfrey Tearle, and to the right, the inimitable Lenore Ulric.

8

LEFT: Backstage at New York's Martin Beck Theatre, in the dressing room I shared with Miss Ulric, taking one more puff before I sailed down the Nile.

9

RIGHT: Again appearing with Miss Cornell, this time in the touring company production of *The Barretts of Wimpole Street.* Again, playing the maid.

10

Playing the alcoholic wife of Melvyn Douglas on Broadway in *The Bird Cage,* 1950. The part of an alcoholic was a stretch for me at that time.

11

After thousands of readings and auditions, Eli Wallach and I finally got the leads in Tennessee Williams's play *The Rose Tattoo*, 1951. Landing the role of Serafina was my big break.

12

At table 2 with the Number 1 playwright, Tennessee Williams, and his good friend and mine, the wonderful Frank Merlo.

13

Years later, Tennessee, who had taken his knocks, wrote this to me.

Dearest Maureen —
I do not say fuck the drama critics because fucking is too good for them!
Love
Tennessee.

14

ABOVE: Off-Broadway at the Phoenix Theatre production of Chekhov's *The Seagull*. What a cast: June Walker, Will Geer, Judith Evelyn, Kevin McCarthy, Montgomery Clift (standing), and George Voskovec.

15

RIGHT: In 1952, I appeared in another Broadway production by Tennessee Williams, *Orpheus Descending*.

16

LEFT: In the 1960 film version of the play, retitled *The Fugitive Kind*, I had to surrender the role I'd played on Broadway to Anna Magnani, but I finally got to work with Marlon Brando.

17

ABOVE: My favorite role.

18

RIGHT: Continuing my favorite role, now with a complete cast, Danny and Kathy.

19

One of these two women was once called "The Most Beautiful Woman in Hollywood." Now I ask you, do you think it was the one on the left (Dolores Del Rio) or the one on the right?

20

RIGHT: The one and only Mr. Broadway—George Abbott.

21

BELOW: Here I am with Lynn Redgrave, Ten, and my beloved friend and the softest touch in show business, Colleen Dewhurst.

22

Johnny Carson's version of *Cat on a Hot Tin Roof* with George C. Scott as Big Daddy.

23

To the best of my memory, the only time I played a cockroach was on *Saturday Night Live,* with *SNL* regulars Laraine Newman, John Belushi, and Gilda Radner.

24

To honor one of my reluctant arrival in California, Carol and Walter Matthau arranged to have a band meet me at the Pasadena train station.

A departure for me, *The Secret Affairs of Mildred Wild* gave me a chance to portray both Scarlett O'Hara and Shirley Temple, although fortunately not at the same time. That's Doris Roberts on the left.

Getting to play Big Mamma for real in *Cat on a Hot Tin Roof* on TV, with the great and glorious Sir Lord God, Laurence Olivier, my Heathcliffe.

Though we are not related and have never actually performed together, people often confuse me with actress Jean Stapleton of Edith Bunker fame. Maybe this picture will clear it up once and for all.

28

On board the *Wu Li,* where there was always a party.

29

With my daughter Kathy in London at a party, during the filming of *Cat on a Hot Tin Roof.*

30

Ruby Keeler we ain't, but my pal Zoe Caldwell and I brought down the house with our unexpected little dance number.

31

ABOVE: The darling, wonderful Milton Goldman, the best friend and agent a girl could ever ask for.

32

LEFT: It must have been a party for this group to ever appear together. That's Vanessa Redgrave towering over Luise Rainer, next to columnist Earl Wilson, with me clutching my pearls.

33

Another party shot: Hermione Gingold and I are the bookends, with the gorgeous Arlene Dahl and the glorious Helen Hayes squeezed between us.

34

ABOVE: Three's company: the odd couple—Walter Matthau and Jack Lemmon—and me.

35

RIGHT: Clockwise, that fast actor Henry Fonda, followed by Martha Scott, Lillian Gish, Lynn Fontanne, Cloris Leachman, Christine (Mrs. Roger) Stevens, and me at the 1979 Kennedy Center honors.

36

Some of my best friend are actors. Here are thre of them, Jason Robards Eli Wallach, and Ann Jackson.

37

ABOVE: Tim Hutton looks like he's
rying to get back the Oscar that I
ust won for *Reds,* but I hung on.

38

IGHT: The irrepressible Eloise
Vhite, flanked by me and my
riend and fellow actress Elizabeth
Vilson.

39

Sharing some beauty tips with Elizabeth Taylor as Lillian Hellman supervises.

40

Elizabeth Taylor collecting one of her many deserved awards. Looking on, clockwise from top left, are Senator John Warner, Roger Moore, Gregory Peck, Roddy McDowall, Mr. and Mrs. Richard Brooks, Julie Harris, Bette Davis, and me.

41

It may look like the Supreme Court in session, but it's actually the cast of *Nuts*.

In dear Maureenie . . . . I would be proud to have you as my mother any day . . . Love – Barb

42

The all-star cast of *Cocoon*.

43

Pete Simonian with two Jeanette MacDonald and Nelson Eddy fans, First Lady Barbara Bush and me.

44

Maureen of Troy, back on First Street.

45

The one and only Neil Simon.

This is what it's all about—my grandchildren Max and Alexandra.

47

RIGHT: Max Allentuck and me, friends always.

48

BELOW: Reminiscing with Joanne Woodward at Canyon Ranch in Lenox, Mass., while working on this book.

wasn't in the cards. The day Danny grew indifferent, I called Max in tears.

Max kept saying, "What's the matter? What happened?"

"Nothing happened," I sobbed. "Danny left for school this morning and loved me, and he come home this afternoon and he hates my guts."

After my conversation with Max, I sat down and bawled some more. The phone rang and Eli Wallach was on the other end.

"Maureen, what's the matter?" he asked.

"I'm never going to have any more children," I cried.

"Who asked you?" Eli replied.

Danny despised me for about two years, and it sure knocked me for a loop.

Around the time Danny began hating me, I had a little brush with Simone Signoret, a heavenly woman. We had lunch together one day, and she told me that some friends of hers were putting on a production of Tennessee's *Sweet Bird of Youth* in London and they wanted me to play the Princess Kosmonopolis.

"Are you kidding?" I sputtered. "They gotta be nuts!" I'd seen the original Broadway production with Gerry Page as the Princess and Paul Newman playing opposite her, and they were fabulous. Gerry's was a known quality, but we never appreciated Paul Newman enough. His Broadway work was limited, but boyoboy, was he ever good!

"Listen, Simone, I don't have one single itty-bitty clue as to how to play that part. I can't do it."

Signoret then proceeded to give me a lecture. "You must do it," she concluded.

I lectured right back and said that I had nothing to add to Gerry Page's performance, which was sock-o great. Simone got carried away and lit into me. She said it was the duty of an actress to accept any challenge and I should extend myself. I let her prattle on and the whole business ended at the luncheon. Flash forward: A few years later Simone was in New York, and I joined her and some of her buddies for drinks. They were jabbering away in French, and though I don't understand the language, I thought I was hearing something and broke into the conversation.

"Hey," I said to Simone, "are they saying what I think they're saying."

"What's that?" asked Simone.

"It sounds like you were asked to do *Sweet Bird of Youth* in Paris."

"Oui," said Simone.

"Did you do it?" I asked.

"Non."

"Why didn't you?"

"For the same reason you didn't do it in London," smiled my friend.

"You miserable sonofabitch, Simone. You made me listen to all that crap about my duty as an actress. And I felt bad about it, too, and you go and pull the same shit."

Max and I lived together for a few years even after the marriage was, to all intents and purposes, over. We went our separate ways. Our marriage was kaput every way but legally, and long before that legality took place, I entered into another relationship, with David Rayfiel. Both David and I were married when we met. David's wife was an actress in the touring company of *The Rose Tattoo* and we socialized as couples. David and I were passionately drawn to each other, although I never could figure out what David saw in me. He had movie-star looks and was smart and funny and caring. We began to get very serious as my first marriage was gurgling its swan song. I didn't know what was going on with David's marriage and wasn't about to ask him. I'm not pleased that I carried on in this manner. I didn't see myself as the "other woman" type, but hell, I didn't see myself as a confirmed alcoholic, either. And by this time I really was "off the wagon."

Looking back, I think my guilt over treating Max so abominably provided yet another reason for my drinking—as if I needed more reasons. How hard it is to explain the anxiety that threaded its way underneath our seemingly contented marriage. The only clues to the underlying uneasiness were my drinking and the fact that I'd found another man. I believe that if everything's okay in a marriage, you're not looking for anyone else; it's not possible to have an affair. This is the way I feel, though, admittedly, I'm hardly an expert on such matters. I'm so dumb about things like that. Some of the most tumultuous romances and liaisons have been going on right around me and I've never known. Unless people are pawing each other in front of me, I don't get it. Max and I were at a party once and I sensed that hanky-panky was going on between two of the partygoers, a big producer and a big star, both of whose spouses were also in attendance.

"Max, look at A and B," I told him proudly. (I'm using letters to protect the not-so-innocent.) "They're up to something."

"Maureen, you've got it all wrong," laughed Max. "They're not interested in each other. They're using each other as shields. A is after C and B is after D, and they've been fooling around for years. Everybody knows it."

When it came to affairs of the heart, even when I thought I got things right, I didn't. Christ, I didn't even know guys were flirting with *me* until we got to the altar. I don't know why I felt the way I did about my marriage to Max. He was a good, kind, smart, funny man, and he put up with a lot of outrageous alcohol-induced behavior from me. Maybe I couldn't bear his tolerance. Our marriage already was pretty shaky when Max and I had another child. We'd both wanted more children; we loved kids, and maybe I felt that it would help bring us together or something like that. So Kathy was born, but, instead of perking up, the marriage really began to go downhill. For one thing, I was seeing David a lot. Finally Max moved out of the house, and still we didn't divorce. I think Max and I were able to hold on as long as we did because we were both in the same line of work and went about our business. We never had major fights. How could we; I wouldn't fight. I'd seen too much fighting when I was a child, and I'd go around the world to avoid confrontation. I had to have driven a couple of husbands crazy because I wouldn't fight or at least address our problems. No, my solution was ever the same—don't fight, drink—and I honestly don't know why. I only know I spent fourteen years in analysis and I still don't get it. All that money and time trying to find out why I did what I did, and I don't know. I blew it.

After Max moved out and got his own apartment, David moved in with me and we each pursued our careers. David divorced his wife, and we lived together for about seven years before we actually got married ourselves. David was a different cup of tea altogether from Max Allentuck. Max and I at least had some things in common; David Rayfiel and I were just about exact opposites. He got up early in the morning and went to bed early in the evening, he was fastidious, he didn't drink, he didn't smoke, and I don't think he swore that much. (He wanted to write, and he did go on to achieve great success writing for the stage and screen.) As opposite as we were, a powerful attraction drew us together. Unfortunately, when it came to the business of sharing my life with another, I still didn't have a framework. Bottom line, I loused up two marriages. But I'm the greatest ex-wife a man ever had.

Whatever the magic is in matrimony, I don't know how to wave the wand and make it happen. Although I knew the stuff technically, "wife" was never my role. By the time I'm seventy maybe I might have a bead on it. Who cares? I wouldn't marry again. Hell, I really don't think I'm capable of being married to anyone. I'm too screwed up. I don't know how to use the tools, plus I've got that good old Catholic guilt, which I can liberally splash over all my woes. Living with David made me feel tremendously blameworthy, probably because our relationship had come out of my deceiving Max. I had naively clung to the notion that life was like MGM movies—you get married and live happily ever after. I've always been nutso that way. I may have had an MGM mentality, but I lived in a Warner Bros. world, where happy endings were iffy at best. I mean, you'd have thought I'd learned something from being married once. Instead, after I married David I got worse and worse. Fortunately for Danny and Kathy, David was a wonderful stepparent. From the beginning, he was considerate and loving toward my children. To this day, much as they love Max, they look upon David as a second father.

After Max and I separated, he visited with the kids regularly and for that very long time, divorce didn't enter the picture. Sometimes David wanted to get married and I didn't; other times it was the reverse. It's possible I was still holding on to my first marriage; somehow it made me feel less guilty. Then one day Max dropped a bombshell: He told me that he'd met someone else and wanted to marry her. He asked me for a divorce. Wanna hear something funny? I was bullshit. Me, who'd been the chief screwer-upper of the marriage; me, who'd been living with another man for years; me, who started the whole damn business —that little old me was furious at my husband because he wanted a divorce. I listened calmly to Max as he made his request and was as polite as Emily Post. The minute he walked out the door, I went into a screaming fit that was quite bewildering to David Rayfiel.

"That miserable bastard Max. Who the hell does he think he is asking me for a divorce! That sonofabitch. Can you believe this shit?" I went on and on and on and ended with a flourish: "Okay, I'll give that mother a divorce, but I'll never speak to him again, I'll never look at him, again." David had listened to my entire performance and at the end looked up and said quietly, "You're absolutely right, Maureen, you mustn't see Max again. It's bad luck."

I was the guilty one. I had no right to hold anything against Max, and yet I felt betrayed. I was the rat fink and yet took him to task. I never could understand why I reacted that way. My mother threw my father out of the house, but she had good reason. I was the double-crosser in my first marriage, and Max had left the house because I made it impossible for him to stay. God, it's so complicated. I was furious at Max for wanting a divorce; however, I wouldn't say anything bad about him to the children. No way would I knock him.

We got our divorce, Max remarried, and he and his wife, Vaughan, took an apartment on 81st and Riverside Drive right near Calhoun Lower School, which is where Danny and Kathy went to school. Over the next years the children alternated between the two households, the "zoo" at West 70th Street and the residence at West 81st. Max and Vaughan had three children together, and as I mentioned at the beginning of this book, we became, and continue to be, an extended family. Although we have no blood ties, Max's kids, Joshua, Rachael, and Zachary, look upon me as a kind of aunt and I regard them as niece and nephews.

Back to the early sixties. Okay, now I'm living with this tall, handsome, talented man who looks like a WASP movie star, and instead of trying to make the arrangement work, I proceed to smash it to smithereens. I was so crazy about David but so ashamed about what I'd done to Max that I went berserk-o and systematically began destroying my ill-gotten relationship. I drank and ate my way into monstrosity. I OD'd on my favorite food—bacon and Franco-American spaghetti—and got fatter and fatter and fatter. In the end, I had zoomed well over the 200-pound mark and was closing in on 250. At five foot three, I resembled nothing more or less than the Hindenberg.

The nutty thing is, for the longest time David Rayfiel stayed with me and, I guess, continued to love me. I did everything to make myself unattractive, and still this guy hung around. I know from fourteen years of dealing with psychiatrists that there were subterranean reasons why I behaved as I did. Unfortunately, I still don't know what the reasons were—fortunately, I don't much care anymore. Thank God, I don't have to worry about such things. David and Max are both nice guys and they should live and be well and be happy and, hallelujah, I'm out of the loop. I took the goodness from all the muck, and the goodness was my children and now my grandchildren.

As far as those fourteen years I spent in analysis go, they went. I got so bored with myself and so bored with the whole business, I'd take different buses and go different ways in a cab just to keep myself awake.

Kathy and Danny are convinced that David "saved" their young lives, and maybe they're right. Danny's certain he'd have been psychologically damaged if his mother had remained alone or gone with someone who didn't care about him and his sister. Danny scarcely remembers the original family unit when Max and I were together. His memories, and Kathy's as well, start with me being with David. Kathy didn't even realize things were not "normal" until some kid at school said one day, "Your mommy and daddy aren't married. They're divorced." "Oh," said Kathy as the light bulb went on over her head, "I guess you're right." Being younger, Kathy was more protected than her brother. My drinking shook up Danny much more than Kathy when they were kids because he was older and saw me in some pretty terrible stages. Once, I stumbled in the bathroom, hit my head on the tub, and fell to the floor. Poor Danny discovered me and thought I was dead. The kids now know that thanks to the old Irish peasant stock that is my heritage, I probably could survive a direct hit by an atomic bomb.

David was a rock for the children because they could count on him. The guy had a built-in metronome and was orderly about everything. He went to bed around eight-thirty or nine in the evening and got up early in the morning to work. He'd make breakfast for Danny and Kathy and get them off for school. I, on the other hand, didn't rise until I absolutely had to. I'd taken to mixing sleeping pills with booze, and that combo knocked me out good.

One Christmas morning, Kathy and Danny wanted to open their presents and came bounding into my room to get me up. Nothing could wake me. They screamed in my ears, jumped up and down on the bed, and when none of these tactics worked, they literally dragged me out of the bed across the floor. I bounced along the carpets clutching the bedding, which had been ripped from its mooring along with me, and cried out, "Give me five more minutes, just five more minutes." Mrs. Santa I wasn't.

If West 70th Street was a madhouse, two things kept it from blowing up: love and laughs. Whatever traumatic situations arose were accompanied by laughter, even the worst of them. Gallows humor, perhaps; still, the sense of fun permeated our home. God, we laughed a lot, and that laughter was the saving grace.

The kids were with me during the week and went to stay with their father on the weekends. Max's home provided the antidote for mine. Unlike me, Vaughan was a classic mother. She cooked, she sewed, she went shopping and did all those little tasks that mothers are supposed to do. Kathy and Danny had their half-siblings to play with, and since Eli and Annie Wallach lived in the same building, Kathy spent a lot of time with them and their children, Peter, Roberta, and Catherine. I tried to keep up with the kids' school activities, but I couldn't always be there because of my own career demands. I'd even try to fix up their lunch pails, with varying degrees of success. On Mondays Vaughan always prepared perfect little sandwiches neatly covered in Saran Wrap. I didn't do sandwiches; I used what was at hand. Kathy loves to tell about lunch period in Calhoun. The teacher asked the students to open their lunch bags and show what they had been given to eat. I guess they must have been trying to check the nutrition or some such. Anyway, the kids opened the containers and displayed the contents. Sandwiches were the order of the day: the peanut butters, the fluffernutters, the tuna fishes, the egg salads, et cetera. Kathy Allentuck emptied her lunch bag on the desk, and the teacher stopped short when she spied the Maureen Stapleton version of a school lunch. I'd ordered in food at three in the morning and slapped the remains together for my daughter before I went to bed. On her desk lay a couple of barbecued ribs, a half-container of chop suey, and a shriveled slice of pepperoni pizza.

Aside from the nutritional value of their lunches, I think my kids adjusted okay to my working life, although there were a few incidents where things got a little hairy. I was asleep in the bedroom when Kathy saw me on a television show. She knew I acted on the stage and was used to the idea of the theater. This was the first time she'd ever viewed me on the small screen. I forget what the program was; I only know my character was in big trouble. I think I might have died, and little Kathy was shaken up by my death scene. She couldn't quite figure out what was happening and went tearing into my bedroom.

"Mommy, Mommy, get up, get up," she cried and began shaking me. As usual, it took a while for me to respond; meanwhile my poor little girl was sobbing. Reality and make-believe had collided, and she panicked when she couldn't rouse me—maybe Mommy really was dead. I came to at last and had to reassure her I was okay. I explained that the television was just "pretend" and that Mommy was alive and kicking. It's the only time I can recall her being upset by something like that. She never carried on about my theater appearances; they were an accepted part of the routine. When I was working and it came time for me to go to the theater, David would take Kathy and Danny in tow, and the three of them would escort me out into the street and either put me into a cab or onto the bus. We'd wave our good-byes and David would take the kids back home and put them to bed. The ritual was comforting. Mommy had gone off to act on Broadway. Seeing me on television without any explanation or preliminary warning, however, was not part of the routine, and seeing me there—especially watching me die —frightened Kathy to death.

Many, many people hung around our West 70th Street home, and lots of those people became residents at one time or another. I used to have a weekly poker game at the apartment on Thursday nights. I went to a fabric store and bought a big piece of pink felt (there wasn't any green available) that I threw over the dining table. David would go to bed and I'd stay up all night with my pals, drinking, smoking, and playing. We didn't use chips—when you're nickel-and-diming, you don't need chips.

I found poker very relaxing. I'd been a bridge player in my twenties but was never crazy about it. Colleen was a bridge fiend. She had marathon rubbers at her house. I was crazy about poker. We'd often gather at my place to play *after* an evening's work in the theater. I'd order takeout to feed my card-playing crew and to provide those nutritional lunches for my children. The regular contingent included Jimmy Coco, Janice Mars, John Baragrey, Ralph Roberts, and Lucille Benson. Lucille was a slightly nutty lady, but a helluva poker player. Janice Mars was something else. She'd be playing along and then stand up and go into the kitchen. "Keep me in," she'd say on her way out of the room. We'd keep her in, and every single damn time, she'd win! She practically never won a game when she was at the table; it was only when she left the room that luck ran her way. She should have played every hand sitting on the stove.

Aside from the poker players, an endless parade of diverse personalities drifted in and out of my house, ranging from Marilyn Monroe to Oona O'Neill Chaplin. One evening Oona was picking me up at the house, and I was purposely a bit late and told her to come on in. She stood in the entrance hall as I screamed for Danny to make an appearance. He came to the top of the stairs and I called up, "Danny, I want you to meet Oona Chaplin." "Hi," Danny called down and disappeared back into his room. Oona was living history as well as one helluva fine lady, and I thought it would be kind of nice for my son to be able to say years later that he'd met the daughter of Eugene O'Neill and the wife of Charlie Chaplin. Well, Danny met her, but I'm not so sure if it's ever come up in any of his conversations. I didn't know Oona very well; we got together a few times over drinks because we'd been introduced to each other by her best friend and the woman who became the best and dearest friend to me, Carol Marcus.

In 1958 I appeared on Broadway in S. N. Behrman's play *The Cold Wind and the Warm.* I was thirty-three years old and, naturally, played the part of an older spinster aunt, a Jewish one at that. I liked ethnic roles and fell into Italian, Irish, and Jewish ones with a measure of ease. I think it's because of the neighborhood I came from; all those accents and cadences were part of growing up on First Street in Troy. Conversely, I never did French, German, or English characters as well, because I didn't have those rhythms of speech in my head.

Robert Whitehead was the producer and Harold Clurman was the director of *The Cold Wind and the Warm.* The cast included my old pal Eli Wallach (this time, Eli did get first billing), and wonderful pros like Morris Carnovsky, Sanford Meisner, and

Sig Arno. Suzanne Pleshette and Vincent Gardenia were in the company, too. They still hadn't cast the role of the ingenue when Carol Marcus read for the part—her stage name was Carol Grace. I'd met Carol years ago, probably at parties, and we had gotten fairly friendly. Carol had been married to William Saroyan (twice!), and had two children ages fifteen and twelve. Danny and Kathy were eight and four, and Carol was slightly older than I, and still she got the part of a sweet young thing.

Harold Clurman and Carol did not hit it off, however. Carol says he was angry because he wanted his girlfriend for the part. Knowing Harold, this is quite possible. Anyway, Carol was a bit nervous because of the antagonism between her and the director. Her part was small, but that didn't keep her from blowing her fears way out of proportion. She came to me for help.

"Calm down, Carol," I advised her. "You're not exactly playing Hedda Gabler. Don't drive yourself crazy. Just get a lot of sleep, talk loud, and keep moving." My standard advice must have helped. She was terrific in the part, and working together in *The Cold Wind and the Warm* clinched our special relationship. We became great friends.

Not long ago Carol published her autobiography, *Among the Porcupines.* She came to New York City on a publicity tour and forced me to come down from Lenox and stay overnight in her hotel suite. I tried to wriggle out of it, but she wouldn't let me off the hook. Put it this way: Carol is one of a handful of people for whom I'd make the trip to New York City. *Among the Porcupines* is delightfully and wonderfully entertaining, just like its author. There's a bunch of stuff about me in her book, and while I don't want to repeat those stories, a few are extremely important in my life and have to be mentioned. Anyway, my version of what happened may have a different slant from my beloved friend's, and you're welcome to cross-check. Carol and I could be each other's publicists. She goes around telling everybody how lovely I am and refers to me as an old-fashioned valentine with terrific legs and a great décolletage. Her eyesight is okay, so I don't know where the hell this crap is coming from. We do enjoy each other's company and always have and still get on the phone and "dish" for hours. Trouble is, even though she's in Los Angeles where it's three hours earlier, Carol doesn't think anything of calling me at eleven at night—*her* time.

I could go on and on about this amazing woman, but I'll cut it short. In my humble opinion, Carol Matthau is nothing short of brilliant. I'm knocked out by her dazzling and attractive mind and amazed at her "takes," her humor, her all-out radiance. She is utterly fascinating and absolutely beautiful, and she comes by her beauty honestly. Rasheen Marcus, Carol's mother, was something else again. That lady was gorgeous and didn't do anything to keep up her looks with either surgery or fancy cosmetics. Someone once asked Carol, "How old were you when your mother was born?"

Carol was dating Walter Matthau during the run of *The Cold Wind and the Warm.* They had met when both were appearing on Broadway in *Will Success Spoil Rock Hunter?* They'd fallen head-over-heels, and the romance continued when Carol came into our play. Then they had some sort of row and broke off; Carol started seeing Kenneth Tynan. That didn't last, though, and she went back where she belonged, with Walter. They lived in an apartment on 81st Street and West End Avenue, and David and I and Danny and Kathy had the best of family times with them. Later, the Matthaus would share the worst of family times with me.

Chapter Seven

I knew Lillian Hellman socially off and on for years. Max worked for Kermit Bloomgarden, who became Lillian's producer after she left Herman Shumlin. I read for a part in Kermit's production of *Montserrat,* Lillian's translation of a play by Emmanuel Robles. Lillian Hellman was a formidable lady and I found her a bit terrifying at first. Her aspect was powerful and her looks were impressive. I mean, she wasn't a Barbie doll, but there was something tremendously appealing about her, including the way she carried herself, the way her mind worked, and the way she wore clothes. As for the last point: as a rule, you gotta be wearing your wedding gown before I notice that there's anything special. I only began to notice Lillian's wardrobe when Carol Matthau pointed out to me that the playwright was a helluva dresser.

Lillian wrote *Toys in the Attic,* and I was sent a copy of the script. The play concerned the dynamic interplay between two sisters and a brother, and it was terrific. I called the Bloomgarden office and told them I wanted to try out for the part of one of the sisters. I went over to the office, did a reading, and loused it up pretty good. My penchant for picking the wrong part never let up. I was bad and I knew it. After I flopped on my face, one of the guys said, "Well, Maureen, none of us would have thought of you in that role anyway. As long as you're here, why don't you read the other sister?" I read for Carrie Berniers and got the part. Anne Revere, Irene Worth, and Jason Robards were also cast. Arthur Penn directed and he was terrific—fast and smart. One day we were rehearsing a scene in which my character came home just after being fired. I started talking and began to cry . . . it just happened. Arthur took exception to my tears. "That's wrong, Maureen; she wouldn't cry."

"She wouldn't? I could give you five thousand reasons, beginning with she's not married and she's just lost her job. And you don't think she'd cry?"

"No, no," said Arthur, "what she feels is rage, cold hard anger."

I really thought my character would cry, but Arthur didn't and I respected him enough to listen to his criticisms. Even if you can justify your actions logically, a good director can tell you if you're off the track. I thought I was right on target with the tears, but I couldn't see the whole picture. The director could. "Do it for me," I asked. "Show me." A lot of directors will give you something without actually demonstrating. Arthur was willing to show me what he thought Carrie would do, and I trusted him enough to go along with what he felt was correct; I imitated him till I got it. He was right.

It was during the tryout run of *Toys in the Attic* in Boston that I stopped being afraid of Lillian Hellman and we became great pals. Lillian had been a prodigious drinker in her day, but by the time we became buddies, that was all behind her. According to what I was told, she'd been diagnosed as an alcoholic and stopped drinking for some ten years. After that, she went back to social drinking and never drank to excess again.

What she did do to excess was smoke. She smoked so damn much that when she was dying in the hospital with an oxygen tent covering her, she still had to have her cigarette. She'd pull the tent away and light up. I used to go over and read to her and

I saw her puffing on a cigarette with my own eyes—right under the sign that read, "Danger. No smoking." Peter Feibleman, her close friend, said she smoked four packs on the day she died.

I know the feeling. Last summer I had to go into the Berkshire Medical Center in Pittsfield for a hernia operation and nearly went berserk-o without my cigs. You can't smoke in hospitals anymore and they're pretty strict about the rules. Nevertheless, I managed to find a couple of nurses and a volunteer worker who wanted their puffs as much as I. After the operation, at my request they'd load me into a wheelchair and push me into the open courtyard, where we'd have our little smokes together.

At the same time that I was doing *Toys,* my divorce from Max came through, and even though I had David to keep the home fires warm, I raged against my ex-husband to Lillian—and anyone else within earshot, *except* for my kids. Funny, I never told Max how violently I reacted, and if he reads this book, I think it'll come as a shock to him that I was so pissed. Lillian Hellman had definite ideas about divorce. "For two years," she said, "you're entitled to want to pull the teeth out of the head and let the blood out of the veins of your ex. After that, it's unseemly." I was being pretty unseemly because I was goddamn upset that Max remarried. Time has taken care of all that. One thing I realized: If you put too much energy into rehashing a failed marriage, you easily can become a professional ex-wife. The lesson I learned is simple: When a relationship—marriage or otherwise—is over, you've got to kiss it good-bye and get on with your life.

Lillian and I had a great deal of fun together in Boston. I'd really been carrying on about my divorce, and she decided that I needed a pick-me-up; for Lillian, "pick-me-up" meant wardrobe. We were staying at the Ritz-Carlton, and she dragged me down Newbury Street and into Bonwit Teller. "I picked out a dress for you, Maureen," she announced and had the saleswoman bring it for me to try on. The dress was perfect and expensive. I balked at the price; Lillian *made* me buy it. Once that was purchased, she turned to the next order of business. I had made the mistake of telling her that what I really wanted someday was a black alligator handbag. But for me, "someday" didn't mean Thursday, which was the day she got me into the store. "Look at this, Maureen, look what I've found for you," said Lillian, triumphantly swinging a handsome black alligator bag under my nose. "And look!" she gloated, "it's on sale." She was thrilled because the bag was reduced from $300 to $200. I wasn't so thrilled, because $200 was still a lot of dough. However, there was no way I could get out of that place without buying the bag. In fact, she continued to accessorize me with scarves and gloves and hankies and everything the store had to offer. If clothing saleswomen had a special god, they must have prayed to her for customers like Lillian Hellman. The purchases were wrapped up to be sent to the hotel, and Lillian and I left the store.

"Never again," I said as we stepped onto the sidewalk. "I'm never going shopping with you again. This is *it!*"

"That's funny, Maureen," Lillian laughed. "Dorothy Parker said the same thing. She told me she'd only shop with me in the five-and-ten."

And I never did go shopping with Lillian after that, not even to Woolworth's, but still hanging in my closet is the dress she made me buy. Hell, I have just about every dress I ever bought hanging in my closet—except for the ones I gave away. I've been giving away clothes all my adult life because my weight's fluctuated so much my dresses run from size 6 to size 600.

Lillian Hellman continued to look down her nose at my wardrobe and my possessions in general and my jewelry in particular. I didn't have a grand collection of gems; however, I did have some things my mother had given me and a few baubles I'd received as presents. I often wore some of the pieces, but Lillian never made any comment. One night my hotel room was broken into and my jewelry was taken. The next evening I had dinner with Lillian and Irene Worth and mentioned the theft. Irene commiserated; Lillian just said, "What jewelry? I never saw you wearing any."

I didn't mind Lillian's digs; I loved to spar with her. I don't know why the hell Lillian and I were so friendly, except that we made each other laugh. As far as anything else was concerned, I wasn't in her league. Lillian used to invite me to dinner parties at her place. She was a gourmet cook and an elegant hostess. I'd come in and find myself surrounded by intellectuals and real upper-crust types but, except for yours truly, no theatrical folks. "Why do you invite me to these dinners?" I asked Lillian. "What am I, your token moron?"

Her friendliness toward me really was extraordinary considering that Lillian Hellman loathed theater people in general and actors in particular. I can vouch for the fact that she held actors in contempt. She sure was tactless when it came to dealing with the casts of her plays. I went with her to a final run-through of the touring company of *Toys in the Attic*. I thought the actors did fine; Lillian didn't. When they had finished, Lillian turned to me.

"I'm going to tell them a thing or two," she glowered as she started up from her seat ready to do battle. I grabbed her arm and pulled her back down.

"Lillian, don't talk to the actors. You should never be allowed to talk to actors. You just don't know how to speak to them." All of which was true. In the guise of advising companies, Lillian Hellman would annihilate them. Although I wasn't going on the tour myself, I didn't want her doing a hatchet job on my colleagues. "When you go down there, don't you dare give them the benefit of your truth and honesty; just tell them they're wonderful."

"I can't do that!" Lillian exclaimed. "Dash used to tell me to do that, too, and I never could."

"Just try it," I said. "The company will respond if only you'll temper your remarks."

"Oh," growled Lillian, "and do actors have to be pampered and babied all the time?"

"No, that's not what it is. It's that some people, like directors, know how to talk to people. You don't."

She fussed and fumed and finally agreed to try a little tenderness. She started down the aisle toward the waiting performers and was halfway to the stage when she turned around and came back to me.

"I can't do it!" she said through clenched teeth, "I just can't."

And down the aisle she stormed, right up to the proscenium where she proceeded to rip the hides off the poor actors. Lillian did not pussyfoot; she was tough and could get really furious if she was crossed. In the matter of that celebrated feud between her and Mary McCarthy, I tried to get my friend off the case. Lillian was very ill at the time, so ill that going blind was the least of her disabilities. She hated television, but since she could no longer read she decided to turn on the TV set, and that's when she heard Mary McCarthy call her a liar on some talk show. Lillian's blood boiled. She was wounded and she wanted revenge. "Stay out of it," I told her. "Don't you get it? It's so simple: The woman is jealous of you. Why give her the benefit of making this a big deal? She's just looking for publicity." My words cut no ice, however, and the donnybrook was on. I meant what I said. It's okay to be jealous of someone, but don't make a goddamn fool of yourself, which is what I thought Mary Mc-Carthy did. Like most writers, Lillian Hellman used poetic license. So what? That's the way she remembered things. She wasn't always right. I mean, she'd sometimes tell about things I did, and I knew damn well I hadn't done them. That's the way she saw it, though, and the way she remembered it. She interpreted events and if her explications weren't true to the letter, for Pete's sake, it was just part of her being a creative writer!

She was also a crusader and wanted me to clean up my act. Her advice was succinct: "Get in shape, Maureen, and snag yourself a rich husband!" From her own experience, Lillian thought this was the cure-all. She had a long relationship with Dashiell Hammett, who wasn't rich. She took care of him and now was convinced that a smart young woman should use her wiles to cop a winner. Dash was still around and, like Lillian, had been an A-number-one drinker. I liked Dash Hammett. I remember being at some opening night parties with him; he wasn't drinking. I was. He didn't drink that much anymore, while I, of course, did, and Lillian got on my case. I brushed her off. I was willing to tidy up and go for a rich husband, but I wouldn't under any circumstances give up my booze. My resistance was her challenge.

Lillian went to London for a production of *Toys in the Attic* and just before she left asked a favor from me. She was in a hurry and a bit flustered and blurted out, "While I'm gone, keep an eye on Dash, will you? Call him and take him out for a drink or something."

"Lillian, do you hear what you just said? You want me to go drinking with Dash? I never thought I'd live to see the day you'd say that."

"My God," Lillian cried, "I never thought *I'd* live to see that day."

After *Toys in the Attic,* I began a ritual with Lillian. Once a year I'd take her out to a restaurant of her choice. "I'm not picking it," I told her, "because if I choose the joint, you'll find something to bitch and complain about." She'd select the place, and I'd order a limousine and take her out in style. One time, after a splendid meal during which she smoked four hundred packs of cigarettes, we got into the limousine and she started to light up again. Jesus, the woman had emphysema. I couldn't help it; like a schmuck, I reached over and took the cigarette away from her. Lillian glared at me. "Do I take the wine out of your hand?" "I'm sorry," I said, handing back the cigarette. "I lost my head. Here, smoke."

Lillian and I kept up our friendship until she died. Everything went kaput at the end—her eyes, her lungs, her legs; everything except that brilliant mind and that sublime wit. At the end, she couldn't see, she couldn't walk, and she could barely breathe. She was hospitalized and lay blind and bedridden in her smoke-filled room. Peter Feibleman told of going to see her toward the end; he walked in and asked, "How are you feeling?"

Lillian turned her head. "Terrible!" she groaned. "Oh, Peter, I have the worst case of writer's block I've ever had in my life."

Too bad there isn't such a thing as "drinker's block." I sure could have used it back in the early sixties when I was totally out of control. Desperately and, I have to say, valiantly, David Rayfiel continued to try and help me. He begged me to go to Alcoholics

Anonymous, sometimes even offering to take me. I did go to a few meetings, with David and sometimes on my own. They were terrific people but it didn't take; the only time I didn't drink was when I was at the meetings. My drive to drink was stronger than my drive not to drink.

I managed to hang on during those years and always could pull myself together enough to work. In 1959 I made *The Fugitive Kind,* the film version of Tennessee Williams's *Orpheus Descending* in which I'd starred because Anna Magnani wouldn't commit to a long enough run. The Italian actress had been signed for the film and Marlon Brando was to play opposite her. Once again, Magnani and I played see-saw with movie roles and she came out on top. Hell, I didn't put myself up there with her, anyway. Once Magnani was signed I didn't think about the movie until I heard through the grapevine that the producer wanted me for a secondary role. Since I had been the star on the stage, he was afraid I'd bust his balls if he offered me a minor part. I called and told him I'd be happy to do it. And I was. I made the movie and made good money and had the pleasure and thrill of working with Bud Brando and Anna Magnani.

After *The Fugitive Kind* I worked on a film version of Arthur Miller's *A View from the Bridge.* Sidney Lumet was the director and I really liked working with him. I've been extremely lucky when it comes to directors and, in fact, can recall only one with whom I didn't enjoy working. I think it was a television show and Bob Preston was also involved. I was having a tough time and just didn't know what was going on. Naturally, I looked to the director. Well, this guy talked and talked and talked. He was a major pain in the ass. I turned to Bob.

"Oh Christ, what the hell's this jerk going on about?"

"Turn it off," Bob advised. "That's the way I do it. Whenever I'm with a director I don't like or can't work with, I just turn it off. Nod your head and say 'yes' but don't listen." These were like words from the Delphic Oracle. I'd never thought of doing such a thing. It was the perfect solution. The director went on and on and on and I sat there nodding my head like one of those dunking birds on a glass of water. Meanwhile I'd tuned the guy out and didn't hear a word. The only problem was that I kept nodding even when he wasn't talking to me. The director was so wrapped up in himself, though, that he didn't even notice and couldn't have cared less.

I've never forgotten Bob's trick, although fortunately I never had to use it again, at least not with directors, and especially not Sidney Lumet. Sidney and I have worked together about three times. He's so very easy to work with and has so much energy, it's like he should be doing two movies at once. All the waiting around required for the movies is not his style. Some people and directors can do "fritter time," but it drives Sidney crazy. He really knows the camera and is one of those directors you can rely on totally. His eye and ear are infallible. He doesn't say much, but when he does you know something is wrong. Then he gives you a bit to make it clear and you can be sure it will be right.

I've been damn lucky when it comes to directors. Most have been terrific, and if I have one regret in that department, it's that I never worked with Elia Kazan; he's great. I've been fortunate in my dealings with fellow actors, too. Some stand out a bit more than the rest for various reasons, good and bad. Remember Jean Seberg? She was the beautiful youngster from the Midwest who won the contest for a newcomer to play Saint Joan in Otto Preminger's film. Jean was a darling and really a misplaced saint herself. At the time we were working together in *Airport* she was helping this Black Panther guy who'd recently gotten out of prison. Jean got everyone to help, and people were breaking their backs to be nice to this downtrodden human being. The guy was a shit; he abused Jean by taking advantage of her and her connections and then sticking it to her. He'd telephone her on the set and let her have it. One day Jean was talking on the phone to him and getting more and more agitated. Tears were in her eyes. I walked over, took the phone, and barked into it, "You know what, buster, you're a sonofabitch. You are a miserable human being and you're sucking the blood out of everybody. I really don't care what happens to you. You get yourself a job from nine to five and then I'll be concerned." I said my piece and handed the phone back. Jean was saying, "Oh God, oh my God," as she put the phone back to her ear. Poor little Jean was shivering into the phone, and you know what the guy said to her? "Who was that woman who just cut me up? I liked her." Go figure!

While working on *Bye Bye Birdie,* I went to some picnic kind of party and took along my six-year-old Kathy. Jennifer Jones Selznick and her daughter Mary Jennifer were also at the picnic, and the two little girls hit it off. The next day, Jennifer called and asked if Kathy could come over and play with Mary Jennifer. Kathy was eager to go and off she went. The upshot was, she and Mary Jennifer became buddies and my daughter was over at the Selznicks' for the entire summer. Later Mary Jennifer's daddy brought his family to New York City and checked them into the Waldorf Towers. Kathy went to the Towers every week and the Selznicks took her to everything, from first-run movies to Broadway plays. They wanted to take her on jaunts down South, too. I wouldn't let her on an airplane, so those trips were out, but the Waldorf visits went on for quite a while.

"This is a little unbalanced," I told Mary Jennifer's mother one morning when she came to pick up Kathy. "My daughter's always going over to your place; it's time for Mary Jennifer to play here."

"Oh, I'm afraid she can't," said Jennifer. "You see, David is very concerned about safety, and I don't think your home is protected enough." I didn't think we were a danger zone, so I suggested she check it out. Jennifer said okay and looked over my brownstone with a fine-tooth comb. At the end of her inspection she told me it was no go.

"David would never allow it," she said. "It's just too exposed."

"You could station guards on the roof across the street," I suggested. Mrs. Selznick was unmovable and little Mary Jennifer never did come to our place.

David O. Selznick may have been the genius behind *Gone With the Wind,* but my contact with him exposed me only to the doting father. He was crazy about his kid and wouldn't let her out of his sight. He'd been married first to Irene Mayer, the daughter of Louis B., and they'd had two sons, Jeff and Daniel. I saw Daniel a few times, and he said he didn't spend that much time with his father when he was a kid because David was so busy running the studios. It was a whole different number with Jennifer Jones, his second wife, and their daughter. Kathy told me how David would take her and Mary Jennifer on icebox raids and sit down and talk with them at great length. He was a caring and concerned daddy, and Mary Jennifer was the apple of his eye. She and Kathy kept up their friendship for a few years and then distance and time separated them. How tragically and ironically things worked out for the child who was so idolized by her dad; in her early twenties, Mary Jennifer Selznick committed suicide.

In 1962 I returned to Hollywood to work on *Bye Bye Birdie.* Following *Birdie* I didn't work on a film for seven years. I wasn't exactly being kept busy with television or radio, either. Frankly, I'd reached a critical point in my personal life and nearly went down for the count.

Have you ever seen a bullfight? If you have, you know there are guys who work the bull over, jabbing him with spears and things like that. Then, when the animal is running around with bloody sticks in his back, the toreador steps in for the kill. In 1963, after years of sticking it to each other, David Rayfiel and I got married and that marriage killed our relationship. Things between us had deteriorated badly, yet for some crazy reason, we decided to go all the way. Looking back, it's obvious that we should have gotten "divorced," not "married." True confession: I'd been faithful to Max until David and only strayed then because things were over between Max and me. On the other hand, from the beginning of my association with David Rayfiel, I had had affairs—not big deals, because I truly was nuts about David, but "affairs" nevertheless. Don't ask me why. It was sicko, wacko, and dummo and I think it happened because in some demented way I figured I owed it to Max to be unfaithful to David—convoluted as that sounds.

On the subject of "affairs," I recall a conversation I had with Carol Matthau. She asked me how many men I'd slept with, and I said, "Oh, I don't know; about a hundred, I guess."

"A hundred?" she gulped.

"Yeah, give or take a few. How many have you slept with?"

"Six," she answered.

"Six? Jesus, you haven't slept with anyone."

I don't think I really slept with a hundred guys; I just said it to shock Carol. Furthermore, I have no intention of naming any of the "hundred" in this book, other than the important ones, and with one notable exception, they're almost used up. Even though I'd "drifted" in the early years, by the time David and I *married,* I'd stopped having romances. Besides, I'd grown so grotesque that I'm sure no one wanted to have anything to do with me.

David and I tied the knot legally in July 1963 in the Triangle Diner in Lake Luzerne, New York, where we had a summer place. The owner of the diner was also the justice of the peace. Carol was my bridesmaid, and if she hadn't been, I might never have made it to my own wedding. The day dawned and I didn't; I stayed in my bed. David got into a boat and went out into the middle of the lake, where he floated around until late in the afternoon. Carol kept after me and eventually dislodged me from the covers. She got me on my legs and into the bathtub, which already was a novelty. I wasn't keen on bathing in those days; it was part of my peculiar reaction to being with David. I think I was doing everything possible to repulse that man, and not bathing seemed as good a method as any. One afternoon David came home and I stood at the top of the stairs and called down to him proudly, "David, I took a shower today."

"What happened," he called back, "the canary died?"

Walter and Carol were our witnesses at the Triangle, and after the ceremony we returned home. A few people dropped by to offer congratulations; it should have been condolences. Carol says my cousin Red knocked at the door, took a look at me, said he'd forgotten something, and, explaining that he'd be right back, left. He never returned. At last the few people who had appeared departed and Carol and Walter retired to their room. David and I went into our bedroom. He closed the door, turned to me and said, "Alone at last. Except for you of course." Carol and Walter overheard that line and passed it on. I've been told that "Alone at last. Except for you, of course" was quoted by Broadwayites for years.

In a very real sense, David Rayfiel *was* alone. My relationship with him was not as strong as the one I had with the bottle, and after our marriage I sank like a stone.

David's play *P.S. 193* had been produced in 1962, and a few years later he wrote *Nathan Weinstein's Daughter*. He wanted me to play Rachel, the play's main character. I read the play and told him I wouldn't do it. I didn't like the part or the play and felt I had to keep my professional life separate from my personal one. I know David was hit pretty hard by my refusal, and I'm not so sure that I wasn't being more spiteful than critical. Danny is convinced that part of the Rachel character was David's vision of me, or at least the me he wanted me to be. Be that as it may, I didn't play it. Someone else was cast in the role. David was a nervous wreck opening night and begged me not to drink, just this once. I promised I wouldn't. I did, and he was devastated by my behavior. I'm not a quiet drunk, as I've proved on many occasions. I spoiled his night.

My frustrations were aggravated by my suspicion that David was having an affair. My doubts were raised by a number of incidents, including the arrival of a postcard addressed to my husband and obviously written by a woman. I confronted him with the evidence, and he denied any hanky-panky. I accepted his disavowal, grudgingly. I desperately wanted to believe nothing was going on and suspended my disbelief to keep my sanity. Then one evening Carol and Walter and I were going out for dinner. We were driving down Madison Avenue on our way to the restaurant when I saw a familiar figure walking along the sidewalk. It was my husband, and he was strolling hand-in-hand with a young woman. In a flash I recognized her as the actress playing Rachel in David's play. As the car sped by I let out a bloodcurdling scream and fell off the seat onto the floor. I have a natural tendency to dramatize real-life situations; no way was I overacting then, however. I felt as though I'd been punched in the heart and in trying to gasp for air, shrieked like a banshee. I imagine boxers must have the same kind of feeling when they're struck by a powerful body blow. I lay on the floor of the car and became totally hysterical. Carol had also seen the couple and knew what set me off. She did her best to comfort me or at least get me to calm down.

"I can't believe it. I can't believe it," I kept saying over and over. Carol helped me back onto the seat. I fell back, wrapped my arms around my chest and rocked back and forth. Carol took me to her home and sat with me while the others went off to dinner.

"He cheated on me," I moaned, "he cheated on me. He lied, there was another woman. I knew it, I knew it."

Carol tried to help by explaining that there was nothing else David could do; I'd driven him away. I hadn't realized that David confided in her. He told Carol that he was going insane because of me. We didn't have sex anymore and I had let myself go completely to seed. He loved me but needed and wanted the comfort of a woman. "Tell Maureen how miserable you are," Carol advised, "but for God's sake don't cheat. She won't be able to take it. She won't forgive you." Carol was right—only in the past year or so have I reached some sort of détente. Up until then, I really hated him.

I desperately wanted to get drunk that night and couldn't drink. I didn't want to drink; I wanted to kill myself. I just wailed and cried and scared poor Carol to death. Carol realized that I was too far gone for her to help and called Bob Whitehead for reinforcement. Bob was always there for me; he immediately came to the rescue and told Carol to pack up some of my clothes and get me ready while he arranged to put me into a ritzy little East Side hospital. He arrived at my place and along with Carol helped me into a car. We held hands on the way over to the East

Side. Remember what I said about gallows humor? Well, it was much in evidence throughout this extraordinary evening. I was in total agony and out of my mind with anxiety, and yet when I checked into the hospital, I made certain the admissions officer got my health insurance number and arranged to be charged directly for my stay. I found out afterward that Carol and Bob each attempted to take on the hospital bill and were astonished when they were told that the basket case they'd brought in had already spoken for it.

I was sedated and put to bed. I lay there in a half-stupor and was about to drift off into much-needed oblivion when Carol, who sat by my bed looking like a covergirl from *Seventeen* magazine, took my hand and spoke to me.

"Maureen, can you hear me?"

"Yes, I can hear you," I murmured weakly.

"When this is over, and one day it will be over, there is one thing you have to do."

Even in my semicomatose state I responded with interest. Carol must have the answer. She was smart, she'd found happiness with Walter; she was the fountain of knowledge. She could tell me. "What is it I should do, Carol, what?"

"You must get a full-time maid, Maureen."

This was the answer to my problems? I was going out fast but managed to hoist my two-hundred-plus pounds of agony onto my elbows and cry, "A what?"

"A full-time maid."

"I have somebody who comes in three times a week," I sighed, falling back onto the pillow.

"No, no," she said, "it's got to be a full-time maid." And with these words buzzing in my ear, I went off to dreamland. Even though I was barely conscious, I recall this interchange quite clearly. I might not believe it actually took place except for the fact that Carol tells the same story. I was a drunken wreck, but all I needed was a full-time maid.

The Greeks have a word for it, and I can't come up with it. It translates into a "reversal of fortune" and that's what I went through during the next few days. Finally, I'd hit bottom. I'd been looking for it for years, and now that I was there, something inside forced me to pull myself up and out. Maybe it was the old Irish peasant stock asserting itself; maybe it was just the life force. I don't know. I do know that after a few days in the hospital, I decided I wanted to change my life; I wanted to live. Something happened to me during that traumatic experience, something so completely *con*structive it was almost scary. I took charge of things and systematically began to organize my life. With Bob's assistance, I made appointments to see a doctor who worked with alcoholics. She had treated a number of them successfully, and I hoped to join their ranks. After a few sessions at the doctor's office, at her suggestion and with her support, I agreed to put myself into a psychiatric facility in Roxbury, Connecticut, where the controlled environment would make it easier for me to dry out. The next Saturday, Bob Whitehead drove me to Roxbury and I walked, of my own volition, into the funny farm.

This joint wasn't just for alcoholics, it was for assorted nuts. That first weekend lots of wacko people were walking around mumbling to themselves and I thought all of them were patients. Come Monday morning, most of them were gone. The people I thought were inmates were actually visiting doctors. You could have fooled me; I was sure they were nuts.

We were a diverse group at that place: alcoholics, depressives, and schizophrenics. We had private rooms and you had to take care of your own quarters. There was no drinking but, thank God, you could smoke. Everything at the funny farm was considered therapy, even swimming in the pool. There were private sessions with the main doctor once a day, and in the evenings Gestalt therapy classes were held. I thought Gestalt therapy was screwy. I didn't want to go and was informed I had to. A visiting therapist conducted the class and her job was to get you going about your past. I tried to cooperate and mentioned the memories of my childhood, like the fights between my mother and father.

"Good," said the therapist, "that's good material. Now let's work with it."

Working with it meant I was supposed to go back into my past and relive those traumatic scenes. Again I resisted. Reliving that crap was about the last thing on my "I want to do" list. "No thanks," I told the therapist, "I'll sit this one out."

The therapist argued, "You've got to go back because you've got to release all that built-up anger. The best thing for you would be to let it all out. Scream it out!"

"I don't think you really want me to do that," I told her.

"Yes, I do," she persisted, "it's very important for you to do it. You must go back to your childhood. And when all those scenes pass before you, just scream. It will release you."

This broad kept at me about going back to my childhood and "screaming" and I continued to decline her kind invitation. We played Alphonse-and-Gaston with my childhood for weeks. The daytime doctor, who happened to be the director of the place, also urged me to do what the therapist suggested. The insistence of the two doctors finally wore down my resistance, and one night I decided to take the Gestalt plunge.

"Okay, I'll go back to my childhood," I said to the therapist. "But I'm telling you, you're going to be sorry." I began to talk about First Street and my mother and dad and the fights and I relived them and then I screamed. *Oy vay,* did I scream! You can't give a trained actress that kind of opportunity without expecting to get spectacular results. My scream raised the roof of the funny farm. I screamed so loud the people in the room with me went momentarily deaf. I screamed so loud I could have raised the dead in the nearby cemetery. I screamed so loud they called the director in from her home. I screamed so loud the police came from their headquarters two and a half miles away to see who'd been murdered—and that's a fact. How did I feel after the big blast? My throat was sore, and that's about all I remember.

The next day at my regular session, the doctor said, "What on earth happened last night?"

"Listen, Doctor," I told her, "I did what you asked. You told me to go back and I was just following directions." I was rather pleased with myself because I was pretty sure they wouldn't ask me to try that little exercise again.

While I was in Connecticut, I had the support and love of so many friends to bolster me. Arthur Miller lived nearby with his wife, Inge, and their daughter, Rebecca. Arthur would come once a week to the funny farm and take me to his house. I'd spend the day and have dinner and then he'd take me back. They were so wonderful to me.

Bob Whitehead was a regular visitor. He came to see me every weekend and wrote me letters and called me during the week. He was my Rock of Gibraltar. Max was stalwart, too; he took charge of the children. Kathy was at camp and Danny went with Max to Amagansett. Occasionally Bob would bring Danny up to visit me, and I'd try and talk to him as though everything was just hunky-dory. He didn't buy it. How hard this must have been for my children. Both kids knew something had hit the fan. Not only was mama in the nut house, they were about to lose their beloved step-papa, and even though she was off at the camp and away from the battle scene, Kathy became more and more suspicious. David bombarded her with letters. He always was a big letter writer and now was outdoing himself by writing every single day. He desperately wanted to stay in touch and even in my advanced state of wrath, I recognized his importance to the kids. Danny and Kathy knew I was furious at David, but while I didn't want his name mentioned in my presence, I still didn't slam him or even tell them the reason for my anger. In fact, for years my children were full of resentment toward me because they believed I was completely at fault and had forced David out. I knew Danny took David's side more than mine, and still I didn't push. I continued to make every effort not to let my personal animosity toward David color the children's feelings toward him. Hard as it was for me not to defend myself, I never wavered from that position. Many times I was tempted to say, "Now listen, I'm going to tell you what really happened." I'm not sorry I didn't. While I had cause to dislike my father, my children didn't have any reason to dislike either their stepfather or father. Both men were good to them. I may have screwed up my marriages, but I sure as hell wasn't going to be responsible for screwing up my children's relationships with their two dads.

If you listen to my children and my friends—Carol, Zoe, Annie, and some others—they'll tell you I drove David Rayfiel away because I couldn't handle my feelings. Carol chided me for "testing" him all the time. I revert to my old position—marriage was not my best arena, and being a wife was not my best role. The separation from Max was remarkably tranquil compared to the situation that developed between me and David in the next few months. Without going into all the ins and outs of my experience at the funny farm, I'll just say that I went into that place a drunk and two months later came out dry as a bone. What's more, for the next three years I never touched a drop of liquor. I left the sanitarium clean and sober, and what's more, I was one hundred pounds lighter! I looked like a human being again.

In December of 1966 I went into a revival of *The Rose Tattoo* at the City Center and then at the Billy Rose Theatre; Harry Guardino played Mangiacavallo. The play did okay. In any event, it kept me off the streets. At the same time, David and I were discussing our divorce and I got this notion in my little brain that I was going into that procedure like Miss Mary Pickford, thin, elegant, soft-spoken, and totally adorable. In order to achieve this goal, I began taking tranquilizers—Placidyls, I believe. In my effort to be Miss Mary Pickford I was eventually popping those little guys at a furious rate. I'd show David Rayfiel what he had lost! I got thinner and thinner, and toward the end of the *Rose Tattoo* run I outpilled myself. I may not have been drinking, but I definitely was on another substance-abuse track. I never understood people who said that they didn't know how many pills they took; I mean, you take a pill and maybe another one, but how can you forget? I became a believer when I reached that point myself. I swallowed pill after pill and couldn't keep track. Pills pretty much were all I was consuming; my glorious appetite died. My weight continued to drop and the Hindenberg blimp, née Lois Maureen Stapleton, now hovered on the threshold of malnutrition. I weighed an unwhopping 108 pounds. Between the pills and the starving, I Mary Pickforded myself right into the Morris Bernstein Wing of the Beth Israel Hospital. I had overdosed on the Placidyls. I had to be detoxified and there, in the Morris Bernstein Wing, began one of the weirdest experiences of my life. All my life I'd been looking at the scales, praying for the numbers to go down, and for the first time, my problem was to get those numbers up. I could eat anything I wanted, but I didn't want anything. Not since that flight from California had I been so put off food. They actually had to force me to eat. What a strange sensation it was to be put on the scales and have everyone stand around and cheer if I put on an ounce.

Again, I found myself among some really nice people—they were charming, lovely, and addicted. I became friends with one particular young woman who had tried to commit suicide three or four times. Sunday was visiting day in the Morris Bernstein Wing. I had been in for about three weeks, and on the third Sunday I went into the big reception room where the patients waited for their company. Harvey Orkin was there, as were Lucille and Danny. We were sitting and chatting when way down at the end of the hall, the elevator door opened and out stepped Marlon Brando. I have always called Marlon a "foul-weather friend." You don't see him as much when everything's going your way as you do when your world is falling apart. To prove my theory, he came to call on me in the loony bin. Marlon began the long walk down the hall and as he approached, he smiled that incredible grin of his and then raised his finger to his mouth, brushed it up-and-down his lips, and began going, "blub blub blub blub." Right in the center of the nut ward he's making noises like a crazy person. I started laughing even as I called to him to cut it out. Marlon reached our group and hugged and kissed me and shook hands with Danny and Harvey and the others. We all went off to my room and sat around. My physician, a wonderful man named Aaron Silver, also joined us, and, before you could say *sayonara,* a half-dozen nurses rushed in and stood around waiting to be introduced to Bud. He was adorable and proceeded to charm everybody. Boy, did my stock go up in that joint! The little girl who'd attempted suicide came to my door and I invited her in. She was carrying a package and offered it to me.

"My mom made some ziti and it's delicious. You've got to eat some."

"Sure, I'll eat it later."

"Nope," she answered, "I want to see you eat it now." This kid who'd tried to knock herself off wanted to make sure I got healthy.

"Okay," I replied. I took the package from her and while opening the bag proceeded to point out the visitors. "These are my family and friends," I said, and began the introductions. "Lucille Bensen, my son, Danny Allentuck, Harvey Orkin, and Marlon Brando."

This kid was nodding her head and saying "howdoyoudo, howdoyoudo," and when I got to Bud she stopped and said, "No. Are you really Marlon Brando?"

"Yes, I am," he said.

"No," she said again.

"Yes," Bud answered.

"Are you really Marlon Brando?" she repeated.

"Yes," laughed Bud. He jumped up and gave her a big hug and kiss. This kid was so flustered that she forgot about watching me eat the ziti and ran out the door.

Marlon stayed for the rest of the afternoon and was the last to leave. I was on my way to the dining room when my young chum fell into step with me.

"That was really Marlon Brando," she said.

"Yes it was."

"Well," she sighed, "I've been thinking it over and I don't think I'll tell my doctor. If I told him Marlon Brando kissed me, he'd put me in a straitjacket for sure."

The rest of my stay at the Morris Bernstein Wing was uneventful socially. Physically, I successfully detoxed and left Beth Israel in great shape. I'd gone up to 118 pounds and, if I do say so myself, looked terrific.

Over the years that I'd been futzing around, an American playwright had been turning out wonderfully entertaining material for Broadway, and in 1968 my opportunity came to get on the Neil Simon bandwagon. Doc had written four one-act plays, all of which took place in the Plaza Hotel, and Saint-Subber was going to produce them under the umbrella title of *Plaza Suite.* Mike Nichols was the director, and he cast me and George C. Scott in the lead roles. The first play in *Plaza Suite, The Out-of-Towners,* was way too long and had to be dropped; eventually it was made into a movie with Jack Lemmon and Sandy Dennis.

I love Mike; he's so bright, and I'm not saying that just because he cast me. On the first day of rehearsal the participants gathered together. Usually at this time the director does a lot of talking and explaining about the play and its meaning. Not Mike. As soon as we were seated, he said, "This play is about the discovery of the world. Let's read." Mike was a funny guy and Neil Simon was a funny guy. Early in the run I came to the theater with a terrible head cold. I looked awful and felt awful. Neil came by my dressing room half an hour before curtain and found me sniffing, wheezing, blowing my nose, and inhaling.

"What's the matter with you?" he asked.

"I'm fighting a cold," I explained.

"Win," said Neil on his way out the door.

George and I took the main roles in each of the three plays and had the chance to create three entirely different characters in one evening. During an early rehearsal, George announced to Mike that he wanted to do something different in the second act. "I want," said my costar, "to play the whole act offstage." George suggested that we run across the stage, shout at one another, and then run off into a closet and finish there. In other words, we'd play the entire second act out of sight. Mike listened to George's plan and without saying anything to me said, "Okay, we'll try it that way tomorrow." Rehearsals finished and after George left I grabbed hold of Mike.

"Much as I love George, and I do, I gotta tell you something. There is no way, *no way,* that I am going to play an entire act offstage."

"Of course you're not," laughed Mike.

"So why the hell did you say we'd rehearse that way?"

"I have to give George enough rope," answered Mike. "You watch, he'll come in tomorrow and tell us it can't be done."

"Why didn't you give me the high sign?"

"In front of George? Are you kidding?"

The next day George marched in and rather solemnly said that he'd thought it through and felt we should do the scene in the old way. His experiment was noble but wouldn't work. Mike was right on about George and he sure knew how to handle him.

George has a photographic memory; he can simply look at pages and know them. Not me. I have to go over and over the lines. Lots of times during the rehearsals I'd cry out, "Hey fellas, wait for me. I'm not as fast as you." I wasn't kidding. I had a bit of trouble mastering the dialogue, and as everyone knows, when you're doing Neil Simon, you've got to be fast and precise. If you go off, it kills the rhythm. I'd fumble something terrible in rehearsals.

"I just got my breath," I cried out in one run-through.

"I *finally caught* my breath," screamed the director from the back of the house.

Instances like that one occurred over and over and I have to say that while Mike constantly corrected me, Neil never said a word. At last the whole thing gelled and I was letter-perfect. I never fought with Mike over it, either, he was right. The lines Neil Simon wrote were more specific and much better than anything I improvised.

Plaza Suite was unusual for me in one particular way; it was the only time I didn't do my own makeup. The three separate episodes called for three totally different looks and there's only so much time during intermission to redo your face, put on a wig, and change costumes. I didn't have time to pee, let alone get out of and into character. We had professional makeup artists for that show and we needed them. As far as the costuming is concerned, I usually don't give two hoots about what I wear. I mean, I started out in a slip for *The Rose Tattoo,* so whatever followed was bound to be better. Most of the time I was so grateful someone else was decking me out that I just accepted what I was given and rarely had an opinion one way or another. I did, however, like the dress I was supposed to wear in the second act of *Plaza Suite*. It was kind of sexy and fit me just right, and I thought I looked great. We'd started a dress rehearsal and George called for a stop.

"Mike," he called out, "Maureen can't wear that dress."

"Why not?" asked Mike.

"She looks like a hooker," answered my costar.

"George," I said smiling, "that's the sweetest thing you've ever said to me."

After the rehearsal, Mike came into my room and closed the door behind him. "What'll we do about the dress, Maureen?"

"Change it," I said. "I don't want George to be unhappy. Hey, I like the dress, but it ain't worth it if it's bothering him."

I adored George, but occasionally there were little glitches in our relationship that usually were fueled by alcohol. There's a particular incident I'll never forget. We were in Boston for try-outs, and after the performances some of us would gather in George's hotel suite and play word games. George would drink a lot and sometimes get testy. One night he got real mad at me for some reason and stormed out of the room. Everything else that happened that evening is a blank. The next morning, when we assembled together on the stage, Mike Nichols came in carrying what looked to be the swamp-infected remains of some poor, drowned animal. It turned out to be my mink coat. George had been so furious, he'd stuffed my beautiful fur into the toilet, where it languished, absorbing water, until it was discovered and given to Mike. The coat was ruined, and the fact that I could laugh and forgive that big pussycat George C. Scott gives you a good idea how much I love him.

Plaza Suite was a hit, and a comedy at that. I don't think tragedy and comedy are that far apart. You start from the same place; it's just that comedy is so much more precise. I didn't act any differently in Simon than I did in Williams or Hellman. Comedy is so marvelous. Sometimes I think it's pure mathematics. You establish certain things, like laughs, for example, and then they come at the same place every night, every time. I do, however, remember that after months of playing *Plaza Suite,* I lost a solid built-in laugh. I mean I *just lost it.* I tried everything I knew to get it back but it wouldn't come. I called Mike and asked him to come and watch the show and see if he could figure out what I should do. Mike came to a performance and afterward said, "Just take the second half of the line an octave lower." I did what he told me and like music to my ears, the laughter rolled over the footlights. He's so smart and has such an infallible ear, I bet Mike Nichols could have helped me wrest the laugh back from Lenore Ulric in *Antony and Cleopatra.*

Bob Balaban was also in the cast of *Plaza Suite.* He was a recent college graduate and had just arrived on Broadway. He was a kid, and that's partially why I took him under my wing; that plus the fact that I thought he was poor, a mistaken impression, as I mentioned earlier. One evening, a few weeks after we opened, we were taking a curtain call and as we smiled and bowed to the audience, I whispered to Bobby, "Come over to my house, now. I've got to talk to you. I've got big trouble. My son's lost in Europe."

Later Bobby came over to my place and listened to my story. "I'm terrified something's happened to Danny," I wailed. "He went on this overseas trip and was supposed to return a few weeks ago, and I haven't heard a word from him. I think he's dead or something." Bob comforted me and told me he was sure Danny was okay. He suggested I contact people overseas. So I called up every embassy and the assorted friends I could think of and alerted them to Danny's disappearance. The upshot was that they placed ads in the papers, and throughout Europe little notices were appearing in the dailies reading: "Danny Vincent Allentuck, telephone home at once. Mother." When Danny got back—never having been lost at all, of course—he was fit to be tied; everywhere he went, people walked up to him and said, "Danny, call your mother."

Around the time of *Plaza Suite,* I began making television talk-show appearances. I was on the *Tonight* show quite a bit (it was still broadcast from New York then) and really got a kick out of it. Johnny Carson had come to see *Plaza Suite* with his wife and invited George and me on his show. It's mind boggling when you think that more people knew me from those appearances than everything else I ever did combined. Later, anytime I went to California I'd be on the show. You'd think I'd get used to it. Not me. I'd get nervous and carry on before the airing. Johnny was always comforting and put me at my ease. I must have driven him nuts, though. I still have a postcard he sent. "Dear Maureen," it reads. "If you're through wringing your hands now, you were great as usual and thanks for making it so much fun. Best, Johnny."

I did a lot of television in those days. Hey, I even played a bee on *Saturday Night Live.* The funny thing is, with all the stuff I've done, a great many people who hear my name still think I'm the broad who slept with Archie Bunker. I can clear it up right now. Edith Bunker was played by Jean Stapleton, a wonderful actress and no relation. I'm always mistaken for her. Moreover, while I'm constantly asked if Jean and I are related, as far as I know, that's happened to her only once, but what a once. Jean herself told me she was introduced to Lynne Fontanne and that great lady of the stage asked, "Oh, are you a relative of Maureen's?"

Besides the joy of appearing in a smash hit, during the run of *Plaza Suite* I had the joy of meeting one of the most exceptional men I've ever known. Talk about legends—George Abbott was *the* legend of "The Big Street"; he was actually called "Mr. Broadway," a title given to him a long time ago. He was also referred to as "the most practical showman in Broadway history," and was a performer, author, "play doctor," and director. In one or another of these capacities, he was involved with classics like *Three Men on a Horse, On Your Toes, Damn Yankees,* and *The Pajama Game.*

Not long after George Abbott came to see *Plaza Suite* I received a Christmas card from him. "That's nice," I thought and let it go at that. Next he sent me an invitation to attend a run-through of a play he was doing. I couldn't go. Again I didn't think much of it because I was sure he sent cards and invitations to everybody in the theater. The next thing I remember is that I'm at a big party at Gracie Mansion. What the hell I was doing there I don't remember; I do remember I was seated at George Abbott's table. He was just the kind of tall skinny guy I go for, except George was Protestant rather than Jewish. I told him I'd read his autobiography, *Mr. Abbott,* and liked it very much. He thanked me and then asked if I had come to the party with anyone.

"Nope," I answered, "I'm here by myself."

"Well, you must allow me to take you home," offered Mr. Broadway.

"Sure," I agreed, "but I have to stop at a party for Jimmy Breslin on the way." I had promised to put in an appearance and George was perfectly amenable. We left Gracie Mansion and went to an apartment on the Upper West Side, where the party was in full swing. Maybe you remember that Norman Mailer ran for mayor of New York with Jimmy Breslin as his running mate. Anyway, this gathering was a Mailer-Breslin fund-raiser. We stayed briefly and then George took me home. The minute we got in the taxi, he began to make moves. His arms went around me and I kind of backed off and then his arms went around me again, and after the third or fourth maneuver I questioned him.

"George, what are you doing?"

"I'm trying to go to bed with you," said Mr. Broadway.

"Oh, all right. Why didn't you just say so."

He took me home and into the bedroom and, if I recall correctly—and I know I am recalling correctly—we stayed there quite happily for a good long time. This may not sound like such an unusual occurrence—boy meets girl, boy beds girl—however, I must point out that George Abbott was not a boy. Mr. Broadway, in fact, had been around longer than Broadway. He was eighty-one years old when we met and I was forty-three. And you know something? Despite my friends' assessments of who my "grand passion" was, George Abbott was the object of my greatest passion for the very simple reason that for all the years I knew him, he made me laugh inside.

What an extraordinary man he was; a different cup of tea from any I'd known. He was long divorced when we met and was a straight shooter from the word go. He'd been married twice before and had a daughter by his first wife. On our first date he took me out to dinner and after a wonderful evening made arrangements to see me again.

"We'll have dinner Friday," said George, "because I promised this friend I'd take her dancing on Saturday, and Sunday I have a date with another gal."

"George?"

"What?"

"Are you trying to tell me that you're seeing other women?"

"Oh-oh," replied Mr. Broadway, "you're not one of those jealous females, are you?"

"As a matter of fact, I am."

"How terrible for you," said George sweetly and matter-of-factly. The ball was back in my court. Mr. Broadway didn't mince words. He played everything on the level. I wanted to see him and so did a lot of other broads whom he'd been dating. The message was simple: If I wanted to be with him, I had to accept him on his terms. I did want to see him and accepted the terms. Gradually the other ladies fell off, and it was just him and me for about the next ten years.

Danny was sixteen and Kathy was twelve when I began dating George. The day after the post–Gracie Mansion escapade, I had dinner with my children and spoke up.

"Kids, I met a man last night and I like him very much."

"Gee, Ma," said Danny, "that's wonderful."

"Yeah," echoed Kathy.

"You'll meet him this weekend," I explained, "and I want to tell you right now that he's eighty-one years old."

"You gotta be kidding," said my son.

"No," I replied, "I'm not kidding."

The kids looked at each other and smiled and from then on the joke in the house became the following exchange between my children. They'd catch each other's eye; one of them would hold up eight fingers and the other would flash one, and they'd start giggling. One evening I was preparing to go out when

Danny walked into the room fresh from studying his American history and said quite seriously, "Mom, do you realize that George Abbott was alive during the Johnstown Flood?"

"No dear, I hadn't realized. And maybe you don't want to mention that fact to Mr. Abbott, either."

Hal Prince and his wife, Judy, were great friends of George's. They'd been in Europe for the summer and when they returned we met on the street.

"I hear you're seeing a lot of George," said Hal.

"Yes, I am."

"You must go dancing a lot."

"No," I said. "Actually, we've only been dancing once."

"You must be a terrible dancer," said Hal.

"No, I'm not."

"Well, George is terrific on the dance floor and loves to go out dancing, and if he's not taking you to the clubs, well, something's wrong."

Later that day I told George about the exchange with Hal.

"And," I finished with a flourish, "Hal said I must be a terrible dancer." I expected a compliment from George to bolster me up.

"No," said George, "you're not terrible; you're adequate."

"Adequate?"

"Yes, adequate." This was not the compliment I'd been anticipating.

"I'm not an adequate dancer," I huffed. "I'm a very good dancer."

George would not upgrade his evaluation, and much as I argued, adequate it was and adequate it remained. It got my goat to be termed adequate, and I began to wage a little campaign. Over the next weeks I sent him a series of letters, most of which said, succinctly, "Maureen Stapleton is the best dancer on the block and the best partner I ever had." The letters were signed by various people, including Gene Kelly, Fred Astaire, and Rudolf Nureyev. I stopped short at Valentino and Nijinsky because they were dead.

"Keep those letters coming," laughed George. And I did, for a helluva long time.

In 1974 I received an Emmy Award nomination for my portrayal of Bea Asher in the PBS film *Queen of the Stardust Ballroom,* and, more delightful for me, I was praised for my dancing.

"Well, George," I said at dinner after the nominations were announced, "I did okay for adequate."

"I can't imagine anyone calling your dancing adequate. Whoever could have said such a thing?" said George, smiling innocently.

"I'll let you know when I find out."

Nossir, George wasn't big on gooey flattery. Once I said to him, "You never say sweet nothings to a girl. But you know that if you do, it doesn't bond you to me or mean you're committed in any way; it's just that occasionally a girl likes to hear a sweet nothing."

George thought a bit and then smilingly offered his idea of a sweet nothing. "Would you like a piece of candy?"

Another time we were walking hand-in-hand and I turned to him and said, "George, please say something flattering. Can't you think of something nice to say?"

He continued walking, put his head to one side, and appeared to be thinking. "Okay, I've got it," he said. "You know, Maureen, one thing I really like about you . . . your hands don't sweat."

"There you go, George, turning my head again," I said.

My romance with George Abbott rocked the theatrical community. We were the "talk of the town." Norma Crane, my close friend and fellow actress, thought I'd flipped my lid.

"Maureen, what the hell's the matter with you? The guy's too old."

"Haven't you ever heard of a May-December romance?" I asked.

"Forget it," said Norma. "I can see him for December but you're no kid."

"How about December-August?" I offered.

Norma would not be put off. "What the hell can you do with a guy that old anyway?"

"Honey, he's not that old. He's only eighty-one and he's fabulous."

Norma thought about it for a few seconds and then asked, "Does he have an older brother?"

I took a lot of flack from everyone about the disparity in our ages; I don't know what George heard from his chums. I'll tell you the truth: George was in remarkable shape throughout our years together. The only physical problem he had was with peripheral vision. He was about ninety when he had an operation to correct it. After the surgery we were scheduled to go up to his summer place in the Catskills and George was determined to do the driving. This had me worried. I called up his daughter Judy and asked if she would drive the car.

"He won't let me," she complained.

I was nervous and called up my pal Norma. I told her the story and she laughed. "Don't worry Maureen, that's not the way George Abbott's going to die."

George picked me up and we drove along the Henry Hudson Parkway. I could see he was straining to take in everything. I was really on edge and didn't stop worrying as we drove over the George Washington Bridge. It was very evident that George was uncomfortable behind the wheel, and, to his credit, he pulled the car over and said to his daughter, "I don't feel like driving anymore, Judy."

"Okay, Dad," she said and took over.

That was the last time he attempted any long drives. He still got behind the wheel for short trips, and I was nervous as a cat every time I got in the car with him.

If George had any flaw, it may have been his legendary thrift. Throwing money around definitely wasn't his thing. The first summer we were together I was appearing in *Plaza Suite,* and George invited me to join him in the Catskills for the weekends. On the first Saturday night, I hired a limousine to pick me up at the theater and take me to the mountains and arranged for the limo to take me back as well. During the weekend George said, "It's ridiculous for you to hire a limo to go back to the city. I'll drive you to the bus stop. You can take the bus, and don't worry, I'll pay your fare." And that's exactly what he did. For the rest of the summer I'd pay for the limousine up and George would treat me to the bus ride back.

I was drinking again, but very moderately for me. I had to be careful around George because he was practically a teetotaler. On those weekends in the country, we'd dine and he'd sometimes take a swallow of wine and then spit it out. I never figured out why, though I suspected he did it so that my breath wouldn't knock him out. One time we were in a restaurant and someone sent a bottle of champagne to our table. George politely had a glass, and I, politely, finished the rest. The next day he complained about a terrible headache.

"But George, you only had one glass of champagne."

"I know it's mother's milk to you, Maureen," said George, "but I have a headache."

In 1970 we did a show together, *Norman, Is That You?* George was a joy to work with, an absolute genius when it came to comedy. He could illustrate how to get a laugh and make it happen again and again. Sometimes in comedy you can get three different laughs in one line or sentence. You might think the laugh is only at the end of the line, and then you discover that there are two more. The trick is to get all the laughs you can, and you can do this only by finding out where they are. George had a real feel for pulling out each chuckle. He'd say things like, "Walk behind the couch, stop at the third pillow, look down, count two, look up, and say the line." In *Norman* I recall a particular sentence that I thought had only one laugh—at the end. George milked it. He had me say the first half of the line facing the audience, then turn around and say the second half with my back to them. I got two laughs for the price of one every time. Of course, in comedy you never can be dead certain how the audience will react. The lines you thought were so amusing in rehearsal may not play funny to the audience. The reverse is often true, too. That's why comedy is harder to play than drama.

We rehearsed *Norman, Is That You?* for four weeks, opened,

played for two weeks, and closed. I was sorry that it didn't last, because I really loved my part. "Beatrice Chambers" was on stage for less than half an hour, whereas most roles I'd played had me behind the footlights for the better part of the evening. When I saw the original poster for *Norman,* I had a fit because my name was featured. I was afraid some people might come expecting to see me starring, and I wasn't on stage long enough to warrant real top billing. I told them to take my name off the poster and pay me less money. My requests turned out to be unnecessary.

For ten years George Abbott and I were an item and, God, what larks we had. Toward the end of our decade of fun and games, I realized George, who was now ninety-one, was "stepping out." He'd invite me to places and his granddaughter, Amy, whom he adores, would be there as well, along with another woman named Joy. It became increasingly obvious that though I was invited, George was with Joy, who, by the by, is five years younger than me. Eventually that sonofagun threw me over and married her. George and Joy Abbott settled in Florida and really lived happily ever after, just like an old MGM movie, until he died peacefully on January 31, 1995, at the age of 107. My memories of George Abbott remain fresh and joyous. I never felt slighted or jilted by him, because he always played things straight. And while we were together we had such fun. What a guy!

After George went out of my life, according to Zoe Caldwell, I never lost my fascination for older men. Zoe's father, Edgar, was crazy about me and I adored him. Edgar came from Australia for long visits and stayed with Zoe and Bob in the Whiteheads' fabulous home in Pound Ridge. When they married, Bob and Zoe bought this piece of property on a mountain ridge and built their home. It's a forever place, and they'll be there for the rest of their lives. Anyway, whenever Edgar Caldwell heard I was coming up to Zoe and Bob's place, he would stop what he was doing, shower and shave, and get all dolled up—just for me. Of course, he was a kid compared to George Abbott (everyone was!) and nothing ever came of this infatuation. Still, to this day, if Zoe gives me any lip, I tell her to treat me with respect, if only because I could have been her stepmother.

Milton Goldman of ICM became my agent for *Plaza Suite* and remained my agent until he died, which was shortly after my last Broadway appearance in *The Little Foxes*. Milton was probably the most celebrated agent of his time and was as beloved as he was famous. He positively adored his work and because he was so happy at what he did, really enjoyed life. Milton was the protégé and lifelong companion of Arnold Weissberger, a theatrical lawyer and gifted amateur photographer. Milton and Arnold regularly gave fabulous parties in their superbly furnished New York apartment. The guests would assemble and Arnold would get out his camera and record the event; his pictures were eventually published in a book. Every summer, Milton and Arnold went to London and stayed at the Savoy Hotel, where they continued throwing parties just about every night. The place was packed with the biggest names in entertainment—Peter O'Toole, John Mills, Rex Harrison—all of whom I assumed were his clients. You might not see someone for years, but you were sure of bumping into him or her at one of those Savoy bashes.

The mainstays of Arnold and Milton's New York galas were Lillian Gish, Helen Hayes, Hermione Gingold, and me. We were known as Milton's Groupies, and why not? Although he never talked much about what he did, Milton was a damn good agent, the best, and he was a real upper, a whirling dervish of activity and always for good causes. I know for a fact that he raised plenty of money for Martha Graham, and God knows how many other companies or individuals benefited from his generosity. He loved parties, and if he weren't giving one, he was going to one. He was still partying and swinging when he died at seventy-five.

Milton Goldman's social life didn't slow down his business activities; he was the kind of agent who looked out for you. He sure took care of me; hell, he even looked after my family. When my daughter, Kathy, had an opportunity to appear in the movie *Summer of '42*, Milton went right to bat for her and she got the part. He did this for you and he did that for you; he simply couldn't stop doing something for somebody. Yes indeed, Milton Goldman protected me and pushed me. What more could an actress ask from an agent? He also filled in as my escort when I was without a suitable partner. One time we were at a theater party and I'd gotten rather tight. I had by then fallen from grace and gone back to heavy drinking, not hard liquor—never that—but wine and beer and lots of it. Anyway, I wanted to leave and needed my escort to take me home. I found him standing with a bunch of people.

"Boy, am I glad to see you!" I cried, throwing my arms around him. "I love you, Milton. I wanna go home."

Milton smiled, politely extricated himself from the group, and started steering me toward the door. I was overcome with affection for him, and as we left the room I gave him what I considered my biggest compliment: "Milton, you're a doll. I really love you, and if you ever decide to fuck a woman, I'm your man."

Chapter Eight

Do actors instantly recall every single role they've ever played? Maybe some do; I sure don't. Certain roles I'll never forget doing; others, for whatever reasons, don't come tripping into my brain. I guess I could name them all with a little prodding and poking into my memory bank, although I'd have to work on it. Last winter I received a letter from *Who's Who* or *What's It* or whatever that book is called, containing a list of my Broadway appearances. This was the final manuscript copy and I was asked to make sure all the titles were included. I read the list, thought it looked okay, signed the release, sealed the envelope, and was about to mail it back when a friend dropped by for "tea." During the course of our sipping and chatting, she brought up my appearance in *27 Wagons Full of Cotton,* a play that I instantly remembered had been omitted from the "final" list. I reopened the envelope, made the addition, and mailed it off. If that friend hadn't brought up the subject, my CV would have been incomplete. It's kind of scary if you think about it, maybe not in my minor case, but in the big picture you hate to think a momentary lapse could result in incorrect or incomplete information.

I forgot Flora in *27 Wagons Full of Cotton* not because it wasn't exciting and interesting for me at the time I played her; it just wasn't uppermost in my thoughts nearly thirty years later. Two roles, Serafina delle Rose and Evy Meara, will never slip my mind, not in a hundred years. The former you already know about, and the latter is the protagonist in Neil Simon's 1970 play, *The Gingerbread Lady*. Evy Meara is an alcoholic singer who returns from a drying-out place and in the course of three acts tries to get rid of her abusive younger lover and hold on to her teenage daughter. According to the gossip of the day, *The Gingerbread Lady* was an amalgam of the lives of Judy Garland and guess who? Frankly, that rumor was pure bull. I don't think Doc Simon was talking about either of us when he wrote the play. I knew Judy Garland—she was a great woman, a superstar. Evy Meara is a night club singer, not a big star. Judy's name never came up at rehearsals, not even once. As for Evy being me, well, I may have had a drinking problem but *never* when I worked. Evy couldn't work; I've always been able to. Nobody in this wide, wide world can rehearse, try out, and play a role different from herself eight times a week and be a real problem drinker. Oh, another important point: Evy tells her daughter to get out; that drunk I would never get. I'd never throw them out. I'd die for my kids. *The Gingerbread Lady* wasn't my story, not by a country mile. And as far as I know, it wasn't written *for* me any more than it was written about me. Anyway, what does it matter if the play was about Judy or me or Genghis Khan if it's a good play? I loved *The Gingerbread Lady* and still do. What I liked best was its humor; one critic called it "a sort of tragedy with wisecracks."

The Gingerbread Lady was beset with problems from the start and nearly didn't make it to Broadway. Bob Moore was the director and, as usual, the first rehearsal was smothered in tension, aka fright. I can't emphasize this aspect of the profession enough. You're stepping into the arena again and there are no guarantees available. No matter how many times you've gone on stage, there's no assurance that this time at bat you're going to get a hit. That's the way it was, is, and will be; the uncertainty goes with the territory. No actor can ever be cocksure, and if he ever is . . . he's wrong.

We gathered together for that first sit-through and began the reading. Given the regular amount of nerves and attendant woes, I thought I was perfectly calm. We went through the play and Bob Moore listened and made a few suggestions and discussed some of the details. The rehearsal ended and I was getting ready to leave. Bob came over to say good-bye.

"Were you a bit nervous today?" he asked.

"No more than usual," I answered.

"Really," chuckled the director. "Take a look at your handbag, Maureen."

I looked down at my purse. I'd been sitting there twisting the handle all afternoon and had finally pulled the damn thing off. I'd never realized what I was doing; I'd thought I was calm. What is calm, anyway? As a rule I'm a nervous wreck every time the curtain goes up, and I don't think I'm alone. Some actors have rituals or use lucky charms to keep the butterflies out of their stomachs. I've never gone those routes and just sort of tough it out. I've never got over being frightened, especially on opening nights. Still, I've never let my fear paralyze me. You have to do a bit of adjusting to make yourself as comfortable as possible, and that can take years. I made a particular modification which had to do with my eating habits. I used to have dinner between shows on matinee days. I'd go to a restaurant, eat a splendid meal, return to the theater, and throw up. I couldn't keep the food down, and it was expensive food, too. So I stopped going out; instead, I had a few bites of cottage cheese and a cup of tea in between performances. That was the most I could handle. After the show I could eat the side of a cow.

During my theater days I also had to modify my behavior, especially in the area of criticism, good and bad. After a *Rose Tattoo* performance a bunch of people came back to see me, and as they walked into the dressing room I greeted them with, "If you have any constructive criticism, keep it to yourselves." At a certain stage in my career I became "paranoid" about people complimenting me on a performance when I knew I'd been lousy. Someone would say, "nice work," or words to that effect, and I'd be terribly rude and tell my flatterer where to go, where to get off, or what he could do with his compliment. I had a chip on my shoulder the size of a 2 × 4 and indulged myself in childish behavior for a long time. I ate my guts out when I received unearned praise. One night after giving a fifth-rate performance, I was walking down the stairs when a man called out, "You were wonderful, Miss Stapleton." I walked right over to the guy and punched him. Later I thought about what I'd done and became very contrite. Okay, I said to myself, that's enough; you've got to stop this crap. Do the best you can and let it go. Even if you've given the worst performance of your life, when someone compliments you, just smile and say thank you. My pep talk worked and I got over the nonsense of lashing out at others.

I learned a lot of lessons in the theater, some that aided my personal life and others that were more professionally helpful. Through my experiences in *Plaza Suite* I became aware that you can never paraphrase Neil Simon. Consequently, I had to go over the lines in *The Gingerbread Lady* again and again to get them letter-perfect. Early in rehearsals I asked a friend to cue me. As I recited the lines, he kept stopping me to correct my readings.

"Stop nagging!" I screamed in agony. "Just let me get through it. I'll get it straight later."

"Oh no," said my friend. "It says on this script Maureen Stapleton *in The Gingerbread Lady,* not *The Gingerbread Lady by* Maureen Stapleton." My friend was right. Bottom line: When you're doing Neil Simon, "if it ain't on the page, it ain't on the stage."

The Gingerbread Lady went to Boston for its tryout. We bombed. The audience didn't like it; in fact, they more than didn't like it; they hated it. A lot of that loathing had to do with the language Evy used; it was pretty explicit and probably contributed to the rumor that the play was all about me. Honestly, I think Evy Meara was more outspoken than I am! The fact is, you can't come out and hit people over the head with a barrage of four-letter words and expect them to like you—and that's equally true in writing a book. The audience was upset over Evy's vulgarity; I could hear their groans when I spoke her lines. The answer might seem simple—just get rid of the expletives. Not possible; you couldn't cut out all the rough language, because it was so much a part of the character.

The company was worried sick, but we trusted each other totally and trusted our ability to get this play right. Bob Moore was a painstaking director and a very sweet man, and Neil Simon remains one of the gentlest gentlemen in the world. He really was bothered by his inability to repair *The Gingerbread Lady*. "If it were a straight comedy," he confessed, "I could go home tonight and fix it. But I don't know what to do with this play." Doc valiantly tried to get at the problems, first by cutting out Evy's crude stuff from the opening and gradually adding it in acceptable doses, sort of like spoon-feeding. Once the audience got used to Evy and began to like her, she could say anything and not alienate them—which is as true in life as it is on stage.

The language may have been corrected, but the play still wouldn't fly. Whatever the reasons, the last few days of previews were dreadful. We decided not to go on to New York. *The Gingerbread Lady* officially closed in Boston and after the last, sad performance, I returned home. Two days later, Bob Moore telephoned. His message was terse and terrific: "We're on." It seems that on the train back from Boston, Neil Simon picked up the script and began a full-fledged hatchet job. He threw out one act entirely and rewrote a good portion of the remainder. Bob liked the result and called us all together again. We rehearsed the "new" version and premiered on December 13, 1970. Neil wrote me on opening night, "Dear Maureen, if it weren't for your dedication, inspiration, and complete love for this play, I could have been in Barbados for the last six weeks."

The Gingerbread Lady was luck for me; I won a Tony for Best Actress. After the ceremony I was asked how I felt about getting the award. "What the hell," I answered, "it's better than getting hit with a wet fish." How did it feel to be a star? Don't ask me. I never considered myself one. I'll tell you what a star is, though. Lana Turner came backstage after a performance with her manager, and we went out to some nightclub in the Village. We walked in the door, and the minute Lana was spotted, the orchestra began playing a song from Lana's movie *Ziegfeld Girl*.

"Jeez," I said to her, "they're playing your song."

"Yes," Lana Turner explained with a dazzling smile, "it happens a lot." I'll consider myself a star when I walk into a room and the band starts playing my song.

I did receive a few special acknowledgments for *The Gingerbread Lady,* including a fan letter that I never threw out.

Dear Miss Stapleton,

Recently saw your wonderful performance in *The Gingerbread Lady* and enjoyed the show immensely. It left me thinking about you when I left the theater. I would like to have the pleasure of dating you sometime in the near future. I am thirty-eight years of age, six foot one and weigh about 190 pounds. Enclosed you will find a photo of myself.

Thanking you I remain . . .

I got this response before all those personal ads started appearing in the newspapers and magazines. I should've answered the damn thing; the guy looked pretty cute.

We were still out of town in New Haven with *The Gingerbread Lady* when my mother died. Max called and told me after a performance. Mother's death took me by surprise. She'd retired and had kept busy with ceramics classes and furniture making. I have some of her handiwork, including a graceful little side chair. We talked at least once a week on the phone and, as I said, she'd not been sick. I don't even remember what she died of; it must have been a stroke or a heart attack or something of that nature.

I left for Troy the next day, and the play closed while I attended the wake and funeral. Now both my parents were gone. Looking back, I barely remembered my father's passing some ten years before. My mother had called to tell me he was dead, and I did return home to attend his funeral. If I'm not mistaken, his pallbearers were American Legion buddies. I don't think I shed any tears; his death, like his life, left me cold. On the other hand, I truly grieved for my mother. She'd been a major force in my life, and in her own determined, forthright way, one helluva lady. So many thoughts crowded into my brain, so many scenes from my childhood. Yes, my mother was straightlaced and circumspect; yet she eased up in her later years, especially with my children. During the Vietnam War, Kathy was in high school. She had tacked a poster on her bedroom wall that read FUCK WAR. I thought it was a good poster. My mother was visiting once and dropped into Kathy's room. "I don't like that word," she said to her granddaughter. "I don't like that word at all." She didn't like the word but she didn't order Kathy to take the poster down, and it stayed on the wall. Years earlier when I was growing up, the poster would have been torn down and my wings would have been clipped.

It's so difficult to assess the life of a parent, especially a much beloved one. I believe that while my father didn't do anything for my welfare, my mother really tried to give me a jump start. I drove off in a direction that she might not have chosen herself, but at least she saw me attain a measure of accomplishment. I'm grateful for that.

I went back up to Troy awhile after the funeral in order to sort things out at the house. I discovered that my brother had had a tag sale of all mother's possessions on the front lawn and a great many of them were gone. I was pretty shaken. The material things may have been lost, but I still have my memories of her, and most of them are pretty damn good. Of course, I have no idea how old she was when she died, which is exactly the way she'd have wanted it.

• • •

Whatever its worth as a piece of dramatic literature, *The Ginger-bread Lady* was very special for me both because of my role and because it afforded me the opportunity to work with my own daughter. Kathy was in the eleventh grade when I toured with the play. She'd already made her acting debut in *Summer of '42,* and after auditioning, she was cast in the role of my daughter for the *Gingerbread* tour. Although I hadn't pushed my kids in the direction of the theater, I was thrilled to be appearing on stage with Kathy. It was a mother's dream and a daughter's nightmare. Kathy alternated playing the part with Lucy Saroyan, Carol Matthau's daughter. I had fun doing it; I can't speak for Kathy. I know she thought her character was incredibly whiny.

The fact is, Kathy really wasn't that keen on being an actress. God knows, you've got to be keen with a capital *K,* or else you ain't gonna do it. As I said, I never pressured my kids to go into the theater; I just figured if they wanted it, they'd go after it. Forget Danny—he wouldn't touch acting with a ten-foot pole. For a little while Kathy did toy with the idea. I know she enjoyed her success with *Summer of '42.* The excitement of it, however, didn't overwhelm her; her heart never was set on acting. Eventually she was completely turned off; according to her, because of a visit to a casting agent's office. Kathy walked in; the agent took a look at her and said, "Do you always wear your hair like that?" For Kathy, this was the last straw. "I thought it was rude and horrible for someone to pick on me before I opened my mouth," my daughter told me. "I'm not cut out for acting, Mom." And that was it. Kathy dropped her career like a hot potato. "I saw you exert the kind of energy that has to be expended," Kathy explained to me, "and I couldn't do it." At first Kathy didn't fall completely away from the theater. She took a job in Bob Whitehead's office for a couple of years, then, tired of the New York pace, she moved up to Lenox, married Rick Bambury, and had my two fabulous grandchildren, Alexandra and Max. If nothing else, my daughter proved I was right in saying that you have to have blinders on and be stark raving mad to go into the theater.

During the summer stock tour of *The Gingerbread Lady,* I became a yachtsman of sorts. We were someplace in Massachusetts or Connecticut; I don't remember which state exactly, I only recall that we were near the water. A woman connected with the theater invited me and the girls to go out for a sail on her husband's boat. Kathy, Lucy, and I accepted her invitation and it was so wonderful I immediately fell in love with boating. We went out on that sailboat quite a bit, even after evening performances, which was unusual because boats generally are moored at night. I had such a feeling of tranquillity on the "low" seas that after a couple of those jaunts, I got a bee in my bonnet; I thought it would be nice to have my own boat. I thought about it and talked about it till one day my buddy Pete Simonian said, "Well, if you want a boat, why don't you just get one?" So, with Pete in tow, I went boat shopping along the Mohawk.

I'd been on a sailboat all summer, but I never could have handled one of those things; I was looking for something more tailored to my nonskills as a sailor. Pete and I went to a boat dealer in Troy and found just what I wanted—a houseboat. At the time, I knew nothing about the hierarchy of boats. Put simply, it goes like this: The sailboat without a motor is the most elegant, the king of the water. Then comes the sailboat with a motor, a little less regal, still a majestic craft. Next is the cabin cruiser, and so on down to the dinghy. Below the dinghy—and probably below a rubber tire—is the houseboat. No matter how big or how beautiful or how much it cost, the houseboat is the slum of the waves, a floating tenement. Sometimes I'd get into conversations with folks in the marinas.

"Oh, you have a boat?"

"Yep," I'd answer proudly.

"What kind?"

"A houseboat."

"Oh," and there'd be this perceptible beat while the information was weighed and classified.

"That's nice," they'd say politely. I finally figured out that in their eyes it wasn't "nice." They were a mannerly group and would never tell me to my face that I was the captain of a hunk

216

of junk. Let's face it, you're not really a sailor if you have a houseboat, at least not to yachtsmen.

I learned something else when I purchased my boat—it's not like buying a stove or a refrigerator. When you buy a boat, you're buying the shell and I do mean shell. The extras, things like the motor and the furnishings, have to be purchased separately. What's that old story about the guy who went to buy a yacht and asked the dealer the price? "If you have to know the price," said the dealer, "then you can't afford it." I could afford my boat and the motor and furnishings, too, but it didn't come easy. The guy I bought it from was a sweetheart of a man. He took me to the shop in Glens Falls, where the boats were built, and I gave him a partial payment check right then and there. The boat was supposed to be delivered immediately. So I go back, and I'm waiting to hear that my ship is in the water, and I hear nothing. Pete and I go up to see the guy again, and he's real nice and explains that something happened to the other check and I have to make out a new one. Okay, I make out another one. Did I know that he owed the guys in the Glens Falls shop a lot of money and had used *my* original check to clear some of his debt? Can you believe I made out another check? The guy was a real sweetie; courteous, knowledgeable and softspoken. Who knew the police were after him? He was not my idea of a con man. Even so, he skipped off. Fortunately I got my boat. I was lucky. One of the guys on the dock told me later that the salesman really was a nice guy and did a lot for boats—until he went "bad." I'm telling you, I can't even buy a boat without getting into a Tennessee Williams plot. Somehow everything worked out, and I took possession of my sturdy craft and called it the *Wu Li*. Why? I can't for the life of me remember. I think it had something to do with Tai Chi. If anyone recognizes what "wu li" stands for, let me know. I'm curious.

When I bought the *Wu Li* I was told that it slept ten, but I realize now that they always say that. Sure it could sleep ten: ten very tiny people all madly in love with each other. Actually, the boat could comfortably sleep four, maybe five, down below.

The *Wu Li* was moored on the Mohawk. We loved to sail along the Hudson, and in order to get to that river you had to go through a series of five or six locks because the Mohawk is something like ninety feet higher than the Hudson. I could start the boat, get it in the channel, then go up and down the river, but no way could I dock the damn thing. Word got around, and people used to gather at the docks when I was attempting to moor; it was quite a show. All the folks in their big fancy boats would come over to the little wooden dock where I was heading. I'm telling you, every other dock was empty. The burning question was, "Would Captain Maureen be able to secure the *Wu Li?*" I'd come putting up to the pier and then I'd freeze. Everyone would start yelling directions, and I'd get more and more rattled and finally turn over the reins. The fact is, I never successfully docked the *Wu Li* myself. I never went out alone in it, either; there always were passengers. Pete took it up and down the Hudson a few times, and then we got a buddy of his to be the official captain. No mutiny, I assure you. I was delighted to turn over the helm.

The *Wu Li* wasn't that big—about thirty-five feet, I think—and I really loved it and so did my family and friends. They'd come aboard and we'd go on picnics. Zoë and Bob brought their two boys and took a couple of sails with me up and down the Hudson. We'd drop anchor, and the boys would jump in the river and take a swim for themselves. My aunts and cousins were willing passengers, too. There always were crowds, from the people watching on the docks to the people on my boat. For six years I spent most of my summers living on the *Wu Li.* My kids would visit, but they didn't like it as much as I thought they would. I mean, they liked it, but not enough to want to stay on board.

The *Wu Li* was a helluva lot of fun and a helluva lot of work. People usually put a great deal of time and energy into their boats, which I didn't know when I bought mine. *You* have to clean the boat every day, which is something I thought the air and water took care of. I didn't mind swabbing the decks, but you can do that for just so long. Plus you have to put the boat in mothballs for the winters and get it scraped and painted, et cetera, et cetera. About the sixth summer, my ardor for boating began to wane. By then I was on board the *Wu Li* only two or three days a year. If you're only using a boat for a matter of days, there's too much upkeep to warrant owning one. I thought about the rewards and weighed them against the drawbacks and figured out that I'd had my fun. I sold the *Wu Li* with no regrets. I have a lot of happy memories of my nautical days and there's a swell picture of the *Wu Li* on my bathroom wall—and that's about as close as I want to get to any boat at this stage of my life.

There was a time when boats were essential to my career. I'm not talking about houseboats; I mean *big* boats, the ocean liners and freighters that took me back and forth across the Atlantic Ocean on voyages that will never, I repeat, never, happen again.

In 1976 I signed a contract to appear as Big Mama in a televised version of Tennessee Williams's *Cat on a Hot Tin Roof,* with Bob Moore directing and Natalie Wood and R. J. Wagner playing Maggie the Cat and Brick. The array of talent in itself was terrific, but the whole deal was lifted into the realms of heaven because Big Daddy was being played by Laurence Olivier. I, me, Lois Maureen Stapleton was going to appear opposite the greatest actor in the world and the guy who'd been married to and appeared opposite Vivien Leigh. The concept was so thrilling that I almost forgot that England, where the play was going to be done, couldn't be reached by my preferred modes of transportation, train or car. I wouldn't fly, not even to Laurence Olivier, but nothing could prevent me from sailing to him. I booked passage on the *QE 2* for myself and Kathy. I thought the trip would be a special treat for my kids, and while Kathy was able to come along for the whole deal, Danny and his then girlfriend had to join us later on. Before sailing to London, I had a farewell lunch with Colleen and a couple of other actress friends. The conversation never left Laurence Olivier. At one and the same time my pals were happy for me and pea green with envy. At the end of the meal I stood up and took my leave. "Remember, girls," I announced, "I'm doing this for all of us."

The trip over remains a bit of a blur; the seas were high and so was I. We reached Southampton and proceeded up to London, where the rehearsals were scheduled to take place. The actual filming would be in Manchester. Kathy and I checked into the Athenaeum Hotel and I tried to get a night's sleep. All I could think of was that I'd be meeting and working with Laurence Olivier within hours. The next day I reported to the studio at about noon. Olivier had already begun rehearsing with Natalie and R. J. Wagner, both of whom I had known before their first marriage. They were darling, just darling. She was so beautiful and such fun to be with, really terrific. And R.J., of course, is the dearest guy in the world. Everybody loves him, you can't not love him. It's like Elizabeth Taylor; it's impossible not to like her much less love her. R.J. and Natalie were now in their second marriage—they'd divorced each other, married others, then divorced them and gotten back together. Hooray for Hollywood. Natalie was a great friend of Norma Crane's, and I remember that when R.J. and Natalie were dating for the second time, Natalie was talking gooey gooey ga ga about R.J.

"What's with this goo-goo talk?" I asked Norma. "Doesn't she know they were married once?"

"She forgot," Norma answered. It's amazing how you can be in a repeat situation and play it like an innocent. Natalie was positively wide-eyed and acting like a giddy teenager. One time in Hollywood, we were going to a preview or something and she leaned over and said with a sly smile, "I'm bringing a big surprise for my date tonight."

"You're coming with R.J." I told her. "What's the big deal."

"How did you know?" asked Natalie.

"The word is out," I said matter-of-factly. Natalie responded with a faint "Oh." I mean what the hell did she think she was keeping secret? Anyway, they were an adorable couple and I loved them both dearly. I still love R.J. Poor Natalie is gone now but never forgotten. Roddy McDowall asked me to do the caption for her photograph in his book *Double Exposure*. I wrote,

"Natalie is every great song in the world starting with 'the most beautiful girl.'" Amen.

Kathy and I arrived at the London studio just in time for the lunch break. Olivier came over and we were formally introduced. What a scene. I stood there with my jaw hanging open like some drooling fool. He, of course, pretended not to notice and couldn't have been more cordial.

"How do you do, Maureen. What a great pleasure it is to meet you." Thus spake the world's premier actor, at which point the world's most flustered actress dropped a curtsey and mumbled, "How do you do, Sir—I mean, Lord—I mean, God." I didn't know what to call Olivier and ended up calling him everything. From then on I to referred to him as "Sir Lord God" and he got a big kick out it.

The introductions over, we headed down the corridor toward the cafeteria. I walked with R.J. and Natalie, while Olivier fell behind to accompany my daughter. I overheard their conversation.

"I'm terribly sorry, my dear," said Sir Lord God, "but I didn't get your name."

"It's Kathy."

"Oh," he said, "then you must call me Heathcliff." When I heard him say that, my jaw once again flapped open and strange sounds like "aah aah aah" came out of my throat. Kathy didn't blink. What the hell did she know? She'd never seen *Wuthering Heights.* Even though Kathy didn't catch the full glory of the Heathcliff reference, Olivier took a shine to her. At the end of every rehearsal session, he'd say goodnight to me and add, "Give my love to Kathy." I'd go home and say, "Heathcliff sends his love." I'd have sold my soul to be the recipient of that message.

Olivier's wife, Joan Plowright, was appearing in the West End, and one afternoon he invited Kathy and me to go to the theater and have dinner with him and the Mrs. I don't know why, but I said, "Oh, we'd love to be with you, but we've got tickets already." I may have been trying to show him that I was interested enough to see Joan Plowright perform without freebies. Who knows? I felt like an asshole after I said it and immediately ran to the phone to get Kathy. I told her to run out and get two tickets for the play. We went to the theater and afterward had dinner with the Oliviers.

I grew very fond of Larry: still, there always was that in-and-out thing. I'd be talking to him as if he were just a person and then suddenly I'd think, "Oh my God, it's Laurence Olivier." Joan Plowright's terrific, too, and we had a lovely dinner that evening. Sir Lord God was ordering wine up the gazzu and, naturally, I drank a *lot* of it. I was so busy guzzling that I didn't notice that Kathy was drinking a lot as well. She told me later that Olivier watched her down the wine and then leaned over and said, "You're drinking all that wine yourself to keep Mommy from getting drunk, aren't you?" The guy was smart, all right.

We rehearsed at Fox Hall in London for about three weeks and then went to Manchester to shoot. The first evening in Manchester, Lord Olivier hosted a gala dinner party for the entire cast and crew in our hotel. What a joint that was, one of those enormous places that's two city blocks wide, with huge public rooms, endless dimly lit corridors, and lousy plumbing. They even had one of those blue-and-white plaques in the lobby, the kind that tells you what historical figure lived there or what historical thing happened there. The plaque in the Manchester hotel read, "In this lobby, Mr. Rolls met Mr. Royce." Trust me, that damn lobby was big enough for the Messrs. Rolls and Royce to drive in their cars with space left over for Mr. Mack and a few of his trucks. Olivier took over one of the dining rooms. He gave the dinner party to put everyone at ease and, believe me, enough booze was available to put the entire British Isles at ease. I dined and wined and wined and wined and by the end of the dinner, I was really easy. I was so easy that I was just about the last guest at the table. Only Larry and George Rondo, Bob Moore's friend and assistant, remained, and those two gentlemen escorted me to my room.

On the first day of the shooting we were in the BBC's huge television studio and the whole crew was assembled on the set.

All eyes were on Lord Olivier. Poor Larry really had two jobs when he worked: one was his own, and the other was to make everyone feel at home and not be in awe of him—which everyone included yours truly. Larry and I walked around the set together and familiarized ourselves with the surroundings. After a bit, he went to the center of the set, reached up, and pulled down the microphone hanging above us.

"Robert, can you hear me?" he asked. Bob Moore was in the director's booth way at the other end. He clicked on and said over the loudspeaker, "Yes, Larry, I can hear you. What is it?"

"Maureen and I were wondering whether we should go around the table two or three times," said Sir Lord God. I looked at him in bewilderment. I didn't know why he was questioning Bob. We'd gone around the table twice during rehearsal and it was no big deal. Bob Moore called out over the loudspeaker.

"Twice, go around twice."

"Right," answered Olivier, "twice it is, Robert. Thank you."

The lightbulb went off over my head. I realized what Larry was doing. He was letting everybody know from the start that Bob Moore was the director and the director, not Lord Olivier, was in charge. Larry did it very casually, but the whole crew got the message and Bob Moore was established as the boss. I remember thinking, "Very classy, Sir Lord God, very classy indeed."

"Classy" really is too small a word for that man. Everything Larry Olivier did while we worked together was on a higher, smarter, kinder, and better level. Two of the minor cast members in *Cat* were Americans who'd lived in London for many years. At the beginning of the rehearsals, Larry, in his quest to put everyone at ease, had gone over to them and requested their assistance. "Could you help me with my American accent?" he asked. Let me tell you, those two guys grew one hundred inches taller; and why not, Lord Olivier needed their help. As if he needed their help; he could do *any* accent. That was the kind of thing he did, though, and it was only to make others feel com-

223

fortable in his presence. There was nothing condescending in his manner, either; he was quite sincere, and, I might add, still terrifically attractive. He'd been really ill and was in constant pain, especially from his leg. He'd have to sit with it raised during the breaks, and though he never complained, you knew he was suffering.

Olivier remained ill for the rest of his life, yet pushed himself into his work right up to the end. He did Othello and practiced for months to get his voice an octave lower because he felt the Moor required a deeper voice than his. When I heard that, I remember thinking, "Who would have noticed? Who would have cared? It's Othello, do it any way you want to do it." Not Larry. *He* wanted his voice lower and worked for months to get it that way. Years later, at the end of his brilliant career, when he did *King Lear* for television, he was close to enfeebled by his illnesses and, from what I heard, spent weeks and weeks at the piano playing scales and following them with his voice to get it supple enough to tackle those great arching speeches. All that effort, and simply because he thought it necessary. No wonder he was the best; no wonder he was Sir Lord God.

Larry had a very calming effect on me. I wanted to do my best for him; like a schoolgirl, I wanted to impress him. We'd lunch together and he'd talk with me about Big Mama and Big Daddy and their relationship and the various ways it could be played. He was a soothing presence, no question. And yet he went through hell during the shooting. Big Daddy has huge long speeches, sometimes a full page and a half of dialogue, which is back-breaking stuff to learn. He learned them, and then, during rehearsal, the network reps would come in every day and make changes, horrendous changes as far as memorization goes. They didn't lop off the whole first paragraph or the last section or even hunks in the middle; instead they did "interior cuts," which are murder. It's so much easier to cut out a whole speech than to change little bitsy words, yet they did this to him every single day. They were censoring, and I'm pretty sure it was because the broadcast was scheduled for America as well as Britain. I don't think the BBC was as uptight as our television in those days.

Every day when Larry came in, someone would hand him a revised script, and it was painful to watch him wrestle with the constant picayune alterations. He really struggled.

Meanwhile, dear R.J. and Natalie were letter-perfect in their roles; they'd learned their entire parts before they came to London and none of us had to deal with the extensive cuts that Olivier faced. Now, I don't care if you are the greatest actor in the world; when the other members of the cast know their lines and you're still fumbling, it's an extra added pressure. So here's Lord Olivier pushing and pushing with script in hand, and here's R.J. and Natalie spouting their lines with absolute assurance. About the second or third day of rehearsing, I had dinner with R.J. and Natalie.

"Look guys," I said, "I know Larry's the greatest living actor and all that, but he's having a hard time. You two have your lines down pat, but his are being changed every day and he's got to keep up with the revisions. It's got to be offputing for the man. I think if you could just hold the scripts or pretend that you don't know every word, it might help."

"Oh my God, of course," said R.J. "I don't know why we didn't think of it."

The next day when I came into rehearsal, R.J. was holding the script in his hand, and later Natalie did the same. Larry was still breaking his back to get the changes, and was it painful to watch. Sometimes I had to go out in the hall because I couldn't bear to stand there and watch him wrestle with the dialogue. Mary Sweet, another cast member, went with me. We thought if we stepped out, he wouldn't feel the pressure of other actors looking at him while he tried to find the words. One time I was on the set and he went through one of those big, long numbers. At the end he was leaning with his hands on the table and his head hanging over.

"Larry, excuse me," said Noah, the dialogue coach. "Do you want it exact?"

Olivier lifted his head and sighed. "Settle for what you get, darling, settle for what you get."

That was the extent of his complaints. Every time he got

through a damn speech, even though they'd bring in another batch of tiny cuts, he never screamed or threw a fit or said, "No, I can't do this anymore." Lots of actors, lesser ones than Olivier, might have done just that.

I've been asked if I thought he was the greatest actor of our day, and I have to say that while he was certainly great, John Gielgud and Ralph Richardson weren't exactly chopped liver. Even so, I might tip the scale to Olivier for the simple reason that I never had the honor of appearing with either Gielgud or Richardson and, more important, Laurence Olivier was Heathcliff, and baby, that did it for me.

When *Cat* was in the can, I took my kids on a sentimental journey, a boat ride across the sea to Ireland. I was in search of my roots and thought it would be a kick to visit the land of my ancestors. I should have stayed in bed. It was the trip from hell. In the first place, the kids didn't want to go; after all, it was only half their roots. I pushed for the trip, which already was a big mistake; whatever happened was my fault because they never wanted to be there. We went to Dublin first and checked into the Royal Hibernian Hotel. We walked into the lobby and went to the front desk, where I was asked to open my purse while they checked for guns. My feeling is that if someone wants to bring in a gun, I don't think she'd be stupid enough to put it in her handbag. Anyway, just the idea that somebody might be checking in armed to the teeth was rather disconcerting.

The next step on the agenda was to hire a car so we could drive to Momma Walsh's birthplace, County Mayo. We got the car and began the drive. Now, the atmosphere in the automobile was not the greatest, because my kids were still miserable and letting me know it in no uncertain terms. We stopped overnight someplace on Galway Bay. Well, I'd heard the song "Galway Bay" many times in my life and it was romantic and beautiful, and we hit a town that was so honky-tonk it made Coney Island look like Maui. This wasn't our finest hour. The next day we got back in the car and were ten minutes into County Mayo when we ran into a huge flock of sheep. We didn't run into them so much as we were forced to follow them; livestock and automobiles shared the road in Ireland. I suggested that we wait it out, but the flock was the last straw for Danny and his girlfriend. They said they'd had it with Dublin and Galway Bay and Mayo, period. I couldn't fight anymore. We turned around and drove back to the rental office on the outskirts of Dublin.

Now, I'm going to illustrate the brain of Ireland. It was Friday afternoon when we reached the city and we had rented the car through Sunday. I walked into the rental office and gave the guy behind the desk my papers.

He looked them over and then looked at me and said with great concern, "Oh dear, oh dear, you can't return the car. You see, it's Friday and you're not supposed to return until Sunday. You can't return the car until then."

"It's okay," I said. "I'll pay for it through the weekend."

"No, no," said the guy, "you can't return it today; you have to bring it back Sunday."

"But I'll pay for it!"

"No, no. Sunday."

"But, but . . ." I started sputtering, and the kids sat there listening to this exchange with looks of amazement on their faces. I could see I wasn't going to get anywhere with this joker, so I changed my tack.

"Is there a garage nearby where I can put this car till Sunday?"

"No, no, there's no garage."

"I'll pay for the garage," I informed him.

"No, no, my dear, there's nothing to pay for; there's no garage."

"Well, is there somebody I could leave it with?"

"No, no, dear." I tried to figure out something to do or say and whatever I came up with, this guy cheerfully kept saying, "No, no, dear." The more cheerful he got, the more angry I got.

"Listen," I finally said, "I don't understand why, if I'm going to pay for it, you won't take this car back."

"Because," smiled the man, "this is Friday, and it's Sunday you have to be bringing it back."

227

"Okay," I said, "I know what I'm going to do. The car is parked across the street. I'm going over there and burn it."

"Ah, and you wouldn't be doing such a thing now, would you?" he smiled.

"You bet your life I would!" By this time I'd lost it and the kids were laughing.

I would have torched the damn car, too, had not another man stepped out from the back room, where I assume he was hiding. This guy joined Mr. Potato Head behind the counter and smiled benignly.

"Please, Madam, calm down, don't worry. We'll take the car back." Why the hell this man waited until I was ready to burn the car and murder his help, I'll never know. I paid the bill and took the kids back to the hotel. They were in a better mood because they knew they were leaving, but I couldn't get over that impenetrable "no, you have to bring the car back on Sunday" routine. I tell you, with all due respect to my ancestors, I couldn't get out of that country fast enough.

When the time came for us to return home, we boarded the *QE 2* in Southampton. I think we were about two days out when the alarms began ringing at four o'clock in the morning and the passengers were herded up to the deck. There had been an explosion and fire on board. The explosion had nearly knocked me out of my bed, so I knew something was up. There were about a thousand people milling around on the deck. Other ships began to appear on the horizon, obviously on their way to help us. I knew exactly where all the lifeboats were because the first thing I did when I boarded was to check them out. After what seemed an eternity, the captain got on the loudspeaker. "Ladies and gentlemen, everything is under control. There was a small fire in the engine room," he announced. One thousand people laughed. Small? The whole ship stank from smoke. "Although we are in no danger," continued the captain, "we must return to Southampton for repairs." We limped back to port. The Cunard Line arranged for air transportation for the thousand passengers. Two hundred of us were D.F.'s (Don't Fly's) and we turned down

Cunard's offer; instead we went back to London and waited until the boat was fixed.

After that fiasco, I never thought I'd be back on the high seas. However, when Warren Beatty offered me the role of Emma Goldman in his production of *Reds,* I had to go to England for some of the shooting. The last time I crossed the Atlantic, Laurence Olivier had been the motivating force; this time, cold hard Hollywood cash provided the catalyst. I liked the idea of working with Warren; he's a smartie and a charmer. Years ago I'd gone with him to a preview of one his pictures.

After the showing we got in the elevator and Warren turned to me.

"How did you like the picture, Maureen?"

"It was too long," I answered honestly.

"Yes, but I mean, how did you like it?"

"Warren, it was too long."

Warren paused and, realizing I might be hedging, said, "Okay, it was too long. How wide was it?"

When I signed for *Reds,* travel arrangements had to be made. Alas, it was winter and the liners—what was left of them—weren't crossing. The only recourse was to find a freighter that was going somewhere near my destination. We found a Polish ship, the *Polarski,* which was sailing to Rotterdam. Rotterdam is not exactly a suburb of London, but it was the closest we could get. What's more, the *Polarski* did not embark from New York City; her port of call was Baltimore, Maryland. Down I trained to Baltimore, boarded the ship, and sailed off to the Netherlands with my son and his wife, Nina—not the young lady who'd been with us in Ireland, but a woman he'd met and married between voyages. We'd been out on the ocean for a day and a night when the *Polarski* stopped dead for twenty-four hours. We sat there on the water until it started again. We made a bit of progress and then the engines stopped again, and we floated pretty much on the same spot for two days and two nights. We rocked a lot but didn't move forward. I will resist making any remarks about crossing the ocean on a Polish freighter. We rocked and rocked and no one would tell us what was going on. One of the other passengers was a lovely young Polish woman traveling with her little daughter, and I struck up a friendship with them. There was only one way to deal with this voyage interruptus: get loaded and let the rest of the world go by. The second time the *Polarski* stopped, I drank all that day and all that night and half the next day, and you know what? I couldn't get the slightest buzz on. All I got was a splitting headache; it was like a tomahawk smacked into my brain. I was cold sober and my head was throbbing. A hangover without the reason for it is not acceptable. I couldn't understand it. I said something to the young mother.

"This is the wackiest thing. I haven't had anything to eat and I've been drinking wine for nearly two days and all I have is a splitting headache. I don't get it. Usually I'd be feeling no pain after all that drinking."

"I guess you would be feeling no pain if you were drinking regular wine," answered the woman, "but the wine they serve on board is only two percent alcohol."

"Two percent!" My God, I might just as well have been chuga-lugging Snapple.

The *Polarski* took fourteen days to get to Rotterdam; eleven days times two percent equalled misery for me. I took a train from Rotterdam, then boarded another boat to cross the channel, and then on to London. By now I had upped the percentage of my alcoholic intake enough to feel no pain. I arrived at the studio and told the powers that be, "Okay boys, I'm here and make sure we get it right while I am, because I ain't coming back for retakes." I made a vow on the *Polarski* and, except for the return voyage on a French freighter, I've kept it. No way is this lady going over the big waves again. Even if Clark Gable, Robert Taylor, and Joel McCrea came back to life and asked me to join them for a bacchanal in London, I'd regretfully decline.

Chapter Nine

Remember how I kept losing out to Anna Magnani in the movie versions of the Broadway shows I did? Well, while I never did get the opportunity to do my Tennessee Williams originals on the screen, I finally got the chance to recreate a theater role—sort of—when *Plaza Suite* was made into a film. In the stage version, George C. Scott and I had played the three different characters in the three separate episodes. In the Hollywood version of Neil Simon's play, only one person got to play in all three sections and that was Walter Matthau. I had to be content with doing one third of what I'd done on the stage; Lee Grant and Barbara Harris took over the other roles. What the hell, I was willing to settle for a solid single instead of a smashing triple; it got me out to Hollywood, and I got a nice bunch of dough *and* the chance to work with Walter. I love working with him except for one minor point; Walter, bless his heart, is a maniac about cigarettes. He can't stand them and doesn't want anyone puffing around him. Carol has to put up with her husband's rules; I don't. I remember visiting him in his dressing room when he was filming *Cactus Flower.* After chatting for a few minutes, I told him I was dying for a smoke.

"Not here," bellowed my pal. "Not in *my* dressing room." Fortunately, his costar rescued me.

"Come on into my dressing room," she said. "You can have your cigarette there." So I followed Ingrid Bergman into her quarters and puffed away to my heart's content . . . and I don't think that Bergman herself smoked. What a doll.

After *Plaza Suite* I didn't make another movie for seven years. These weren't lean years professionally by any means. I was kept pretty busy on stage and television. It was during those seven years that I portrayed Big Mama in *Cat* for television and took the title role in *Queen of the Stardust Ballroom,* a really lovely play with music that did very well on television. (And very miserably on Broadway. They tried to turn it into a full-fledged musical, and even with damn good people like Dorothy Loudon in my role, it wouldn't transfer from one medium to the other. Some things just don't make it in another league, and this was one of them.) In the television drama I played Bea Asher, a lonely widow who goes to the Stardust Ballroom and meets a guy. They fall in love. The fly in the ointment? The guy is married. His wife is an invalid, and though he's unhappy, he won't desert her. He and Bea become lovers. I believe we're talking adultery here. I remember making an adjustment in order to play Bea. I said to myself, "The wife is a sick woman and if anything happens to her, I'd help him take care of her." This was the only way I could justify Bea having the affair. You can always give yourself good reasons when you're doing something fishy—on screen or off. I loved doing Bea. I got to dance and even sang a bit! Guthrie McClintic would have been so proud of me.

There were other shows, too, but I don't want to get carried away and start listing my credits. Let's just say I was working hard and hustling for money. Dammit, I'm still hustling because somehow I never quite made the kind of money that means you can cut out. Anyway, the person who brought me back into movies was Woody Allen.

Woody Allen is brilliant and wonderful and antisocial, just like

Wally Cox. My professional dealings with Woody were just that. I appeared in his film *Interiors* as an outgoing, warmhearted, Jewish widow named Pearl. In the movie, this uptight goy, played by E. G. Marshall, leaves his wife and kids for me. In my first appearance on screen, I wore a bright red dress. Later I wore another bright red dress. My clothes were the only vibrant colors in the film. I'm sure Woody Allen wanted it that way.

Woody's a good director. He didn't talk much and didn't give you a lot of things to work on or with, but he sort of sensed if something was not right. He knew exactly what he wanted and had a perfect eye and ear for getting the desired results.

The first week we shot in East Hampton, Long Island. At the end of the day some of us headed into the bar. I was on my way when I spotted Woody in the lobby. I grabbed him by the arm and said, "Come for a drink." He made some excuses. I don't listen to excuses when I'm on my way to a bar and insisted that he join me. I think I strong-armed him. We went in and sat down, and I had a few beers and we chatted. Although I didn't know it, there were rules on a Woody Allen production, one of which was that you were supposed to give him a wide berth. Woody really didn't socialize with his cast, and later the others were amazed to discover that I'd been shmoozing and drinking with him.

"You took Woody into the bar?"

"Yeah; so what's the big deal?"

"You took Woody Allen into the bar and you were talking with him?"

"Yeah. Is there a law against that?"

I tell you, those guys were stunned. Hey, it's hard to resist me when I'm dragging you into a bar. It's kind of like I know where I'm goin', and, like it or not, I know who's goin' with me. I never let formality stand in the way, whether it's Woody Allen or Prince Charles. One time, Kathy, Danny, Max, and I went to a benefit performance in New York City to raise money for some charity. After the show we went to Elaine's on the Upper East Side for a bite to eat. Mattie, the lady who cleaned house for me at the time, was with us, too. Our taxi pulled up in front of the restaurant right behind this incredible white chauffeur-driven Rolls Royce sedan. The driver was waiting for Woody Allen. Inside Elaine's, Woody was having dinner, and I waved hello over to his table and he waved back. We had our meal and then Mattie wanted to go home. Max was going to put her in a cab when I decided on another route; I didn't want her going all alone. I got up and went over to Woody.

"That's your white car outside, isn't it?" I asked.

"Yes," Woody answered.

"Listen, since you're still eating, could I borrow it for a few minutes and have the guy drive Mattie home?"

"Who's Mattie?" Woody asked looking a bit perplexed.

"The lady who cleans house for me," I answered. Woody shrugged his shoulders and said, "Okay."

Max took Mattie out, helped her into the Rolls, and off she went, courtesy of Woody Allen.

Working on a Woody Allen movie is a special experience, and a great one. He had what amounted to a stock company of crew and cast, which is the way the old directors used to work. It really was a family. I noticed early on that Woody was not exactly a bundle of laughs off the set. The guy had a serious outlook, very serious, and that's all I needed to get me going. I was bound and determined to lighten him up and began looking for a way to do it. The opportunity came from the most unexpected source.

I had among my possessions a certain photograph of a baby boy. This infant was Zoe and Bob's child. When he was born I went to see him in the hospital, and he was the most exquisite, darling baby I'd ever seen. Four days later I went back to the hospital and went to see the baby again before I saw Zoe. I stood in front of the nursery window and they held up this little thing; I was certain they were showing me the wrong kid.

For weeks after that, Bob kept saying, "You know, the baby is really funny looking."

I'd cut him off and say, "Don't say that, c'mon."

Bob called and said he was coming into town, and when I met him, he handed me a picture of the baby. I looked at this photo and nearly lost it. "Oh my God," I said, "you're right." This was the funniest-looking kid I ever saw in my life. The great thing is, I can say what I want because that baby has grown into a handsome young man. Oh, but that snapshot was a number, all right. I used to carry it around with me and every once in a while show it to someone. I'd always preface it by saying, "You're not going to believe this," and they'd say, "Oh, it couldn't be that bad." Then they'd look and break up. I remember showing it to Jack Lemmon while we were at Sardi's; he almost fell off his chair. Anyway, I knew that snapshot was just the thing I needed to break through Woody's reserve.

One day I cornered some of the regular crew members, including Romaine Greene, a hairstylist, and Fern Buchner, a makeup artist. Romaine and Fern were known to one and all as the "Salad Sisters." I advised the girls to be prepared because that very evening in the bar, I would make Woody Allen laugh. They poo-poohed and claimed it couldn't be done.

"You just be in the bar tonight," I told them.

After the day's filming, I pushed Mr. Allen into the bar once again. Fern and Romaine drifted in and took their places at a nearby table. In a few minutes I gave them the high sign that I was about to strike.

"Whaddya think of this?" I asked Woody as I drew forth the picture of baby Whitehead and handed it over. He took one look and burst out laughing. You couldn't help it; the kid looked so damn funny. The Salad Sisters' mouths fell open; I had won. I can't remember whether or not I'd put any money on this bet; I sure hope I did.

Flash forward: A while later, Zoe Caldwell did *The Purple Rose of Cairo* for Woody Allen, and one day she was in the chair getting her makeup done by Fern. Zoe told her that she was my good friend, and Fern started talking about me.

"You know, Maureen Stapleton is the only one who ever got a laugh out of Woody. She showed him a picture of this funny-looking baby and Woody really chuckled."

"Wait a minute," said Zoe, "she showed him a picture of a baby?"

"Yeah."

"Did this baby have big ears, and was he looking at the camera over someone's shoulder?"

"Yeah. —Oh no. Oh my God," cried Fern. "Don't tell me. It's your baby!"

Thank God it was the picture that was so awful and not the kid and thank God that "gal" from Australia has a great sense of humor. Otherwise, I would have been in deep shit.

Zoe's such a good pal; it was so wise of Robert to marry her. We have such terrific times together. Years ago Zoe, Franny Sternhagen, Fritz Weaver, and I did a film version of *The Cherry Orchard* for the schools. I played Ranevskaya and John Colicos played Lopakhin. Briefly, Lopakhin is a lower-class fellow who makes big money and buys Mme. Ranevsky's property and has her cherry trees chopped down. We were rehearsing a scene where Lopakhin enters Ranevskaya's house. Franny's character was very rude to him, and I saw a golden opportunity.

"I don't understand why everybody's so nasty to Lopakhin," I said, interrupting the rehearsal. "Why is everyone so down on him?"

"Well," said Zoe, "it was the Russian Revolution and it was the whole idea of Lopakhin and people like him."

"Yeah, like what?" I asked. Franny Sternhagen went into an explanation of the subtext of the play and I kept saying, "No kidding. Really?" Meanwhile, I'd gotten my mitts on a cigarette and lit up during the impromptu lecture. I kept nodding and saying appropriate remarks for the next ten minutes or so as Franny and Zoe really got off on the play and the Russian Revolution and the symbolism and the whole Slavic spiel. I finished my smoke.

"Hey," I said to my fellow actors as I spit into the palm of my hand and squashed out the end of my cigarette, "thanks for telling me, but I really didn't want to know all that stuff. I just wanted a smoke." I don't think I could pull that kind of stunt on Zoe anymore; she's too wise to my ways.

Zoe Caldwell was responsible for one of my most challenging "turns" on the legitimate stage. When I was taking dancing lessons way back in Troy, I bombed in ballet and did great at tap. Zoe knew I loved to tap dance and got a kick out of my fooling around sometimes doing a soft shoe. Anyway, years back, she got a call from a guy working on a big benefit for Sandy Meisner and the Neighborhood Playhouse.

"Miss Caldwell, we're doing the show at the Shubert Theatre and wondered whether you would read some Shakespeare." Zoe, half kidding, said to the guy, "Oh, I'm so tired of doing readings. How about my doing a tap dance?"

"Okay," said the man, "if that's what you want to do, that'll be fine." Then he added, "Oh, by the way, I understand that you're a good friend of Maureen Stapleton. Do you think you could ask her if she would read from Tennessee Williams?"

"No," said Zoe, "she won't read. She'll tap dance with me." Zoe was being facetious and didn't give it another thought. About two months later the guy called again, reintroduced himself and said, "Miss Caldwell, do you and Miss Stapleton have an accompanist for your tap dance?"

"Hell pecker no!" cried Zoe. "We can't even tap dance anymore."

"Well, do you want me to get someone to work out a routine?"

"That'll be fine," answered Zoe, who then kindly informed me for the *first* time that I was to tap dance at the Meisner benefit. Zoe was convinced I wouldn't do it. The opportunity, however, was too delicious to turn down. I can recite Tennessee Williams anytime—being asked to tap dance was a whole other ball game. Peter Gennaro agreed to choreograph something, and Zoe and I went to his studio to discuss the possibilities. I wanted to do "Gimme the Old Soft Shoe," but Gennaro said no.

"You really have to be a good tap dancer for that," he advised me, adding, "I suspect you're just coming back to dancing, so I suggest a routine to *Forty-second Street*." Zoe and I thought it sounded great and began our preparation. We got a proper accompanist and went to Gennaro's studio three times a week for about a month. I'd put on an old dress and throw a coat over myself and then pick up Zoe at her place. She was dressed similarly. We looked like a pair of bag ladies. There were flights of stairs to climb to the studio and my knees were already bad—they're practically gone now. Somehow I'd drag myself up the stairs and into the studio. We'd take off our coats, put on the tap shoes, and work on the routine. If I do say so myself, we got to be pretty damn good. Zoe claims that while I really knew what I was doing, she "acted" tap dancing.

The night of the benefit arrived and Zoe and I went off to the Shubert Theatre. We took our seats and the show began. Everybody read from plays, and after a while it was getting to be too much of a good thing. We had this idea that we'd come out together as though we were going to do a proper reading and then pull the old switcheroo. The announcer called out, "Ladies and gentlemen, Miss Zoe Caldwell and Miss Maureen Stapleton." I swear to God, you could feel everybody's heart sink as we walked to the center of the stage for what they believed would be another play reading. Behind us was the mirrored set for *A Chorus Line,* which played forever at the Shubert. Zoe and I reached center stage and put our hands behind our backs as the piano banged out the downbeat. Then we picked up our skirts and started in on "Forty-second Street." We brought down the house, maybe because everyone was so glad not to hear another recitation. Whatever the reason, I swear to you that never, never in all my life, whatever part I played, did I ever hear such applause. When we finished we shuffled off; the audience began screaming for us to come back and do more. We didn't. I think Zoe could have danced all night. I was so exhausted that I could barely lift a wine glass, let alone kick up my heels.

I got an Academy Award nomination for Best Supporting Actress for *Interiors*—and that's all I got, a nomination. This was my third nomination in that category; *Lonelyhearts* and *Airport* were the first two. I was a consistent bridesmaid to Oscar. When I was up for *Airport* I got a phone call from the Academy Awards costume consultant, Ron Talsky, whose job it was to tell the ladies what to wear. Talsky advised me that I should be outfitted "not for comfort, not for what was in style, but for glamor with a capital *G*."

"Yeah, right," I told him. "I'm planning to wear a Stavro-poulos gown that I've had for five years. Only I don't know if I can get into it. I have to wear a real tight girdle." I figured I'd be glamorous with a small *g*. George Stavropoulos was a darling guy and had done a couple of sensational dresses for me. The night of the awards I squished myself into my garments and hauled myself over to the Dorothy Chandler Pavilion. All I remember from that ceremony is being a presenter, along with Maggie Smith, for the scientific and technical awards. We did our shtick, and left the stage as Johnny Carson, the host, said, "I'm glad the suspense is over in that category." I forget who got the Oscar; I actually think my girdle should have won for technical achievement.

I'm relieved to report that I finally did receive an Academy Award for Best Supporting Actress. It came in 1981, for *Reds*. Since I'd been up to the plate three times before, I figured maybe someone would take pity on me and throw the Oscar my way. I went on a diet and actually bought a new dress. The Academy Awards were pretty special that year because Barbara Stanwyck received an honorary Oscar. I was thrilled to be in the same world as that lady and now had the privilege of standing on the same stage with her. Want to hear something nuts? Barbara Stanwyck was nominated four times for an Oscar and *never* won; it was such an oversight that they had to honor her.

Best Supporting Actress was the first award and Tim Hutton was the presenter. He read the list and then opened the envelope and announced my name. I jumped up and as I started moving down the aisle I suddenly thought, "Did he really say my name?" Everybody was applauding and Warren Beatty was beaming, so I figured I'd heard right. I made it to the podium, grabbed the Oscar and said: "I'm thrilled, happy, delighted—sober! I want to thank Troy, New York; my children; my family; my friends; and everybody I ever met in my entire life; and my inspiration, Joel McCrea." I went waltzing off waving the statue over my head.

Backstage, I was interviewed by the press.

"Did you expect to win?" was the first question.

"Yes," I answered, "because I'm old and tired and I lost three times before."

"How did Joel McCrea inspire you?"

"Just looking at him—and because he's always been a good actor and because I'm madly in love with him."

The last question was a doozer. "How does it feel to be recognized as one of the greatest actresses in the world?" asked one of the earnest young reporters.

"Not nearly as exciting," I answered, "as it would be if I were acknowledged as one of the greatest lays in the world."

You gotta keep those reporters on their toes.

Chapter Ten

You must have gathered by now that I'm a Democrat through and through, and so are most of my pals. We had a rough ride in Washington for a long time. I supported Adlai Stevenson way back when and was an active campaigner for John F. Kennedy, but I was a rank amateur as a supporter when it came to mega-Democrats like Tallulah Bankhead, who'd been born into politics. I met Tallulah back in 1955 when Bobby Lewis invited me to join them for dinner and the opening of *The Chalk Garden*.

"Oh God, Bobby," I wailed, "Tallulah Bankhead! I don't know what I'll say."

"Don't worry," Bobby answered, "you won't have to say a word." Bobby was right. Tallulah talked nonstop through dinner. When we got to the play she had to keep quiet. At the first act curtain she applauded and applauded.

"It's a mahvelous play, dahling, don't you think?" she asked me.

"I'm not so sure yet; it's only the first act," was my honest answer.

There was a dead silence. "You *don't* like this play, dahling?" thundered Bankhead.

"It's not that I don't like it. I just don't know, because it's not over." Those were the last words I said all evening. Tallulah never gave me another opportunity to say anything. Tallulah lived at the Elysée Hotel, the same place Tennessee Williams kept an apartment. I remember being in her apartment with Tenn a few times. We'd all tie one on, and as I began to get drunk, Tennessee would laugh and say, "Well, Maureen's basic black is slipping up on her."

Tallulah didn't get drunk. She always was high, if not on liquor, then on life. And life for her had a lot to do with the Democratic party. JFK ran for President and Tallulah went into high gear. The show biz Democrats, including Tallulah, Lauren Bacall, and Tony Quinn, went to a big rally out in New Jersey. Afterward we all went to a restaurant in New York City and awaited the arrival of the candidate. He didn't show up for an hour or so. Finally he appeared and the place went crazy. Talk about charisma, that man had it in spades. Tallulah dragged him around by the arm, introducing him to one and all. They reached me and she shoved the candidate forward, saying, "Oh dahling, you must shake hands with this girl. She's absolutely *mad* about you." I honestly think I blushed as that beautiful man shook this girl's hand. A thrill, I assure you, a real thrill, and Tallulah beamed approval like a mother hen.

Tallulah's deserved reputation as a rapier wit wasn't the whole story; she could be a very thoughtful lady. When I went through the hell of my second divorce, we talked a lot, sometimes in person, sometimes on the phone, and she'd bolster me up and give me good old-fashioned chicken-soup comfort. Quite a broad, that Miss Bankhead, quite a broad and a *Democrat* all the way.

After the horror of the Kennedy assassination, I did what I could to honor JFK's memory. I became involved with the Kennedy Center honors and would go with Zoe and Bob to Washington, D.C., every year for the ceremonies. Naturally, I'd get bombed out of my mind and be a source of discomfort for my pals. One year I told them I wasn't going; I think they were relieved. I got the last laugh, though. Zoe said it wasn't the same without me and not nearly such fun. Everybody who usually said, "Oh God, get her out of here," was crying, "Oh God, I wish Maureen were here." One of the reasons I decided not to go on that particular trip was that my arthritic knees were acting up. Of course, if the Democrats had been in, I'd have crawled on my knees to get to Washington. That kind of sacrifice I don't make for the GOP.

The night of the ceremony Zoe called: "Maureen, we're on our way to the Kennedy Center. Do you have any message for the President?"

"No," I answered, "but I do have one for his wife. Would you tell Barbara I'm sorry I couldn't get her the 8 × 10 glossy of Jeanette MacDonald, but as soon as I do, I'll send it to her." There was a pause on the other end of the line.

"Sure," said Zoe, "I'll tell her." Even though she thought I'd blown my lid, Zoe got in the line, walked right up to Mrs. Bush, shook her hand, and gave her the message. "Oh, thank you," said the First Lady, smiling beatifically. "How lovely of Maureen to remember. She's such a darling." I don't know if I'm such a darling, but, hey, we Jeanette MacDonald fans have to stick together, and bless her heart, Barbara Bush is one of us. Remembering this story, I'm wracking my brain to recall whether or not I got the picture to her. I sure hope I did.

I got through the Nixon, Reagan, and Bush administrations pretty well, considering. Forget Nixon; I didn't know the guy. I didn't know the Reagans, either. Put it this way: I liked Ronald Reagan as a person. Politically, well, that's another story. Zoe's an ardent Democrat, too, and had trouble keeping things separate when she went to the honors ceremony without me.

"How am I going to shake hands with Bush?" she complained.

"Just shake," I told her. "What's the big deal? Hell, he's a great-looking guy. I really go for him."

"Come on, Maureen," said Zoe, "who are you kidding?"

"No, I'm serious. He's a tall, skinny, blue-eyed Wasp. I like that."

"Maureen, you're not serious. How can you say that you like George Bush, a Republican?"

"What do you mean how can I say that? Listen, I'm not saying I'd vote for him; I'm just saying I'd fuck him." Hell, in certain instances, I've always been willing to cross party lines. I'm not so sure Joel McCrea, Robert Taylor, and Clark Gable were in my political ballpark, and frankly, I don't give a damn. Nonetheless, I consider myself a tried-and-true Democrat, and so are most of my friends. If they aren't, they're keeping quiet just to keep me happy. Lillian Hellman certainly was a super-Democrat, and we were reunited professionally in the early eighties.

Producer Zev Bufman put together a deal with Elizabeth Taylor to present her on the legitimate stage for the first time in her life. The vehicle had to be perfect, and they chose Lillian Hellman's *The Little Foxes*. Alone of all her plays, Lillian guarded *The Little Foxes* like a hawk and protected her baby from bad acting by preventing major productions that were likely to be seen by the theater-going public. You could perform it in colleges and in high schools, and in the Little Theater Club in Paducah maybe, but definitely not in Boston or Philadelphia or San Francisco.

Of course, every actress who came down the pike wanted to play Regina Giddens, but Lillian wanted to make sure an actress had the proper license before she'd let her ride into that part. She once told me she never liked anyone's portrayal of the role that much, not even Tallulah Bankhead's in the original stage version or Bette Davis's on the screen. Annie Bancroft, of whom I'll say there is no better actress, didn't score on the Hellman rating, either. I don't think Lillian thought anyone was capable of doing it the way she wanted. I honestly don't know why she carried on so; maybe she wanted to play Regina herself. Who the hell knows. She just guarded *The Little Foxes* like a sentry. But when Zev Bufman came to her with his proposal, Lillian couldn't refuse. Elizabeth Taylor's presence guaranteed big box office and big profits and big royalties for the playwright. Once the deal had been cut between Elizabeth and Lillian, the rest of the casting began. Lillian called and told me that that "poor struggling" actor, my old friend Austin Pendleton, was going to direct.

"Maureen," said Lillian, "I want you to play the role of Birdie." Birdie is Regina's gentle, genteel sister-in-law who finds refuge in the bottle. Hmmm, sounded vaguely like typecasting to me, give or take a couple of adjectives. Lillian and I had gone through this routine once before, back in the mid-sixties when Mike Nichols was set to direct a revival of *Foxes* at Lincoln Center. Lillian asked me to read for Birdie then and I did, along with a number of other ladies including my good pal Elizabeth Wilson, who "stood by" for Birdie and Regina. Elizabeth had recently finished working on *The Graduate* with Mike and wanted to see the tryouts, and I remember her telling me she couldn't get over how thin I was. Skinny as I was, I didn't get the part; Margaret Leighton did. Now Lillian was on my case again.

"Me? I can't play Birdie," I protested, "I'm too fat. And besides, she's an aristocrat; I'm a peasant."

"Maureen, stop it, this is acting we're talking about."

"Yeah, but I'm not high-class enough to play Birdie and I'm too fat."

"Maureen, you can play Birdie!" Lillian kept at me and I kept making the same excuses until she said, "Wait a minute, Maureen, I know you can play Birdie, but just how fat are you?" Lillian was determined to have me in the play and was the one and only person who thought I could do it. Even Austin had his doubts. When I met with them, she told me right in front of him, "Austin doesn't think you're right for the part." He was embarrassed to death.

"Lillian, no big deal; why don't I read for the part?" I suggested. I had no objection whatsoever to auditioning. And that's exactly what I did; I read for Austin and he hired me. Meanwhile, Lillian had discussed my taking the part with Elizabeth and she said yes. We really didn't know each other, although we had met at a party or two in Washington when she first went there as Mrs. John Warner. What little we knew of each other, we liked. Then we worked together, and now I adore and love that woman, God bless her. I mean, you know she's a big star and she knows she's a big star, so it's not an issue of any kind. Within a short time you're completely at ease with her. She's a straightshooter and about as kind a person as I've ever met.

We started rehearsing and from the first day Lillian was with us quite a bit, though she was physically handicapped. Her eyes were very bad and she was on crutches. Mind you, she still was pretty alert; but because she wasn't in tippy-top shape, she wasn't as vocal. Put another way, she was a helluva lot quieter than she had been twenty years ago and yet remained a presence to be reckoned with.

True to form, Lillian was full of misgivings and suspicions about the "movie actress." She especially bristled at my immediate friendship with Elizabeth. We'd have meals together and spent a great deal of time in each other's company. It's hard to believe that Elizabeth Taylor and Maureen Stapleton had anything in common, but we did: weight. Elizabeth wrote a terrific book of her own about dieting, *Elizabeth Takes Off,* and she looks better than ever today.

I haven't been so successful that I could put down my hints for posterity, although I did have certain "techniques" that worked for a while. I'd go on these fourteen-day regimens with my buddy and fellow actor Billy McIntyre. Billy and Frank Marino have a country place up in Greenwood Lake and at least three times that I can remember, the two of us went up there for a couple of weeks and did nothing but diet. Billy'd bring up tapes of movies and short subjects and we'd watch them to pass the time, or we'd play poker with friends who dropped by. We were up there one winter, and it was so damn cold the pipes had burst. Fourteen days later, when we returned to New York City, I had lost a grand total of three pounds. And though we ate exactly the same things, that sonofabitch Billy Mac had lost seventeen pounds. Men, damn them, always lose weight faster. It's so unfair. When Elizabeth Taylor and I were in *Foxes,* she had come through a stage where she ate out of desperation, and, according to her book, the desperation came from her unhappiness at being a Washington wife.

In the beginning, Lillian had her saber tongue at the ready. She belittled Elizabeth in many ways and complained at the top of her lungs. Realistically, if it weren't for Elizabeth Taylor, the fate of the *Foxes* would have been a lot more iffy, but that didn't keep Lillian from kvetching. At the first dress rehearsal, Elizabeth appeared in a very fancy dress and sported the diamond Richard Burton had given her. Lillian took Elizabeth aside and told her that the getup was too much and probably more suited to a Ziegfeld Follies and further explained that the meaning of the play would be lost if the star glittered too brightly. Elizabeth didn't say a word; she looked at the floor and listened. She was thinking. At the next rehearsal, she appeared in a far plainer dress, without the diamond. Even Lillian was impressed with the way Ms. Taylor accepted and acted upon her criticism. Despite her grudging respect, Lillian did her best to get at Elizabeth, especially after the play began performances.

We opened in Fort Lauderdale; from there we went to Washington and then on to New York for a limited run; then we went to New Orleans and ended in Los Angeles. Elizabeth was pretty damn courageous. By appearing on stage she was setting herself up; the critics might have slaughtered her. I've already mentioned some of the differences between acting for the stage and acting for the screen. If you're exclusively a screen actor, I think the biggest transitional hurdle might be projecting your voice. Elizabeth handled it okay, though we did have some assistance. The theater in New Orleans was the hugest goddamn place I've been in, so vast you couldn't even see the people in the second balcony. My God, they'd have had to electrically enhance Ethel Merman in that joint. Microphones were used and there might have been mikes on the apron of the stage in New York. For sure, we didn't use body mikes in any of the theaters.

Once the performances began, Lillian and her paranoia went into high gear. She didn't like what was happening to her play; *The Little Foxes* had become a star vehicle for a Hollywood icon. As I said, I liked Elizabeth's performance as Regina. She got better and better and it was quite wonderful to watch her take hold of the role. Regina, as interpreted by Elizabeth, had a sense of humor, which is very much part of Elizabeth's persona and, to me, fit very nicely into her character. You have to keep your ears perked when you're around Elizabeth 'cause she slips things in very quietly. I remember one day Austin was giving Elizabeth a piece of direction. He went on and on and on about what kind of person Regina was and how she was this and that and so forth. Forever. Finally he finished and Elizabeth looked at him and said, "What line do you want me to do all that on?"

Lillian was ticked off more by the audiences' reactions than anything Elizabeth Taylor actually did. Her fans were out in force and reacted to every little bitty gesture or movement. Elizabeth would walk across the stage and they'd applaud. She didn't break, not once, and just kept going in her role. Still, it was too much for the playwright. In order to exert control, Lillian called rehearsals even after the play had opened. Again, Elizabeth was a good sport; she did buckle a couple of times and asked politely why we had to have a full rehearsal that ended a couple of hours before a performance that was sold out, as were all the performances in every single city we played. Furthermore, though Elizabeth never said so, the production's unqualified success was definitely *not* because Lillian Hellman was the author or because Maureen Stapleton was playing Birdie. Elizabeth was the big gun and Lillian tried to shoot it out with her. Elizabeth's weapon was, and still is, a remarkable ability to enjoy life, and her desire is to share that joy.

On the first Sunday after we opened in Fort Lauderdale, Elizabeth hired a yacht and threw a party for the cast and crew and anybody they wanted to invite. For those who don't know the normal procedure, this kind of gesture is way out of the ordinary; it's not the behavior of your everyday garden variety star. A lot of parties are given but just for the cast. Elizabeth would never give a party if it didn't include the whole shebang, and she'd never go to one if everyone from top to bottom hadn't been invited. That Sunday anyone and anything connected with *The Little Foxes* boarded the yacht, and I'm sure we all had a great time, although I couldn't exactly remember.

In fact, the next day when I went to work I said to Elizabeth, "Boy, that was a great party. I must have had a great time, except I can't remember coming back. Would it be a lot of trouble to do it again?"

"Great idea," Elizabeth agreed. "We'll do it next Sunday."

I thought I was making a little joke. By God, she actually threw another yachting party.

Once we finished in Fort Lauderdale we went on the road to Washington. Of course, while everyone else flew, I trained. For the short hops, though, everyone took the train, and I had company. I loathed having to travel again; still, I was hustling for my dough and the latter need won out over the former fear. I was never happy riding the rails during the *Foxes* tour and barely survived an especially harrowing trip over the Mississippi River. No one told me that the railroad tracks went over this bridge that was a million feet in the air and had no roadbeds on either side. It was a goddamn roller coaster. Eloise White was with me and the two of us fell to the floor of the car, hugging each other and screaming in terror. The only portion of those train rides that was anywhere near acceptable occurred when we left Washington for New York. Elizabeth hired a special car and had it attached to the train. Inside the car there was food, music, and wine, all for the company and crew. Everybody, including the hodophobic, inebriated Maureen Stapleton, arrived in New York very, very happy.

In Washington, D.C., a reception was held with the President of the United States and his wife, both of whom had been members of the audience. I'd never met Nancy Reagan before, although there was an oddball connection in our pasts—back in her acting days as Nancy Davis, she'd dated Max Allentuck. Lillian Hellman joined the company in Washington and had an accident almost immediately. She'd fallen in her room at the Watergate and struck her head against the coffee table. From the way she described the event, we were pretty certain she'd suffered a small stroke. Lillian was fretful, fearful, and furious at her body for betraying her, but she insisted upon attending the performance and meeting the Presidential party. Although it took all her strength to participate in the proceedings, there was no way she wouldn't attend.

After the performance, the cast lined up in the Green Room. At the end of the line stood me, Lillian, and Elizabeth. Lillian was leaning heavily on a cane. The President and the First Lady walked down the line and shook everybody's hand. I shook his hand and said, "Hello, Mr. President." He smiled and moved on as the First Lady came before me. "Hello, Maureen," she said. "Hello, Nancy," I replied. The First Lady smiled and moved on to Lillian. Everyone had been concerned about what Lillian would say because she was a such a Democrat and all that, and you never knew what Lillian would pull. I remember hearing a general sigh of relief when she graciously accepted the Reagans' compliments. The Reagans moved past her, and out of the corner of her mouth Lillian addressed me.

"You *know* them!" she hissed.

"No, I don't," I answered.

"You called her Nancy and she called you Maureen."

"So what."

"It proves you know her, otherwise it would be disrespectful to call the President's wife by her first name."

Lillian got more and more agitated and would not stop. She kept up her litany of "You know her, you know her" until she drove me to the end of my patience. I turned my head and said slowly, deliberately, and rather audibly, "For God's sake, I don't know her. Max fucked her. We're practically family. That's how I know her."

Lillian Hellman began laughing so hard she barely could catch her breath. She sagged on the cane and crumpled at the knees. Elizabeth and I carried her, wheezing and gasping, to a sofa and laid her down. I could have killed her for making me say what I did, but she really bugged me. Sometimes I'm pushed too far and someone winds up on the floor. Usually it's me; this time it was Lillian.

While appearing in *The Little Foxes* I became an extremely sought after woman. I've never been so popular in my life. I'd be introduced to some woman and the next thing I knew she'd call me on the phone. The names were different, the cities were different, but the conversation was always the same.

"Hello, Maureen. We met last night at dinner. I was calling because I'd like to give a party for Elizabeth Taylor and the rest of the cast."

"Why don't you call Elizabeth Taylor?" I'd answer. Of course, these dames didn't have Elizabeth's number. On the other hand, everyone in the world had mine and telephoned me to get to Elizabeth. Famous people themselves were and are crazy about her. Helen Hayes once jokingly sent a note asking me to get Elizabeth's autograph for her!

Another time in Washington, Elizabeth herself threw a big shindig at the Virginia farm where she and John Warner lived. The entire company, and anyone they wanted to bring, was invited; Elizabeth stopped short of asking the audiences. Buses were hired and jammed to the sides with fathers and sons, mothers and daughters, sisters and brothers, cousins, neighbors, boyfriends, and girlfriends—you name it. My Kathy was there. One guy was a busboy in a restaurant where Elizabeth and I ate; he came with his wife. At least one person was in a wheelchair. What a picnic. Elizabeth simply cannot stop giving. Once I was at a party in Los Angeles and was seated at a table with another actress from the play, Zev Bufman's secretary, another woman whom I don't remember, and Chen Sam, Elizabeth's publicist and a pretty spectacular lady herself. Each of us was wearing a gorgeous designer dress that was a gift from Elizabeth. Giving gifts to her is another matter. What can you give her? I thought I'd solved that dilemma one year; I think it was Elizabeth's fiftieth.

Elizabeth knew how crazy I was about Joel McCrea and she'd been plotting to get us together. She invited him to come for cocktails when we were in Los Angeles, but he was out of town or something. She tried to fly him in for opening night in New York and that didn't work, either. Later, when the Night of a Thousand Stars benefit was planned for Radio City Music Hall and Joel McCrea was in the lineup, Elizabeth asked him up to her place on the top floor of her hotel. After he accepted, I was told that Joel McCrea was ready, willing, and able to meet me. I was so thrilled and excited that I actually rode up in the elevator. It was worth it.

I also came to that particular meeting bearing a gift for Elizabeth's birthday. I'd been racking my brain to come up with something special and finally decided to give her a doll, a miniature replica of herself, dressed in an evening gown and covered with itty-bitty jewels. The doll arrived the morning of my McCrea visit, and when I opened the box, I nearly died. The tiny gown was splendid, but the tiny face was terrible. Billy McIntyre was with me when I unwrapped the thing and was as aghast as I was.

"What am I going to do?" I cried. "There's no time to get anything else."

"You're going to give it to her," said Billy. "She's got a good sense of humor." I clutched the box containing the doll all the way up that hotel elevator and handed it over to Elizabeth.

"Happy birthday," I said, "and don't say anything." I explained to the birthday girl that her present had fallen short. Elizabeth poo-poohed my apologies and gleefully opened the box. She absolutely loves getting presents.

"My God, Maureen," she cried as she pulled out the doll, "that's the ugliest thing I've ever seen."

"Right," I groaned. "Please honey, do whatever you want with it."

"I think I should burn it."

"Good idea," I replied; "let's chuck it into the fireplace." One of the others present, either Joel McCrea or his wife, Frances Dee, suggested that we check with the hotel before we put anything in the fireplace. Elizabeth called down and within a short time the fire warden came to the suite. We explained what we wanted to do, and he looked over the doll.

"I'm afraid you can't use the hotel fireplace," he said. "If you really want to burn this, you could take it up on the roof and we could put it in a wire basket." Elizabeth, the McCreas, and the fire warden hauled the doll up to the roof, placed it in a wire basket, doused it with liquor, and threw in a match. I sat out the immolation downstairs. Elizabeth told me she really loved her present, and I can understand why: It's not every day you get to go on the roof and torch something.

The Broadway run of *The Little Foxes* played at the Martin Beck, the same theater in which I'd trod the boards back in the forties with Miss Cornell in *Antony and Cleopatra*. While it ran, *The Little Foxes* was the top ticket on Broadway.

We'd been playing at the Martin Beck for a while when Elizabeth sent out party invitations to everyone except me. Had I known, I'd have been very upset not to have been included. I was in the dark and that's just the way Elizabeth wanted it. Meanwhile, the invitations made the rounds. The card read on the outside, "Life is not a Cabaret," and inside the message continued, "It's a fucking circus. Elizabeth Taylor invites you to come clown around at the Crystal Room at Régine's, Saturday, June 20th at 11:30 P.M. It's a birthday party for Maureen Stapleton and it's a surprise. See if for once you can keep it that way. RSVP. Love ya."

I had no idea that I was being fêted until I walked into the Crystal Room at Régine's and spotted family members and friends from Troy as well as what appeared to be all of Broadway standing around grinning their heads off. Elizabeth had told me she was taking me for a little drinky-poo after the show, and we drove to Régine's in her limo along with Eloise White and maybe someone else, though I can't remember. Oh, and what a party it was! And to top it off, Elizabeth gave me a diamond for a present. I think she was the first person to give me a diamond and that includes both my husbands!

Chapter Eleven

*T*he *Little Foxes* turned out to be my last appearance on Broadway. I had no idea at the time that it would be my swan song. Nothing else came along, though, and when Milton Goldman died a short while after *Foxes* closed, I lost my career catalyst, my champion. Not only did I adore him personally; I realize more and more how hard he worked for me. Milton would hack his way through scripts and stories, producers and directors, until he'd found something for me. It wasn't just for me, of course; he did the same for all his clients. There was no one like him and there never will be again.

When Milton died, I lost the personal connection. I really didn't pursue parts, because he'd done it all so well and for so long that I'd kind of let my "Office Personality" slide. Equally discouraging, it's gotten more difficult physically to do legitimate stage work. I don't mean memorizing or anything like that; I'm talking about the required discipline. As I said, you have to be, or should be, in tip-top physical condition when you're working in the theater, and unless you're really young and/or you're not responsible for a big part, there's not much else you can do except act. Years ago I could appear on stage and then go shopping or sightseeing or out on the town. I think there's a certain age when you just can't do that anymore; you simply have to direct all your energy toward *getting* to work, period. That age can vary, but basically the whole day has to be spent preparing for an eight o'clock curtain, at least for me.

I don't know why, but it's not the same in films. I can still make movies despite my galloping infirmities, which include those arthritic knees that have plagued me the last few years. I went to an orthopedic doctor years ago who told me that I had to have knee replacement surgery right away. I told him that I'd wait till I couldn't walk and *then* have them operated on. At that moment I began coughing and the doctor said, "Well, from the way that cough sounds, probably you'll never reach that point." I haven't yet. If push comes to shove, I suppose I could load my carcass into a wheelchair and roll around a stage in *The White Oaks of Jalna* or another old potboiler. Of course, there are better plays that allow the actor to remain seated most of the time. Carol Matthau thinks I should do an updated switched-gender version of *The Man Who Came to Dinner*. Doesn't sound half bad to me, either. I'll do it if she'll adapt it!

I had a ball with *The Little Foxes* in and out of the theater. One time I was scheduled to appear on a local New York news program, *Live at Five*. My old pal Liz Smith did a regular gossip segment for the show and conducted an occasional interview. This time she and I were going to chat during the second half of the program. I got to the station and lodged myself in the Green Room to await my call. Meanwhile, Liz went out and did her regular bit. She finished, signed off, and went home, totally forgetting our interview.

Time came for me to go on and everyone's running around looking for Liz Smith, who by then was in a taxi on her way home. The station wanted things to proceed as though nothing out of the ordinary had occurred, so one of the other regulars was dumped into Liz's chair just before our segment aired. The red light went on and I was introduced by the Liz sub—I think it was Jack Cafferty. The camera came in for my closeup, and, unable to resist, I leaned forward, drew my brows together, and blowing the whistle on the smooth transition, said directly into the lens, "Liz, what happened? Where are you? Was it something I said?"

Meanwhile, Liz Smith had arrived at her nearby apartment and switched on the television to catch the rest of the broadcast; that's when she saw my mug looming on the screen. She nearly died. She was so contrite that she sent me a gorgeous bouquet of flowers and an equally gorgeous magnum of champagne. I wrote and told her that the consolation prize was terrific. "In the future," I said in my thank-you note, "we can skip the interviews. Just send champagne."

Life after *The Little Foxes* consisted of bits and pieces of work. I hung around New York and picked up jobs here and there. One big chunk of time went into playing the part of Gloria Vanderbilt's nurse, Emma Kieslich, in the television miniseries, *Little Gloria . . . Happy at Last*. I knew Gloria and learned that she was very upset about the movie. Her distaste for the project grew into a dislike for anyone connected with it. She stopped speaking to me. I felt bad. Gloria's a good woman, and while I can appreciate her distress, I wasn't trying to hurt her; I was just earning my living. If I hadn't played the nurse, someone else would have. It's that simple.

When my daughter, Kathy, tired of New York living and moved up to the Berkshires, I missed having her around, a lot. Then, when my granddaughter Alexandra was born, I lost my heart and my head. I fell absolutely in love with that little girl. I was crazy about that kid and still am. For two years I'd make the trek up to the Berkshires to see them. When Kathy told me she was expecting again, I decided there was nothing holding me in New York City and plenty enticing me to Lenox, so I hightailed it up to Massachusetts for good. For a while I hung out in bed-and-breakfast places and schlepped around looking for a permanent residence. Eventually I found a comfortable condominium and bought it. I brought all my worldly goods along with me, and though a lot of the stuff is out of place and much more suited to a large brownstone than to a garden apartment, I don't care. I never did have taste anyway, and I like having my tchotchkes with me, especially my mother's Imperial Bavarian china.

At first I got to see a lot of my grandchildren Alexandra and Max, then, as they progressed into kindergarten and grade school, their time with me was limited. Now I have to take them when I can get them, which ain't that often. Still, it's worth it. My only regret about leaving New York City is not seeing Danny. I miss him. Fortunately, he likes to come up and visit. I've been here for seven years. It's hard for me to believe, but this is the first time in my life that I've ever lived alone. There was always someone hanging around in New York. Up here, it's a solo and there are times I hate it, especially during the long winters. There's no alternative, though; I ain't going back to the city.

My old friends beat a path to my door, too. Annie Jackson was up recently, and Kaye Ballard, Zoe and Bob Whitehead, and Billy McIntyre, and Janice Mars even dragged her ass in from New Mexico. I did go to New York for Carol Matthau. Life is a helluva lot easier in the Berkshires. One benefit of living in Lenox is its proximity to Troy. I get to visit my hometown often and spend time with my aunts Julie and Jeanette and my old friends Dolores and Virginia. There's something quite special about going back to First Street and strolling around my old neighborhood. I find a kind of peace there. Sometimes I think I'd like to move back and prove that you can go home again.

I've slowed down for sure, but I haven't totally been twiddling my thumbs. I've done movies here, television shows there, voice-overs—that kind of stuff keeps me going. In 1994 I did a film, *The Last Good Time,* with dear Bob Balaban directing. Bob called and asked if he could send a script to me; more important, he said the movie would be filmed on the East Coast. I told him I didn't need to see the script—as long as I didn't have to travel far, if he wanted me, I'd do it. I accepted and then received a copy. I really liked the script, but I knew I would because I trust Bob's judgment. I did have to come down to New York City, and I had to travel over the Brooklyn Bridge to do the shooting. That was the worst part of it.

Lionel Stander was in the movie, too; it was his last film. He died in the fall of 1994. I knew him years ago. He was a good friend of friends of mine, Peter and Nancy Cass, and I saw Lionel at their home many, many times. I reported to the set and found Lionel seated on the sidelines with his wife, a very attractive younger woman. Lionel didn't remember me at all. I would have felt bad except that he didn't remember the Casses, either, and they really were his good friends.

Anyway, except for having to cross over the bridges to Brooklyn, I enjoyed doing the film and Bob was a darling. I did get a bit worried before shooting started because I made the mistake of looking in the mirror. There were bags under my eyes, and I thought I'd become too antiquated to play opposite the star of the movie, Armin Meuler-Stahl. I called Bob right away. "Bobby, you don't have to use me in the movie. You haven't seen me for a while, but I'm really too old for the part." Bobby laughed and said, "Maureen, you're too young for it." I didn't buy it but couldn't argue with him. Knowing how I feel about elevators, Bob was very understanding about a scene in which Armin and I had to ride one. I told him I'd get in the damn thing but he had to swear on his oath that they'd keep it open. If you see the movie, you'll notice that I get into the elevator and the camera switches to a closeup as I *react* to the door closing. It never did. I recently did an episode for Disney's *Avonlea* television show, which was filmed in Toronto.

Lately, I've been talking to people about doing television commercials. Hell, if pitching products was good enough for Sir Lord God, it's good enough for this lady. I've also kept active by doing poetry readings to benefit the Lenox library. It's a beautiful building and like most privately funded institutions, needs a constant financial shot in the arm. Arthur Collins, a retired teacher, started the readings and I've been participating pretty regularly along with people like Dori Previn and Peggy Pope and Kristin Linklater. When I'm not preparing for the readings or movies, I'm doing crossword puzzles, watching *Jeopardy* and *Wheel of Fortune,* and keeping an eye on my grandchildren. My feeling is, work either comes or it doesn't.

A Hell of a Life

Sir John Gielgud said in an interview that acting is half shame, half glory, a combination of exhibitionism and revelation, and I think he's right. Acting *is* such a mixed bag of pleasure and pain. If you had a brain in your head, you'd never choose to do it, but wanting to act isn't a question of intelligence, it's answering a need. I answered the call a long time ago and it's too damn late to hang up. Acting is my job, my work, and the one area of my life in which I'm totally secure.

When I began my career, like 99.9 percent of all aspiring actors I couldn't get to my reviews fast enough. In those days newspaper guys saw the show, left the theater, went to their offices, and wrote their pieces, which appeared the next morning. After the performance, we'd either run to the newsstand or have someone rush the papers to Sardi's, where the reviews would be read aloud by a member of the production. We'd gobble up what this critic or that critic had to say and go to bed in the wee hours knowing exactly how we'd been received. I couldn't believe some of the older actors I worked with who told me they didn't read reviews. I thought they were nuts. How could you not read about yourself?

Many plays later, maybe it was after a so-so review, I don't remember; anyway, at one point in my career, I had an about-face and decided I didn't want to read reviews—at least, not right away. I knew what I was doing on the stage and what I was after in the part; why the hell should I have someone tell me what was wrong—or, for that matter, what was right? I got out of the habit of racing for the papers when the play opened. In truth, as far as reviews went, I stopped reading them and would only take a rare glance *after* the show closed.

I'll never go out on a limb and name any one role as my favorite, in part because of the lesson I learned from that girl who yearned for Saint Joan, and in part because I've had so many wonderful roles. I have to admit, though, that Serafina delle Rose is most dear to me. I created the part and achieved my first big recognition as that passionate Italian lady. And I played her more than once in my professional life. Actually, I did revivals of *The Rose Tattoo* in the 1960s and 1970s. The last one was in 1973, and just as he always did, Tennessee Williams came to check out the production.

"Tenn," I said as we embraced, "do you realize we've done this play together every decade? I guess I have to keep doing it till I get it right."

In the 1966 production, Harry Guardino took the role of Mangiacavallo. Harry is something else. One day during rehearsal I felt faint, which was not usual for me. I excused myself and went out to sit and get some fresh air. Harry came out to see how I was doing.

"I'll be all right," I said. "Give me about five minutes and I'll be back."

Harry looked at me and said emphatically, "No way. That's it."

"What are you talking about, Harry? You can't call off rehearsal."

"I told the director already. You're not working anymore today." Harry always looked after me. The show started out at the City Center and then moved to the Billy Rose Theatre. When we began rehearsals at the Center, the first day the set went up they put a narrow staircase at the rear behind the drop to accommodate an exit and entrance. Serafina and Mangiacavallo go off and do something or other and were supposed to appear on the other side for the next scene. The staircase was constructed to get us off and in position for the next entrance. The first day at the City Center I got to rehearsal before Harry and was shown the stairway. I took one look and said, "That's kind of dangerous. There's no railing." They told me they couldn't use a rail because it would reflect off the back or something. Okay. I started practicing and went up and down a few times. It was pretty damn scary. Harry came in and they were showing him around the set as they had me. He was brought over to the staircase, where he stopped short.

"What's that?" he asked.

"Oh, that's the stairwell you have to take in the third act."

"Hold on, hold on," said Harry. "Oh no, oh no," he continued, "my actress isn't going up that." With those words he gestured toward me. I got such a kick out of hearing him refer to me as "my actress." He *absolutely* wouldn't get on those stairs until they put up a railing. "His" actress was mighty happy when it was added.

Opening night of the 1973 production went pretty well as far as I was concerned, and the audience seemed to be enjoying the play, too. All in all, it felt right. I don't remember much, if anything, of what happened after the curtain fell. My next recollection starts the following evening when I reported back to the theater for the second performance.

At the rise of the first-act curtain, Serafina is sitting on the porch fanning herself while three children play in the yard in front of her. The kids don't have much to do, just some quick dialogue. One of them cries out, "White flags flying, that means fair weather. I love fair weather," then they go skipping off and Serafina begins to talk.

That second night I took my place in the rocker on the porch while the kids lined up downstage. We all were in position and the onstage lights were dimmed when one of the boys turned his head around and looked up at me.

"Didja read the reviews?" he whispered.

"No," I hissed back.

"Well," continued my young colleague, "they said you were too fat and too old."

At that very moment, the curtain rose.

That was twenty years ago; now I'm even older and fatter. But what wonderful parts I did get to play! Like a lady named Mildred Wild. I enjoyed creating the title role of a daydreaming, movie-mad housewife in Paul Zindel's *The Secret Affairs of Mildred Wild* because it gave me the opportunity to do many different characters, including Scarlett O'Hara herself.

I also think I've failed to mention that I appeared in a 1965 revival of *The Glass Menagerie* and had the honor, and chutzpah, to step into the part Laurette Taylor created. Although no one could play the role better than that lady, I figured there was a whole generation of people who hadn't seen Laurette, so her interpretation wouldn't be hanging over my head. Actually, Amanda is such a fabulously written role anyone could play her with the possible exception of Harpo Marx. George Grizzard was in that production and a few years later he and I worked together again, in *The Country Girl* with Jason Robards. What a treat to be with both of them. In 1982 I went down to Texas Women's University in Denton and appeared in a student production of *The Glass Menagerie,* directed by Kim Stanley, and the role still offered such glorious possibilities. It's so hard to go wrong because Tennessee gives you so much to lean on. Amanda Wingfield had been fashioned after Tennessee's own mother. Joanne Woodward, herself a Southerner, told me that after she introduced *her* mother to Tennessee, he said, "Joanne, if I didn't know I wrote *Glass Menagerie* about my mother, I would have thought I'd written about yours." I knew Tenn's mother, but I never used any of her character in my portrayal, because to me Amanda is not a specific person, she's "mother." Tennessee's wellsprings are so deep that he gives you enough to act without your having to go outside the part to find values. There is so much beautiful writing, so much humor, including a lot of belly laughs, but they always come out of character.

I never, ever minded stepping into a part someone else originated. I did it quite a few times, beginning with Sarah Tansey in *The Playboy of the Western World.* Beatrice Straight created the part of Elizabeth Proctor in *The Crucible* and when she left, I replaced her. Who knows how many other women (and boys) played Iras in *Antony and Cleopatra* or Anne in *Richard III?* I've taken over parts that were originally portrayed by such wonderful actors as Uta Hagen and Jessie Tandy, in *The Country Girl* and *The Gin Game,* respectively. Along with my original creations I've been honored to do those re-creations.

I don't believe in sitting around and sifting through your memories all the time. The past is just that; there's no sense in mooning over what was or even what might have been. I did the best I could, and it touches me that there's a Maureen Stapleton Theater at Hudson Valley Community College in Troy. While I won't wallow in the past, I do like to reminisce on occasion about the good times on and offstage. If I had to name one particular moment of my life as the happiest, I think it was just after Danny was born. I was married to Max and appearing in *The Rose Tattoo*. I drove to work with Eli one summer day and remember thinking, "Life is wonderful. I'm so happy." As soon as that thought passed through my mind, I had another one. "It ain't gonna last." It didn't, but I did have that lovely stretch of pure joy.

You can't remember everything; there's so much I've forgotten. One time I was in a summer-stock show and Alan Arkin and his wife were in the audience. We went for a bite to eat after the show and he was such a nice guy and I enjoyed him so much I finally said, "Gee, Alan, I'd like to work in a show with you some day."

"You did," Alan replied. Turns out it was just a quickie TV thing way back in 1960 that I couldn't for the life of me recall.

I wish I could remember all the people I've worked with; I wish I could list them all and I really wish I could acknowledge the audiences, too, all those beautiful people out there in the dark, as Norma Desmond said in *Sunset Boulevard*. Audiences are supposed to be different in different cities, but I never found that. In my experience, they laugh in the same places and they cry in the same places. Sure, some nights the audience can be more enthusiastic than others, but it isn't a question of geography, it's a simple matter of who's out there. I can't name all of you individually, but I give my thanks to each and every one of you who's warmed those seats.

There are so many professionals I've played with whom I haven't had a chance to mention. I worked with Barbra Streisand on *Nuts* in 1987, and she was an adorable girl and a pleasure to be with. She's a straight shooter and you know that about her immediately. Actually, just about everybody I've worked with has been a straight shooter. I've been lucky.

I went out to California to do *Nuts* in 1987. I hated the travel, of course, but a lot of my old buddies, like Eli Wallach and Karl Malden, were in the film, which made the job that much easier. Anyway, *Nuts* went overtime. Some days there'd be a six-hour wait for the camera to get set up. The filming dragged on and, happy as I was to be working and with my chums, I was champing at the bit. One day I took the script into Barbra's dressing room and started talking.

"Look, I've got an idea for the scene that's coming up today."

"Yeah, what?" asked Barbra.

"You know," I continued, "we could cut a lot because we say all this stuff and then repeat it again. We could cut the hell out of this upcoming scene."

"What do you want to cut?" Barbra asked.

"Well," I said, pointing to the open script, "we can cut this page—"

"You want to cut the *whole* page?"

"Yeah, we really said the stuff before." Barbra looked at the page again and then looked back at me.

"Maureen," she laughed, "you just want to go home."

"Well, yeah," I agreed, "but I really think we're overdoing it here." That's the thing about Barbra Streisand, you could go and talk to her and she'd listen. She's another professional with a capital *P* and I'd work with her anytime.

People ask if I miss being in front of the public and receiving its praise. While it's wonderful to gain the approbation of audiences, I've never kidded myself about applause. Whenever I start getting carried away, I think about Adlai Stevenson's assessment. He was running for President and went to a fund-raiser. The guy who introduced him went on and on about how glorious, terrific, marvelous Stevenson was, and the audience went wild before and after Stevenson's speech. Later, Stevenson was going down in the elevator with a friend.

"What's it like to hear all that applause?" asked the friend. "What's it like to know that people love you that much?"

"It's fine if you don't inhale," replied Mr. Stevenson.

So here I am. I'm limping along and so, indeed, is the theater. Things change; the theater isn't like it was when I started, and when I started it wasn't like it was when the previous generation started. My guess is, it'll keep going in some form or another. Is there any thing that I wish I'd done? Oh, Saint Joan, maybe. (!) Actually, I *can* think of one thing—I sure would love to have played opposite Clark Gable in *Red Dust.*

Yep, I've grown way past Evy Meara, Carrie Berniers, Lady Torrance, Flora, Mildred Wild, and Serafina. I'm even too old to play Amanda Wingfield anymore. But hey, there are always parts I can do, like grandmothers and bag ladies. Hell, I'm only back where I began; I started "old" and I'll end up "old." I didn't mind playing it then and it comes a lot easier to me now. Someone recently asked me what I'd like printed on my tombstone and I told her, "a very distant date." It's true; I'd like to hang around for a long time and I'd like to keep working because it's what I know how to do. Whether it's a movie or a television or stage show or a student production or a poetry reading, I'm still eager for that curtain to rise.

Acknowledgments

Thanks to the following:

Daniel Allentuck, Max Allentuck, Vaughan Allentuck, Bill Appleton, Lucy Appleton, Norma Asnes, Bob Balaban, Katharine Bambery, Christine Beith, Zoe Caldwell, Phil Cusak, Virginia Bayer Dunne, John Fahey, Peter Feibleman, Lena Gabriel, Jan and Jeremy Geidt, Beverly Sills and Peter Greenough, Arlene Herman, Marilyn Horne, John Hodgeman, Anne Jackson, Jeanette Walsh Kelleher, Michael Lonergan, Iris Love, Frank Marino, Susanna Margolis, Jordan Massee, Carol Matthau, Julie Walsh Nial, Brian O'Sullivan, George Rondo, Esther Rosen ("Maureen Stapleton, American Actress," master's thesis, University of Arizona, 1983), Chen Sam, Bob Schear, Alan Scovell, Dolores Morano Senick, Liz Smith, Robert Stewart, Elizabeth Taylor, Robert Whitehead, Jeannie Williams, Elizabeth Wilson, Joanne Woodward, The New York Public Library for the Performing Arts, and Canyon Ranch in the Berkshires, Mary Ellen St. John, managing director, and to our editors, Michael Korda and Chuck Adams, and associate editor Cheryl Weinstein, copy supervisor Gypsy da Silva, and our agent, Susan Ginsburg. Very special thanks to Amy Appleton, Billy McIntyre, and Sydney Sheldon Welton.

Some actors I've worked with on stage, screen, and TV:

Jean Adair, Trini Alvarado, Don Ameche, Tom Aldredge, Ann-Margret, Edward Asner, Lew Ayres, Lauren Bacall, Martin Bal-

Acknowledgments

sam, Warren Beatty, Ralph Bellamy, Paul Benedict, Joseph Bernard, Herbert Berghof, Betsy Blair, Ray Bolger, Tom Bosley, Neville Brand, Marlon Brando, Beau Bridges, Wilford Brimley, David Burns, Art Carney, Stockard Channing, Montgomery Clift, Lee J. Cobb, Gary Coleman, Jackie Coogan, Joan Copeland, Katharine Cornell, Hume Cronyn, Bette Davis, Bruce Davison, Dom DeLuise, Brian Dennehy, Brandon de Wilde, Melvyn Douglas, Richard Dreyfuss, Patty Duke, David Dukes, Griffen Dunne, Charles Durning, Herb Edelman, Hector Elizondo, Patricia Englund, Mike Farrell, Norman Fell, Jose Ferrer, John Fiedler, Michael Fox, Victor Garber, James Garner, Jack Gilford, Melissa Gilbert, John Glover, Carol Grace, Sally Gracie, Lee Grant, George Grizzard, Harry Guardino, Steve Guttenberg, Veronica Hamel, Margaret Hamilton, Walter Hampden, Tom Hanks, Julie Harris, Gregory Harrison, Dolores Hart, Helen Hayes, Eileen Heckart, Van Heflin, Marilu Henner, Edward Herrman, Steven Hill, Pat Hingle, Bob Hoskins, Tresa Hughes, Kim Hunter, Mary Beth Hurt, Timothy Hutton, Anne Jackson, Glenda Jackson, Lou Jacobi, James Karen, Diane Keaton, Michael Keaton, Arthur Kennedy, George Kennedy, Burt Lancaster, Hope Lange, Piper Laurie, Carol Lawrence, Wilfred Lawson, Madeleine Lee, Janet Leigh, Michael Lembeck, Jack Lemmon, Michael Lombard, Shelley Long, Myrna Loy, Paul Lynde, Kelly McGillis, John McGiver, Billy McIntyre, Anna Magnani, Karl Malden, E. G. Marshall, Dean Martin, Richard Masur, Walter Matthau, Burgess Meredith, Sanford Meisner, Josh Mostel, Don Murray, Mildred Natwick, Barry Nelson, Laurence Olivier, Jerry Orbach, Geraldine Page, Lila Paris, Pamela Payton-Wright, Mary Peach, Nehemiah Persoff, Suzanne Pleshette, Amanda Plummer, Christopher Plummer, Joe Ponazecki, Don Porter, Stephanie Powers, Tyrone Power, Jr., William Prince, Charlotte Rae, Tony Randall, Burt Reynolds, Lee Richardson, Jason Robards, Jr., Doris Roberts, Cliff Robertson, Mira Rostova, Beverly Sanders, Kyra Sedgwick, Maria Schell, Maximillian Schell, George C. Scott, Jean Seberg, George Segal,

Acknowledgments

Milton Selzer, Charles Siebert, Jaclyn Smith, Lois Smith, Vladimir Sokoloff, Paul Sorvino, Meryl Streep, Barbra Streisand, Gail Stickland, Michael Strong, Kristoffer Tabori, Jessica Tandy, Elizabeth Taylor, Godfrey Tearle, Maria Tucci, Lenore Ulric, Raf Valone, Dick Van Dyke, Gwen Verdon, Betsy von Furstenberg, Robert Wagner, Lee Wallace, Eli Wallach, Sam Waterston, James Whitmore, Nicol Williamson, Elizabeth Wilson, Joseph Wiseman, Natalie Wood, Joanne Woodward, Irene Worth, Anthony Zerbe, Efrem Zimbalist, Jr., Stephanie Zimbalist . . . *and many, many, more. And I love them all.*

Index

Index

Index

Index

Index

Index

Index

Index

Index

Index

Index

Index

Index

Index

Photo Credits